Personal Relatio...
Cultures

In this innovative text Robin Goodwin draws together research from across the world to explore how fundamental differences in cultural values influence the ways in which we form and maintain romantic relationships, raise our children, make friends and communicate with work colleagues and our wider social networks. Common relationship patterns across cultures are examined and competing sociobiological and sociocultural interpretations are discussed.

Robin Goodwin questions the prevailing assumption of an individuating, selfish world, or 'the end of relationships'. He also challenges the current research emphasis on relationships formed by Northern American and Northern European undergraduates and calls for a more morally-driven and applied focus.

Personal Relationships across Cultures will appeal to all those interested in relationships in other cultures and in understanding the ways in which their own values and backgrounds may influence their relationships with others.

Robin Goodwin is Lecturer in Social Psychology at the University of Bristol, England, and specialises in the study of personal relationships and culture. He has conducted research into love, relationship formation, intimacy, social support and sexuality across Europe and in the Far East. He frequently lectures overseas and has published in the leading journals and texts in the field.

Personal Relationships across Cultures

Robin Goodwin

841   Psych

UNIVERSITY OF WOLVERHAMPTON
LEARNING RESOURCES

Acc No. 2248309   CLASS 312

CONTROL
0415128609   302

DATE
19. DE. 2001   SITE   G00

London and New York

First published 1999
by Routledge
11 New Fetter Lane, London EC4P 4EE

Simultaneously published in the USA and Canada
by Routledge
29 West 35th Street, New York, NY 10001

Routledge is an imprint of the Taylor & Francis Group

© 1999 Robin Goodwin

Typeset in Times by Routledge
Printed and bound in Great Britain by MPG Books Ltd, Bodmin

All rights reserved. No part of this book may be reprinted or
reproduced or utilised in any form or by any electronic,
mechanical, or other means, now known or hereafter
invented, including photocopying and recording, or in any
information storage or retrieval system, without permission in
writing from the publishers.

British Library Cataloguing in Publication Data
A catalogue record for this book is available from the British Library

Library of Congress Cataloguing in Publication Data
Goodwin, Robin, 1964–
Personal relationships across cultures / Robin Goodwin.
Includes bibliographical references and index.
1. Interpersonal relations–Cross-cultural studies.
2. Social networks–Cross-cultural studies. I. Title.
HM132.G646   1999   98–43680
302–dc21

ISBN 0–415–12860–9 (hbk)
ISBN 0–415–12861–7 (pbk)

To Janice and David

Contents

Illustrations

Tables

Figure

Acknowledgements

A number of people were invaluable in helping me complete this book. My colleagues, collaborators and friends Sonia Hernandez-Plaza, Roger Baumgarte, Arielle Lehmann, Anastassia Jabarin and Sophia Christakopoulou all made valuable and insightful comments. My thanks are also due to Viv Ward and her colleagues at Routledge for their tolerance of what became a rather late submission. Finally I would like to thank my wife Janice for her excellent proof-reading of an earlier draft.

Robin Goodwin
University of Bristol

Introduction
Studying personal relationships

Turn to any television station, or tune into any radio talk show, and very soon you will appreciate that people are preoccupied with their relationships. Survey after survey has found that personal relationships stand at the forefront of most people's lives, with studies in the US (Klinger, 1977) and the UK (Argyle, 1987) showing that people's relationships are their most highly valued asset. Listen a little harder to your chosen television or radio station and you will be introduced to an analysis of cultural diversity – or at least a portrayal of the prejudices and stereotypes that litter many people's perceptions of relationships in 'other cultures'. You will hear stories of forced marriages, oppressive child-rearing, nepotism and business corruption. You will also hear about passionate (often 'irrational') foreigners who speak quickly, wave their hands around as they speak, and possess fearsome tempers; and about other, tight-lipped peoples who never reveal what they think or feel.

The purpose of this book is not to explore how our everyday prejudices are formed, or the ways in which they are perpetuated. Instead, its purpose is to introduce some of the major themes in the study of personal relationships, and to demonstrate that cultures are both similar and varied in their relationship practices and beliefs. Rather than just noting these similarities and differences, I will try to explain how broader values and economic realities may help explain the relationship similarities/variations across cultures. To do this I will also need to consider some of the claims for universal biological principles primarily associated with evolutionary accounts of development (discussed in Chapter 2). In these discussions, I will try to demonstrate how many of our cherished views of other cultures are becoming less relevant and less accurate – if, indeed, they were ever accurate at all. With many of the world's most populous nations currently engaged in rapid economic expansion, many long-established modes of living and interacting are also undergoing significant changes. These changing patterns of living mean that outdated stereotypes of cultural diversity constantly need to be modified to deal with the present and rather confusing reality – the apparently 'strange' synthesis of 'traditionality' and 'modernity' which now characterises so many of today's cultures.

A brief outline of this book

I begin the first chapter with some considerations of what we mean by personal relationships, culture and the related concept of ethnicity, and give a brief and selective synopsis of some of the major themes in the Western study of personal relationships. I consider why it is important to study personal relationships in a cross-cultural context, and outline some of the particular themes to be repeated throughout the book.

Chapter 2 is concerned with trying to explain why we find both diversity and similarity across relationships in cultures. I begin by considering arguments for universality in personal relationships, focusing on debates about our preferences for a romantic partner. I then turn to consider some of the major ways in which recent researchers have 'dimensionalised' cultural values, to help us make more sense of the findings from our cultural comparisons. I also consider how some of these dimensions of values may be changing, with particular reference to the debate about 'modernisation' and its impact on our personal lives. This, I believe, is best tackled through an understanding of the *ecological circumstances* in which we live our everyday lives, and I consider in particular how migrant groups may adapt their values and behaviours in a new society.

In the next five chapters, specific themes in personal relationships are considered, although inevitably there is some overlap between many of the themes discussed. These various themes reflect the range of relationship dimensions suggested by Blumstein and Kollock (1988): they include the relations of kin and non-kin, of those who are engaged in sexual activity and those who are not, those living together and those not, hierarchical relations versus more egalitarian relations, and cross-sex versus same-sex relations.

In Chapter 3, I consider the formation of heterosexual relationships, and include a discussion of love and love styles across cultures. In Chapter 4, I move on to the developing relationship, considering the meaning of marriage, the growth of relationships, and what happens when things go wrong in a relationship (including a discussion of relationship violence and divorce).

Chapter 5 focuses on sexual behaviour, and the link between sex and societal norms. This includes a consideration of the limited cross-cultural literature on homosexuality as well as extra-marital sexual activities and sexual disease. In Chapter 6, I consider relationships in the nuclear and the extended family, and the nature of family bonds and child-rearing. I also consider the often-vexed issue of marital roles, power in marriage and decision making, and discuss some of the ways in which 'traditional' family roles are changing in many societies across the world.

Chapters 7 and 8 turn the attention to relationships outside the couple and the family unit. In Chapter 7 I discuss relations at work – the role of work for an individual in a society, how cultural values can influence the type of interactions that individuals might have in the workplace, and how decision making and leadership might reflect these enduring cultural values. In Chapter 8 I consider friendship and the wider social network – how individuals might be expected to 'fit in' with others in their society, how social support networks may or may not function, as well as what happens when an individual is isolated within a particular culture. I also consider the role of verbal and non-verbal exchanges in the development and maintenance of social networks. Here I put a particular emphasis on the often-neglected area of relationships under stress – how, for example, those people of Eastern Europe with very stressful lifestyles might use their social networks to help them cope; and the negative effects of social relationships in societies undergoing rapid changes. In the final chapter, Chapter 9, I consider the practical use of what we now know about relationships across cultures, and its relevance to cross-cultural interventions. I conclude with a consideration of how we might best progress in the evolving field of personal relationships across cultures.

Several key themes are discussed throughout this book. One major theme will be the way in which cultural systems (such as values, beliefs and worldviews) help form internalised social norms which are prime sources of relationship behaviour (Pepitone and Triandis, 1987). At the same time, I recognise that not everything that people do, think and feel is determined by culture (Rohner, 1984), and even under conditions where cultural norms and sanctions seem their most prohibitive we are still able to identify individual variations in what people do and think, and how they respond to different circumstances. For example, the attitudes of people in Japan, often treated as one of the most homogenous cultures in the world and certainly highly ethnically homogenous, may vary greatly across age groups and the diverse roles within the society (Reischauer, 1988). We should expect as much divergence in attitudes between a teenager and an octogenarian in Japan as we would between comparable age groups in any Western country (Reischauer, 1988). Thus a key theme will be the way in which a person's culture, social group (such as their occupational class) and individual personality/worldview may interact to influence their personal relationships (Rogoff and Chavajay, 1995).

Another key theme will be that of social change. Cultures across the world are undergoing major economic, political and demographic transitions. The study of social change is one of the major research traditions in the social sciences, yet there is little unifying treatment of the topic (Berry, 1980). One relevant item from the literature focuses on the study of life transitions, usually defined in terms of the changes that occur in a person's position in their environment (Bronfenbrenner, 1970; Trickett and Buchanan, 1997). Here, an emphasis on adaptation and the interdependence of people and their environments (Trickett and Buchanan, 1997) requires us to look at changes at the level of the 'macro-system' (i.e. the political and economic spheres (Bronfenbrenner, 1970)), and the impact of this system on personal relations. I will therefore consider the relationships implications of some of the most dramatic 'macro-level' transitions of the past two decades, focusing in particular on recent work conducted in Eastern Europe and East Asia.

In trying to interpret the meaning of these changes, my approach will focus on the way in which people in their personal relationships adapt to their surroundings. This does not mean that I will be taking a simplistic, 'functionalist' approach to the subject – a perspective often criticised for ignoring large social changes and power differentials (Gouldner, 1971). It does, however, mean that I will try to explain how relationship patterns often 'make sense' within a particular cultural setting: for example, an immigrant family may take on 'fictive kin' (Chapter 6) to help provide needed workers and support in the workplace of their adopted country. Although most of the emphasis of this book will be on the social psychological literature, my approach will also necessarily be multidisciplinary, drawing particularly on the work of sociologists and demographers for my analysis of changes in family patterns, and on research by anthropologists for the consideration of sexual relationships across cultures. While there are certainly some significant interdisciplinary differences in these approaches, a multidisciplinary perspective can offer particular insights in areas which have been of less interest to other researchers.

Of course, the material I review in this book must reflect the topics and areas of concern of the cross-cultural relationships research that has been conducted. During the writing of this book I was struck by the way in which different regions of the world have attracted particular types of research, often suggested by the 'problems' or 'burning issues' perceived to attain to these areas. Thus it was notable that there is now an extensive literature on management/organisational relationships in Japan and, increasingly, in China and other East Asian economies, reflecting the growing investment and economic cooperation between the West and this region (along with attempts to learn the 'secret' of the threatening economic security these regions might present (Rosenberger, 1992a)). In contrast, while there has been very little research on managerial relationships in Africa, there is a large volume of literature reflecting the perceived 'problems' of this continent: population growth (and the concomitants of this apparently 'problematic' expansion) and disease, in particular HIV/AIDS, a sexually transmitted disease which is seen as particularly worrying not only for its large-scale presence in the region but because of its spread outside of African shores (I could find very little reference to the problems of malaria or other 'less relevant' diseases). India, too, has been framed in terms of the 'problems' of fertility/population expansion, although many researchers in this region share the West's fascination with the 'paradoxes' of modernisation in the sub-continent, paradoxes occupying the minds of those also interested in Japan and some of the other Southeast Asian economies. That the coexistence of 'the old and the new' might not seem paradoxical from a non-Western perspective, and that such a coexistence exists in apparently non-exotic Western cultures, is of course rarely noted.

As far as possible in this text, I have tried to avoid what I believe to be the dangerous traps of exoticising practices, but of course I am inevitably rooted in my own cultural Western biases ... I would greatly welcome the comments of readers from other cultures, and invite them to contact me and correct me where I may have erred.

1 The development of research into personal relationships across cultures

Introduction

To begin to understand how relationships vary across cultures, we need first to define our terms. As I will argue below, however, defining 'relationship' or 'culture' is more complex than we might at first imagine, and the kinds of definitions used reflect the type of research which has been conducted. I then go on to describe how particular Western conceptualisations of relationships have restricted the range of relationships examined, this narrowness of focus being just one of the reasons why we might benefit from a broader, more cross-cultural analysis. Unfortunately, this cross-cultural work in itself has often been simplistic in design, mimicking Western ideas and methods. Instead, I will argue that understanding personal relationships across cultures means looking at the nature of people's daily existence in the context of a whole range of historical, social and political factors.

Defining our terms: 'personal relationships' and 'culture'

Personal relationships

What is a 'personal relationship'? When relationship researchers present their considerations of personal relationships, they rarely define their terms. In one of the best-known definitions, Argyle and Henderson describe a personal relationship as a 'regular social encounter over a period of time' (Argyle and Henderson, 1985: 4). A personal relationship is usually seen as one of considerable duration (Kelley *et al.*, 1983), involving a great degree of interdependence of emotions and thoughts (Berscheid, 1994; Kelley *et al.*, 1983) and evolving through a negotiated set of disclosures (Altman and Taylor, 1973).

Unfortunately, such definitions omit perhaps the most critical feature of relationships in Eastern cultures – the centrality of role obligations (Yang, 1995). Such obligations do not necessarily relate to simple frequency of interaction: your relationship with a teacher in an Eastern culture, for example, may remain similar regardless of the number of the interactions you enjoy. Definitions which focus on interdependent thoughts and feelings also tend to neglect the perceptions of others outside of the relationship, ignoring the social stage upon which relationships are performed (Goffman, 1959). These others may play a central part in defining any interaction as a relationship: where there are strict prescriptions about pre-marital encounters, for example, any meeting between the sexes may be defined as a potentially dangerous 'relationship'. Finally, more recent conceptualisations of relationships, particularly those emerging from the literature on social networks, have identified the role of 'weak ties' in linking individuals to other social networks. These may be potentially of great significance during certain pivotal life stages (Trickett and Buchanan, 1997). Reflecting my interest in the centrality of these cultural prescriptions and perceptions, I consider a personal relationship to be *the interaction between two or more individuals located within the context of wider societal and cultural forces.*

Culture and ethnicity

The definition of culture has been widely discussed, and forms a large part of most recent texts on cross-cultural psychology. Originally, culture meant producing or developing something (e.g. crops), and it was only in the eighteenth century that it became synonymous with the 'educated' person, in contrast to the 'barbarian' (Jahoda, 1992). It was not until the mid-nineteenth century that there was a recognition of a plurality of possible cultures (Jahoda, 1992).

Culture is not something we can reach out and touch, nor see or hear: it is something we must infer from the behaviour of others (Rohner, 1984). Some forty years ago, Kroeber and Kluckhorn (1952) identified more than 160 definitions of culture, and a wide number of definitions persist, much to the frustration of some, who have concluded that to search for an adequate definition of culture is fruitless (e.g. Segall, 1984). Looking across the definitions, it is clear that at least one part of culture is the *learned meanings that are shared by a group* (Rohner, 1984). These meanings are likely to have some coherence and organisation (Jahoda, 1992). Hofstede's (1994b: 5) definition reflects this notion of organisation in his use of a computing analogy: culture is defined as 'the collective programming of the mind which distinguishes the members of one group or category of people from another'. Culture can also be defined as the *human-made part of the environment* (e.g. 1948; Moghaddam *et al.*, 1993), a definition which alerts us to the significance of considering cultural products such as houses and other artefacts in defining a culture (Cole, 1990; Jahoda, 1984). Finally, and important for the analysis of relationships and relationship ideas, is the notion that culture is something that is *transmitted across time*, although, of course, cultural messages may be modified from generation to generation (Jahoda, 1992; Rohner, 1984). This is important because culture can then be seen as a kind

of 'social reference point' which helps guide the actions of whole generations of families.

Trompenaars (1993), whose work on cultural values I will be discussing
several times during this text, combines many of these definitions of culture
by suggesting that culture can be seen as 'layered', with the outside layer
being the 'explicit culture' (the 'observable reality' of language, food, build-
ings, houses etc.), the middle layer consisting of norms and values, and the
core layer comprising assumptions which represent the most basic ways in
which groups organise themselves to deal with their environment (allowing
them to deal, for example, with the threat of flood or earthquake). This
means that culture (and, by implication, cultural values) is not a *random* set
of shared meanings, but is the way in which particular societies have come to
deal with particular problems, usually resulting from environmental challenges. This emphasis on the *ecological factors* important in shaping cultures
is considered in Chapter 2.

How might definitions of culture and ethnicity differ? In this book I
recognise the overlap between culture and ethnicity by using the definition
of ethnicity employed by Wilkinson (1987: 185) in her work on minority
ethnic groups in North America:

> an ethnic group is a group of people who are of the same nationality or
> ancestry and who enact a shared culture and lifestyles.

Of course, people can feel differently attached to their ethnic group, as
Wilkinson herself acknowledges and as the work on acculturation (discussed
in Chapter 2) clearly shows, and this may have a considerable impact on who
they meet and marry, and on the nature of these relationships. Nevertheless,
it is always important to remember that others may define these individuals
in terms of their ethnicity even when the individuals themselves would
rather they did not, and that individuals will often react in terms of their
ethnic groups across an array of situations (Berry, 1997).

In this text I will be reporting primarily on how social scientists have
characterised the relationship behaviour and feelings of a particular
geographically defined group. As Smith and Bond (1998) have noted, much
of the research reported gives little detail beyond the name of the country
where the work has been conducted, with 'country' being seen as analogous
to 'culture'. While I, of course, recognise that this is unsatisfactory in some
cases (particularly where there may be a marked differences between the
'cultures' in a particular country, such as is the case of different religious
groups in India) I have relied on the author(s) of the research cited to identify potential differences in the cultural background of the populations they
are investigating. Where this is obviously problematic, I have alerted the
reader to other possible interpretations of the findings reported.

The Western study of personal relationships: a very brief history

When histories of social psychology are written, many writers cite the famous words of Ebbinghaus (1908: 1): 'Psychology has had a long past but only a brief history'. Much the same can be said about the study of personal relationships, with 'the long past' beginning with the Ancient Greeks, and the 'brief history' really only beginning in the 1970s but accelerating in terms of the volume of output in the late 1980s and 1990s. The result is that what was seen until recently as a slightly unsavoury area for scientific investigation is now a major theme for research and features prominently in the most prestigious psychological journals. Here I give a flavour of some of the work on relationship formation and continuation; far more detailed accounts of contemporary Western work can be found in the large number of relationships texts now available (such as the Sage Series on Close Relationships), and in the two large *Handbooks of Personal Relationships* edited by Steve Duck (first and second edition, 1988 and 1997).

Some of the earliest writings on personal relationships are attributed to Aristotle (Berscheid and Walster, 1978). Aristotle discussed a number of topics which have become influential in recent research on relationship formation, including the relationship between receiving rewards and attraction, the role of physical attractiveness in mate preferences, and the idea that we find attractive those who are similar to us (cited in Berscheid and Walster, 1978). Although the ideals of love found in Shakespeare and later romantic literary figures are sometimes misinterpreted as reflecting the longevity of love-based attraction in Western cultures, in reality notions of 'courtly love', as practised among the political elite during the Middle Ages, had little relationship to the dominant practices of marital arrangement, which were largely ordained by pragmatic dictates of politics and economics (Ingoldsby, 1995a). Themes of romantic love from Shakespeare and his contemporaries were therefore examples of wish fulfilment rather than actual behaviour for the period (Murstein, 1986), reflecting a disparity between desire and actuality evident in many contemporary societies around the world.

More 'modern' speculations about mate selection and partner choice really only began in the mid-nineteenth century (Murstein, 1986), with greater mate choice arising in part from the increased mobility following industrialisation. O.S. Fowler's (1859) recommendations (cited in Murstein, 1980: 781) are relatively typical of this period:

> Wherein, and as far as you are what you ought to be, marry one like yourself; but wherein and as far as you have any marked excesses of defects, marry those unlike yourself in these objectionable particulars.

While this may seem quite reasonable (who wants an imperfect partner?), these prescriptions may seem a little optimistic in the real world of the 'dating marketplace'. 'Deficits' such as low social class or poor reputation were likely to influence potential suitors and, as we shall see in Chapter 3, are still important features of mate selection across the world.

It was not until the beginning of the present century that more systematic, theory-based attempts were made to understand personal relationships. Freud was primarily concerned with the abnormal development of object-choice (1910), and later with the tendency to debase the loved object (1912). He suggested two types of love: 'anaclictic' or 'attachment' love (based on the early infantile prototype) and 'narcissistic' love, which represents the seeking out of the individual's own ego in others (1914). He also offered a brief account of the idealisation of love, although this was developed more by later psychoanalysts such as Theodor Reik (1941). Reik saw love as the result of discontent arising from a failure to fulfil our ego-ideal. It is notable that the psychoanalysts' emphasis on need-fulfilment, and their eagerness to trace the origins of partner choice to early maternal interactions, have re-emerged in more recent and influential research into attachment theory (e.g. Shaver *et al.*, 1988).

Another influential psychoanalyst, Erich Fromm (1956), considered relationships to be the 'exchange of resources' (or 'packets of qualities'; 1956: 2), a viewpoint that was to become influential among the more experimental researchers of the 1970s (see Chapter 4 for a discussion of exchange principles). In his book 'The Art of Loving', Fromm claims (1956: 3):

> Two people fall in love when they feel they have found the best object available on the market, considering the limitations of their own exchange values.

Experimental psychological research in the early years of this century was little concerned with the field of personal relationships, although some early studies did compare established partners on an array of different measures, including intelligence (e.g. Schooley, 1936), appearance (e.g. Pearson and Lee, 1903) and opinions and attitudes (e.g. Schuster and Elderton, 1906). After the Second World War, Robert Winch made a series of important attempts to re-examine the issue of need fulfilment (e.g. Winch, 1955, 1958), while Donn Byrne (1971) developed an extensive programme of research systematically examining the concept that 'similars attract'. These contributors are sometimes pitted against one another through the misconception that, while Winch often saw 'opposites attracting' (with the 'opposites' being patterns of needs which Winch saw as complementing one another), Byrne propagated the familiar saw that 'birds of a feather flock together'. In fact, this opposition was a misconception: both Byrne and Winch were suggesting that it is those couplings that are reinforcing to the individuals involved that are likely to succeed. Both writers have attracted strong criti-

cism on both methodological and theoretical grounds: Winch has been criticised, for example, for misinterpreting his own statistical results (e.g. Tharp,
1963), and many point to the artificiality of Byrne's experimental paradigm,
where individuals are forced to rate their attraction to a stranger they have
never met, purely on the basis of rather contrived attitudinal statements (e.g.
Duck, 1986). Perhaps most significant for the rest of this book, such early
work was premised on a simple assumption: that the formation (and to some
extent, maintenance) of a personal relationship resulted from the sum total
of individual attributes or needs, thus neglecting the wider influence of
culture and society at large (Duck *et al.*, 1997). As I will argue, this assumption is a reflection of the individualist bias of much North American
research, and can be challenged as inappropriate even for this society.

The study of personal relationships today

It would be nice to claim that now, several decades later, the field has moved
on to such an extent that complex multilevel models of relationships, which
explicitly allow for the impact of culture and aspects of the social structure,
now dominate the area. Certainly some things have improved: methods are
generally much more rigorous, especially since the development of user-
friendly computer packages which include multivariate techniques. As a
result, researchers are now able to overcome one old methodological criticism in the study of attraction by looking at both the unique and the
combined effects of independent variables, although they are still very much
preoccupied with variables which examine individual differences. Alongside
this, relationships have begun to be conceptualised less as the simple amal-
gamation of the particular characteristics of those involved and more as
phenomena which evolve through interactions (e.g. Sprecher and Duck,
1994) and which involve more complex 'chains' of communication (Kelley *et
al.*, 1983). There has been an increase in longitudinal studies (Berscheid,
1994), although these still form a minority of published studies, and there is
a greater recognition that the couple should be studied as a dyad, rather
than as two isolated individuals (Kenny, 1988).

Consistent with this, the range of topics of study has expanded too, so
that the old focus on initial 'interpersonal attraction' which previously dominated the field (Huston and Levinger, 1978) has extended to the study of
complete relationship progression, from early courtship patterns (e.g.
Huston *et al.*, 1981) to breakdown and dissolution (e.g. Duck's stage model
of dissolution, Duck, 1982; Drigotas and Rusbult, 1992). Some of this work
has at least recognised the importance of the immediate social context (for
example, in the form of the available alternatives in Drigotas and Rusbult's
study). Allied to this greater 'spread' of interests has been the development
of concepts that aim to explain these relationship progressions and their
outcomes. Rusbult and her colleagues, for example (e.g. Rusbult, 1987), have
proposed that there are four modes of response to relationship problems:

exiting the relationship, voicing concern, staying loyal, or neglecting the relationship. This popular taxonomy is indicative of a broader interest in taxonomising that has become a major feature of the field (Berscheid, 1994); we now, for example, have several taxonomies of love (e.g. Sternberg's triangular model, Sternberg 1988), love styles (e.g. Hendrick and Hendrick, 1986); and marriage type (Fitzpatrick and Badzinski, 1985).

So what has been the outcome of this 'long history' of relationships research? While a consideration of relationship alternatives hinted at the existence of a wider social field, the focus is still on the analysis of the individual. An example would be the study of self-esteem, which influences how an individual presents his/her physical appearance (Diener *et al.*, 1995), the love styles of the individual (Dion and Dion, 1988) and how they react to relationship problems (Rusbult *et al.*, 1986). This emphasis on personality reflects a general shift in social psychology towards the personal rather than the social level of analysis, as reflected in writings in the major journals in the field, such as the influential *Journal of Personality and Social Psychology* (West *et al.*, 1993). This has been accompanied by a growing interest in the socio-cognitive processes that characterise interpersonal relationships, the focus of Berscheid's (1994) review of the field. These include relationship schemas and scripts, which represent the expected ordering of events in a situation (e.g. the work of Burnett *et al.*, 1987), and the study of attribution, which largely focuses on the cognitive interpretations and biases in interactions made by couples (e.g. Bradbury and Fincham, 1990). Such analyses largely neglect vital economic factors such as social class and housing (Allan, 1993). Furthermore, although such work *could* be usefully applied to consider broader cultural norms and motifs, relationships research has as yet focused almost exclusively on laboratory work involving the information processing of Western couples (usually students). While we must not neglect the influence of such individual-level variables, we must also broaden our analysis further – to include the analysis of structural factors such as social class and, of course, culture.

Why we need a cross-cultural approach

At first glance, the study of the link between personality and relationships and exchange processes seems a good start for a cross-cultural examination. Surely relationships everywhere can be classified, and there are universal processes that underpin attribution and other cognitive processes?

At the simplest level, this is of course correct; as I will argue in the next chapter, there may be apparent similarities between people who score similarly on various cultural groupings. However, when we look again we realise that these observations tell us relatively little. Gaines (1997) notes how the individualistic obsession with the study of the welfare of oneself in a relationship may provide us with only a superficial understanding when we orient our study towards the shared knowledges, the 'we-orientations' that are necessary for examining interchanges between couples. This may be particularly important when we analyse what we 'get' from a relationship as a predictor of whether we maintain our investment in that relationship (see Chapter 4). Here, broader cultural knowledge which places the couple more firmly in its cultural setting is more likely to be of value in many societies. Notions such as 'relationship blame', typologies of relationship dissatisfaction and concepts such as 'alternative partners' may be of less relevance when power structures and rules in a society limit the possibility of seeking alternatives or dissolving a relationship. Relationships are embedded in societal contexts, which help inform attitudes and strongly influence behavioural norms (Duck *et al.*, 1997).

An imaginary example might clarify this. John from England is travelling alone in one of the more remote regions of mainland China. During his travels he meets Amy, a young single woman of about his age, to whom he is immediately attracted. However, he may well find his interaction with her very frustrating: Amy seems friendly enough and keen to preserve the harmony of their interaction, but her relations with him appear to be heavily influenced by her immediate family members. As a result she views him as a pleasant but definite outsider, and she seems unwilling to go beyond what he feels is the 'stereotype' of the Westerner. In this case, common enough when members of two very different cultures meet, the individual personality attributes of the two people (however 'compatible') may be of far less significance.

Consider too the emphasis in much of the Western literature on relationship exchange. Exchange theory is adapted from economic concepts popular in the late 1950s and early 1960s (Thibaut and Kelley, 1959; Homans, 1967). Such theories are based on reinforcement principles: all actions are seen as 'a function of their payoffs' (Homans, 1967: 31), and simple exchange theory sees an individual as likely to develop a relationship if the rewards offered are sufficient to keep the party involved. Later versions of this theory have examined how individuals' desires may be mediated by their perceived likelihood of achievement (the matching hypothesis: Berscheid *et al.*, 1971), and have stressed the significance of perceived equitability of exchange between the partners (equity theory: e.g. Adams, 1965). However, such Western research on exchange principles may be of limited utility outside Western cultures. As I will discuss in Chapter 4, the 'tit for tat' exchanges that might characterise relations between work colleagues in the West may be less common in Eastern societies such as Hong Kong and Japan, where the principle of equality is more valued (Berman *et al.*, 1985; Leung and Iwawaki, 1988; Yamaguchi 1994).

Such examples illustrate just two ways in which misunderstandings might occur in encounters between people of different cultures. Contact between individuals of different cultural backgrounds is increasing in both frequency and intensity. The businessman who gazes at his Eastern male partner and addresses him by his first name may well give off an inappropriate message

of disrespect (LaFrance and Mayo, 1976). The manager who fails to appreciate the significance of maintaining a collective sense of 'face' is unlikely to
prosper in his or her negotiations in Japan (Reischauer, 1988; Trompenaars,
1993). While such misunderstandings are important, and are likely to have
considerable practical implications for international business as well as for
tourism, we should not stop at simply identifying where things may be
different, but should try to analyse why and how we might learn from these
differences. Cross-cultural research forces us to revise our interpretations of
inconsistencies in results in a manner that could never be achieved by examining a single nation (Kohn, 1987). We should challenge established Western
findings to see how well they replicate across cultures (Kohn, 1987): we
might indeed be disappointed, as Amir and Sharon (1987) found in their
replication of 'classic' social psychological studies. When we obtain the same
findings in very different cultural settings, we can be more sure about the
general validity of our theory: on the other hand, if the results are not
repeatable, we might have to recognise that our original hypothesis is
restricted to those situations in which it was originally derived (Pepitone and
Triandis, 1987). Cross-cultural work also helps us to disentangle some of the
complex sets of confounding variables that make understanding many relationships phenomena so difficult (Kagitcibasi, 1996). Kagitcibasi cites the
problems involved in examining the confounding effects of age and length of
schooling in Western societies (where all children are at school). She notes
how it is often useful to examine cultures where children are not at school to
examine age effects separately in these cultures.

At the level of social policy, we might also try to learn from cultures
where elements of relationships work better – for example, from cultures
where relationship violence is practically unknown (Levinson, 1989). Once
we feel confident that we have isolated those universal variables that operate
in a situation, we can try to extend 'best practice' to other cultures, learning,
for example, from successful programmes in such vital areas as the prevention of sexual diseases. This takes the study of relationships across cultures
from beyond the realms of a party game to a field of investigation with real
importance for the understanding of relationships and their social consequences.

The study of personal relationships across cultures

Jahoda (1992) traces the beginning of modern cross-cultural research to the
work of Tylor (1889), who developed a comparative method of tabulating
the marriage rules and practices of 350 cultures around the world. Despite
these promising early beginnings, there have been few large-scale cross-
cultural studies of personal relationships since that time. Instead, most
studies have been one-off 'fishing expeditions' (Fletcher and Ward, 1988),
rarely guided by theoretical rationale in either their choice of cultures or
variables of study.

Three types of study predominate in the literature. First are those studies conducted by students from overseas visiting one of the academic 'power blocks' (North America, Western Europe and Australasia), usually as part of their training, and working with a more experienced supervisor to produce a two- or three-culture comparison. A second type of study occurs when the research has been the result of a relatively short visit paid by a researcher from a major academic power who has conducted a comparative study during their time overseas. While these studies have sometimes produced real insights, they are frequently the result of a relatively short-term exposure to the country or countries being compared, and their results are thus often open to a wide range of interpretations (see, for example, the controversy surrounding Wheeler's examination of relationships in Hong Kong: Lam and Yang, 1989, Wheeler, 1988, 1989). Finally, we have those studies conducted outside the Western power blocks which aim to replicate old studies first carried out in the West. Such studies often run in to a number of problems. First, the lack of recent material often means that the theories and methods being used in these 'replications' have since been abandoned (or at least heavily criticised) by later researchers. As a corollary of this, the replications are usually only reported in the rather more obscure and lower-status publications. An example is the continuation of work in the 'similars-attract' paradigm (Byrne, 1971) in a number of societies, representing a tradition of interpersonal attraction research largely abandoned by those working in the West (see Huston and Levinger, 1978). Second, the lack of resources for such work, plus (in my view) an overly reverent attitude towards the 'Western' traditions of research, has meant that few researchers outside the West have had the confidence to develop their own indigenous research programmes. This has meant a reliance on Western theories and methods with all the ideological baggage associated with this (Rosenblatt and Anderson, 1981).

Adapting the conceptual frameworks suggested by Doise (1987) and Pepitone and Triandis (1987), we can partition cross-cultural personal relationships research into a number of levels of analysis. The first is a universal level of analysis concerning common human neuro-physiological functioning (Pepitone and Triandis, 1987). At its extremes, the socio-biological research discussed in Chapter 2 reflects some of the theoretical assumptions of this 'level' of research. It is only at the biological level that we can be really confident of universality in relationships, because although there are likely to be common features of the physical world and social structure across cultures which might help form social patternings of relationships (Pepitone and Triandis, 1987) we should not make the mistake of assuming that these commonalities will necessarily lead to the same relationship outcomes in each culture.

Four further levels can be found in socio-psychological research (Doise, 1987). The within ('intra-personal') level is concerned with internal processes relatively uninfluenced by the interaction between the individual and their environment. Little of the research reported in the present text will be at this level of analysis. The 'inter-personal level' is concerned with how individuals inter-relate regardless of their status, while the positional level is more concerned with status effects (e.g. whether you are more likely to help another if you are approached by someone of high rather than of low status). While much of the Western literature on relationships is concerned with analysis of relationships between people irrespective of their social roles, we shall see that relationships in non-Western cultures are far more likely to be predicated upon such roles. The final, ideological, level includes our central interest with cross-cultural norms and variations. There is some evidence to suggest that while socio-psychological research in the US has moved increasingly towards the study of 'lower'-level, intra-personal phenomena, work in Europe (including Eastern Europe) has continued to reflect an interest in the higher levels of analysis (Moghaddam *et al.*, 1993), even if this emphasis has rarely moved on to the highest level to the study of cultural variations (Smith and Bond, 1998).

When we consider this 'highest' level of cross-national comparisons, Kohn (1987) suggests we can also identify four main traditions of research. The first, in which the nation is the object of study, focuses on large governmental systems within countries. We will be using this type of analysis when we discuss cross-national differences in social policies towards the family (Chapter 6). A second type of study is where the nation is the *context* of the study: in other words, where there is an interest in how certain aspects of a social structure impinge on personality. For example, Kohn's own important research (e.g. Kohn 1987; Kohn *et al.*, 1990) is concerned with how social stratification influences psychological functioning, and, in particular, the influence of occupation on the development and transmission of values across generations (see Chapter 6). This approach also recognises that, while nations may provide a great deal of common mental programming for their citizens (Hofstede, 1994b), there is also likely to be considerable diversity within a nation, with major sources of variation including social class, occupation and education.

The third type of research is where nations are the unit of analysis, but where the actual nations themselves are of lesser significance than their scores on particular economic dimensions (such as gross national product). This approach has been used relatively rarely in the study of personal relationships, although its value has recently been recognised by Georgas (1997) in his work on family values (discussed in Chapter 6), as well as by others who follow a broadly ecological approach (discussed in Chapter 2). Finally, a fourth set of studies focus on larger international systems, such as 'capitalism'. Although rarely explicitly discussed in the relationship literature, studies which compare 'modern' with 'traditional' societies (discussed in Chapter 2), and other work concerned with the impact of capitalism on personal relations (e.g. Popenoe, 1988), often implicitly invoke this approach.

One word of warning is necessary when we consider similarities and differences across cultures. Cross-cultural/cross-national comparisons are often principally concerned with differences between cultures – I suspect that few readers of this book were attracted to it by the promise of finding simple universals in relationship behaviour, although cross-cultural consistencies do emerge in my literature reviews. Where we find cross-national/cross-cultural similarities, the unique historical experiences of each country are of lesser concern, and the more varied the social conditions across which we find these similarities, the more convincing they may be (Kohn *et al.*, 1990). When we find differences between nations or cultures, the issues become more difficult, as there are many possible differences in history, culture and political or economic systems which may be relevant to explaining differences in social systems or how these social systems affect people's everyday lives (Kohn, 1987). Here we must turn to the values underlying a culture (discussed in Chapter 2), as well as to the related historical conditions and environmental/ecological concerns that might influence behaviour. Inevitably, too, our interpretations are 'up for grabs', and it is the duty of the researchers to defend their explanations – and for knowledgeable readers to assess how realistic these are.

2 Relationships in a cultural setting

> Culture is like gravity: you do not experience it until you jump six feet into the air.
>
> Trompenaars (1993: 11)

Introduction

For some relationships researchers, the very universality of findings on personal relationships are of interest. For the socio-biologist, mate selection and reproductive behaviour represent 'the first line of evolutionary pressure' (Kenrick and Keefe, 1992: 75). In contrast, other researchers have underlined the significance of variations in cultural values for relationships, tracing the generation of these values to a host of historical and economic factors. One particular set of explanations for the values has stressed their ecological significance, although ecological accounts of relationships often seem less appropriate in a rapidly-changing and apparently 'modernising' world. Two major manifestations of this 'modern' world are the spread of ideas through the mass media, and the flow of peoples between nations, considered in the final section of this chapter.

Universality in personal relationships: a socio-biological approach

The idea that there are fundamental psychological characteristics common to all humans is an old one, which Jahoda (1990) traces back at least as far as Condorcet (1743–94). More recent empirical research has examined universal patterns in language acquisition, facial expressions of emotion and male violence (Archer, 1996; Rohner, 1984). Over the last decade there has been a particular growth in interest in the study of personal relationships from an evolutionary perspective. The great majority of this research has focused on mate selection, and I will focus my review of the evolutionary literature on this topic.

From an evolutionary perspective, whom we choose as a partner, and, to some extent, the ways we go about attracting our partner, are seen as providing valuable insights into the workings of socio-biological processes. Evolutionary approaches assume that each species has a genetically organised set of strategies and tactics for survival, growth and reproduction (Kenrick and Keefe, 1992: 77). Traits that maximise gene replication are considered fit and assumed to be targets of mate choice (Thiessen and Gregg, 1980). Such approaches interpret sex differences in relational practices as resulting from different selection pressures on men and women during evolution (Archer, 1996). The sex investing the most in the offspring is generally assumed to be the most selective in choosing a mate (Thiessen and Gregg, 1980). While males may invest more energy in trying to attract a mate, females invest more resources in parenting (Thiessen and Gregg, 1980).

A number of socio-biologists have seen the development of specific preferences as reflecting adaptational priorities. They argue that a 'selective advantage' is afforded to those who prefer mates capable of reproductive investment (Buss and Barnes, 1986: 569) and therefore potential partners with preferred attributes are chosen for mating (Buss, 1984; Feingold, 1992a). Symons (1995: 81) argues:

> ... human males evolved psychological mechanisms that selectively detect and respond to specific characteristics (such as smooth skin and bilateral symmetry) of women's bodies. These universal mechanisms were shaped by natural selection to have the specific forms that they do because these forms produced reproductively functional behavior in the environments and conditions in which our ancestors evolved.

Women are the more discriminating sex when it comes to mate selection and are likely to be keen to find a mate with good genes, resources and parenting skills (Archer, 1996). Symons (1995) maintains that males have been 'selected' to be sexually attracted by cues of age, hormonal status, parity, fecundity, good health, good 'design' and developmental stability, and information on these variables is available in the specific characteristics of females' bodies.

David Buss and his colleagues (1987; 1988; 1989; Buss and Barnes 1986, Buss *et al.*, 1990) have conducted a number of studies on partner selection from a socio-biological approach. Like Symons (1995), they claim that men should value those features that correlate with female reproductive capability: in particular, female youth and beauty (Buss, 1987, 1988, 1989). Similarly, women should choose men who can 'provide' for the family through the provision of social and material resources, usually reflected through earning potential, ambition and industriousness (Buss, 1988, 1989). To test these hypotheses in a cross-cultural setting, Buss (1989, Buss *et al.*, 1990) gathered data from more than 10,000 respondents in thirty-seven cultures in one of the largest-ever studies of human relationships across cultures. They asked their respondents their desired age of marriage, their preferred age difference between spouses, their ratings of a set of eighteen partner characteristics, and the rank ordering of a further thirteen items. In thirty-six of the thirty-seven samples, females valued 'good financial prospects' more highly than did males, and in twenty-nine of the cultures, ambition and industriousness were significantly more desired by female respondents. In all thirty-seven cultures, men rated physical attractiveness higher than did women, and in twenty-three of them males sought chastity in potential mates more than did females. In each of the cultures studied, men preferred younger females, and women older men. Additional demographic data seemed to support these expressed preferences, with females younger than males at their actual age of marriage.

The 'qualified parental investment model' suggests that, because females invest more in a potential mate, they should therefore be more selective than men in their *overall* partner choices (Kenrick *et al.*, 1990). However, this selectivity is partly dependent on the level of the relationship. For a single date, the lack of commitment means that neither sex invests heavily, but, because the risks are greater for the woman, she is likely to be more careful in her partner choice. As both sexes are likely to invest heavily in a long-term relationship, both sexes are more equally selective in their choices of a long-term partner (Kenrick *et al.*, 1990).

In a further adaptation of socio-biological theory, this time focusing on age differences in partner preferences, Kenrick and Keefe (1992) predicted that males' preferences for young females should be minimal during early mating years, but should become more pronounced as the males age. Young females were predicted to prefer older males both during their early years and as they grew older. Kenrick and Keefe conducted a set of six studies using a variety of different data sources and analysing data across generations and in five cultures (the US, Germany, Holland, Philippines, India) with their results largely supporting these predictions. They provide a relatively complex interpretation of their findings that allows for the combined impacts of individual factors (such as attractiveness), cognitive factors (such as self-perceptions) and environmental influences (such as the availability of opposite sex partners and social norms).

Feingold conducted two meta-analyses of studies investigating the role of physical attractiveness (Feingold, 1990) and non-physical characteristics (Feingold, 1992b) in mate selection. In the first of these analyses, based upon questionnaire studies, he found that men judged physical attractiveness as more important than did women. In the second meta-analysis (Feingold, 1992b), using both questionnaire studies and personal advertisements, Feingold found women more likely to seek those characteristics judged likely to maximise the survival prospects of their offspring (ambitiousness and socio-economic status). It should be noted, however, that this meta-analysis was almost entirely based on US studies.

There are, nevertheless, a number of questions that can be raised about the conclusions reached by these socio-biological researchers, with a number

of critics questioning the extent to which socio-biological arguments illumi-
nate the *social* nature of personal relationships (e.g. Bombar, 1996). The first
question concerns the data reported by the socio-biological researchers.
Buss's own data suggests that both men and women share the same ordering
of mate preferences, preferring a kind, understanding and intelligent
partner. This finding is also consistent with other explorations into mate
selection using other samples (e.g. Goodwin, 1990; Howard *et al.*, 1987). A
closer look at Buss's cross-cultural data also reveals that far more variability
in participants' responses was explained by cultural variability than by sex
differences (Buss *et al.*, 1990). Although for two traits (good financial
prospects and good looks) gender accounted for 45 per cent and 40 per cent
of the variance respectively (far more than geographical origin) for the traits
of chastity, ambition and preferred age difference, gender accounted for only
5 per cent, 16 per cent and 11 per cent of the variance, far less than for
geographical origin (Wallen, 1989). This variability may be linked to degree
of modernity (as Buss *et al.*, 1990, suggest) or societal development (Glenn,
1989). Kenrick and Keefe's (1992) data from five cultures on age preferences
for a partner can also be questioned for its generalisability. This research was
conducted in industrialised societies, and it is questionable whether their
data fit societies such as hunter-gatherers, where older women prefer even
older men whose protective capabilities are highly restricted (Stephan, 1992).
Indeed, Kenrick and Keefe's sample was predominantly drawn from
America and Europe, with the data from India highly restrained by status
and age (the sample was of personal advertisements in a high-status news-
paper, with females aged over forty omitted).

A further problem for evolutionary accounts is the speed at which partner
preferences seem to have changed over the last fifty years. The extensive
partner preference literature shows a growing similarity in preferences over
the years (Goodwin, 1989). At the same time, there has been a marked
increase in the tendency for women to marry older men (Stevens, 1992). This
makes it hard not to interpret these sex differences in partner preferences in
terms of relatively short-term societal values/norms (reflecting social
learning rather than biology).

Socio-biological explanations now form a major area of exploration in
the personal relationships literature. At present, however, it is hard to
disagree with such commentators as Byrne and Kelley (1992: 96), who
conclude that, while socio-biological research on human relationships has
produced some fascinating and rich data, it is still a set of rather 'loosely
assembled principles [that] can be stretched and bent to accommodate
almost any empirical finding'. Thus there is a tendency to assume that the
mere existence of a particular behaviour means that it evolved through
natural selection and that it is adaptive, confusing an observed behaviour
with genetic imperatives (Bombar, 1996).

This is reminiscent of the criticisms of Darwin's own theories on evolution (Chauvin, 1980): socio-biologists often make the mistake of assuming

that the mere existence of a characteristic is indicative of its adaptive value. Furthermore, there is a tendency towards interpreting any similarity across cultures as implying biological causation, an interpretation that Kagitcibasi points out is erroneous. Similarities can imply shared biology or shared psychological/ecological/social/cultural structures, or a combination of biology and shared structures (Kagitcibasi, 1996). For example, men's widespread focus on women's attractiveness may point not so much to biological causality as to social commonalities, particularly those of patriarchy (Bombar, 1996), which is present in many societies.

This is not to totally discard all genetic/biological interpretations and to claim that all is environmentally determined (Kagitcibasi, 1996). The great majority of psychologists would stress an interactionist position for many behaviours, which explicitly acknowledges the interplay of biology and psychological and cultural factors (Abramson and Pinkerton, 1995; Voland, 1998). From this perspective, while the desire for children is likely to mean a desire for partners of child-producing/rearing age, such biological factors should be considered alongside other sociological and proximal psychological variables. To understand sexual intercourse, for example, as simply focusing on the propagation of the genes ignores the role of 'excessive' (non-adaptive) sexual desire, crucial for explaining the complexity of human sexual behaviour (Abramson and Pinkerton, 1995). Before falling into the trap of seeking the false scientific respectability that many socio-biological theories seem to offer, we need to clarify more carefully the nature of the biological imperatives that underline personal relationships, and the manner in which these imperatives may operate in the complex cultural environment in which human beings are located.

Cultural values and dimensions of culture

Suppose your fiancé(e) and your parents do not get along well. What would you do?

This everyday – but potentially explosive – question was asked by Triandis and his colleagues to respondents in four countries: The United States, Australia, Greece and Hong Kong (reported in Triandis *et al.*, 1998). More than half the Australians, but a mere three per cent of respondents in Hong Kong, said they would do 'nothing'. In contrast, more than three-quarters of the respondents in Hong Kong (but less than a quarter in Australia) would urge their fiancé(e) to make a greater effort to 'fit in' with the family.

This book is largely an attempt to explain why these large differences in response occur and persist across cultures. One problem we face when discussing different research findings across cultures is to make sense of our results in a meaningful and coherent way. While the variations in relationships between different racial and ethnic groups are often attributed to cultural differences, researchers have frequently failed to understand what it is about those 'different' groups that influence the different behaviours observed (Betancourt and Lopez, 1993). In this book I will be asking what the differences between cultures mean, and what their origins are – in the words of Lee (1987: 61): 'it is not enough to know that two or more identifiable social systems differ on some criterion ... we wish to know *why* such a difference occurs'.

One way of examining differences among cultures is to focus on differing value orientations, reflecting various dimensions of culture (Hofstede, 1994b). This has the real advantages of allowing us to integrate diverse sets of data and providing us with a basis for generating hypotheses. It can also allow us to select cultural groups for study on a theoretical basis, rather than simply 'casting around' for cultural differences between apparently 'different' cultures (Smith *et al.*, 1996). In the last two decades there have been a number of large-scale multicultural studies which aim to identify the dimensions of values on which cultures vary. Because these help us to 'make sense' of some of the systematic differences in relationships which I will discuss in this book, I will consider this work here and refer to some of the problems that such cross-cultural value comparisons need to address.

Hofstede's work on work-related values

The first, largest and most influential cross-cultural value study was conducted by Hofstede (1980, 1983, 1994a, 1994b). In one of the largest empirical studies ever undertaken in the social sciences, Hofstede (1980) collected data on employees' work experience from more than a hundred thousand IBM employees (referred to by the company pseudonym 'Hermes' in his book). This data was collected across forty countries between 1967 and 1973: in later analyses he added further countries and regions, leading to a total data set derived from fifty countries and three multi-country regions (Hofstede, 1983, 1994b).

Hofstede discovered that four, largely independent, dimensions accounted for almost half of the variance in country mean scores on thirty-two values and perceptions questions. These four dimensions he termed individualism–collectivism, power distance, uncertainty avoidance and masculinity versus femininity (Hofstede, 1994b). Following the work of Chinese Cultural Connection (CCC, 1987; Bond, 1988a) on Chinese values, Hofstede added a fifth dimension, 'Confucian dynamism'. Table 2.1 uses the data from Hofstede (1994b) and Bond (1988a) to list the top and bottom three countries on each of these five dimensions.

The dimensions identified by Hofstede have been used differently in different disciplines (Hofstede, 1994a). In psychology, the two dimensions most widely employed are individualism–collectivism and power distance (Smith and Bond, 1998), with the former attracting the most attention of all (e.g. see the collected volume edited by Kim *et al.*, 1994 and Triandis, 1995). Individualism–collectivism (I/C) concerns the relationship between the

Table 2.1 Top three and bottom three scores on Hofstede's (1994b) cultural dimensions

	Individualism –Collectivism	Power Distance	Masculinity versus Femininity	Uncertainty Avoidance	Confucian Dynamism[1]
HIGH	USA	Malaysia	Japan	Greece	China
	Australia	Guatemala	Austria	Portugal	Hong Kong
	Great Britain	Panama	Venezuela	Guatemala	Taiwan
LOW	Panama	Denmark	Netherlands	Denmark	Philippines
	Equador	Israel	Norway	Jamaica	Nigeria
	Guatemala	Austria	Sweden	Singapore	Pakistan

Source: The table is freely adapted from Hofstede (1994b). The lowest score on each dimension is the final country named.
Note:
[1]This is termed Long Term Orientation by Hofstede (1994b).

individual and the group, with the two values usually presented in the literature as representing opposing ends of one dimension. This distinction reflects a well-established polarity in the social sciences (similar divisions can be found, for example, in Tonnies's (1887/1957) distinction between *Gesellschaft* and *Gemeinschaft*, and Bakan's notion of agency and communion (Bakan, 1966)).

Individualist cultures are those where 'individuals are loosely connected, and everyone looks after their own interests or those of their immediate family' (Hofstede, 1994b: 3). Individualists have personal goals that might or might not overlap with those of their in-groups, but where there is a conflict, they put their personal goals first (Singelis *et al.*, 1995). People in individualistic societies feel autonomous, and members of these societies emphasise the 'I', the 'this interests *me*' (Yang, 1981; Triandis, 1995). In such cultures the stress is on an individual's goals, while emotional dependency is emphasised and people prefer a loosely-knit social framework. Individuals in such societies are keen to detach themselves from family, community and religion: they change friends and marital partners readily, while 'rational' principles and norms form the basis of interaction (Kim, 1994; Triandis, 1995).

Collectivism refers to the opposite pattern, representing cultures

> in which people from birth onwards are integrated into strong, cohesive in-groups, which throughout people's lifetime continue to protect them in exchange for unquestioning loyalty.
>
> (Hofstede, 1994b: 51)

In collectivist societies, the group is all-important, and there is a need for group solidarity and shared activity (Hui and Triandis, 1986). As the 'we' now dominates, obligations and duties can override personal preferences (Triandis, 1995). While collectivist societies are keen to protect and aid their in-group members, they are not necessarily so helpful to those outside this group. Group boundaries are explicit and firm, with collectivism representing an 'in-group egoism' (Hofstede, 1994a: xiii). Relationships are of prime importance, even when they are personally very costly (Singelis *et al.*, 1995), and marriage links families, rather than just mere individuals (Triandis, 1995).

Western European nations, the United States and Canada rate individualism highly, while Asian, Latin American and African nations – and many US minority groups from such regions – are more collectivist (Singelis *et al.*, 1995). 'Modern', industrialised cultures tend to be individualistic, in contrast to the more collectivist, traditional, agricultural societies (Singelis *et al.*, 1995). Hofstede reports a positive correlation between Gross Domestic Product and individualism (Hofstede, 1980, 1994b). The upper and middle classes in a society tend to be more individualistic, lower classes collectivist (although those at the very bottom of society may be more socially isolated) (Singelis *et al.*, 1995). This class pattern seems to hold even where values are undergoing rapid transition, such as in the formerly Communist Bulgaria (Goodwin, 1998; Topalova, 1997).

The identification of cultural variants is not the same as providing a theory. Cultural dimensions are very much 'second order constructs' which emerge from particular cultural histories and conditions; we still need to understand how particular positions on these variants evolved at a societal level, and what underpins movement along them. Several sets of accounts have been developed to explain the differing prevalence of individualism–collectivism across the globe. One set of accounts relates I/C to economic developments: Hofstede argues that when a country's wealth increases, individuals have at hand resources which allow them to develop their own paths, allowing collective life to be replaced by individual life (1994b: 76). In contrast, individuals in poorer countries are more dependent on one another and need to share limited resources. In a complex and affluent society people are financially independent; this leads to social and emotional independence, with priority being given to personal goals over those of the in-group (Triandis, 1989). Economic development may also lead to the development of new social relationships that take people away from their pre-established collectives, and a new emphasis on education that often accompanies an increase in individualism (Reykowski, 1994).

A second set of explanations for the development of individualism focuses on religion (Kim *et al.*, 1994). Confucianism promotes collective welfare and harmony, resulting in psychological collectivism. Individualism and collectivism may follow a Protestant–Catholic divide (Trompenaars, 1993). Thus Trompenaars found that Latin Catholic cultures scored lower on his measure of individualism than those in the Protestant West.

Finally, geographical factors may be significant in the promotion of individualism–collectivism, and there is some clustering of individualist–collectivist cultures by region (Triandis, 1995; Van de Vliert and Huismans,

1998). This might be largely related to climate: countries with colder climates tend to be more individualistic, reflecting a possible dependence for survival on personal initiative (Hofstede, 1994b; Van de Vliert and Huismans, 1998).

One interesting study that combines many of these explanations examined how individualism grew in the former Marxist–Leninist systems of Eastern Europe (Hillhouse, 1993). Hillhouse argues that the Berlin Wall fell because, although East Germany was moving speedily towards an individualistic society, the State system could not adapt fast enough to rapid social transitions. In a longitudinal study of attitude change, Hillhouse examined large-scale public opinion surveys and reports produced by the Central Institute for Research on the Youth of the GDR between the early 1960s and the fall of the Berlin Wall in 1989. A sharp improvement in economic conditions, the restructuring of the economy, the reorganisation and specialisation of work, the emergence of new social groups and multiple group identities outside of the political sphere (such as sporting, religious and other leisure groups), and the high levels of West German media exposure, culminated in a whole range of new social opportunities which emphasised the development of various aspects of individuality. Young people increasingly stressed the importance of personal relationship fulfilment above that of community involvement or political participation, and hankered after individual expression through adventures (which included the formation of new, non-traditional sexual alliances). Ironically, Hillhouse argues, it was the very attempts of the Communist regime to adapt to this individuation, to 'move with the times', that seemed to accelerate its decline, leading to the fall of the regime and the growth of the democratisation movement.

A second of Hofstede's dimensions, *power distance*, is also widely discussed in the cross-cultural literature. Power distance represents 'the extent to which members of a society accept that power in institutions and organisations is distributed unequally' (Hofstede, 1983: 336ff), and examines prevailing norms of inequality within a culture and the degree of respect and deference given to those in superior positions. People in high distance cultures see power as a basic fact of society, and stress coercive power. Those in low distance societies believe power should be only used when it is legitimate.

Individualistic societies tend to be low on power distance; indeed, Hofstede (1994b) reports a high correlation between power distance and collectivism, although this correlation disappears when economic development is partialled out of the analysis (in other words, if rich countries are compared only to rich countries, and poor countries to poor countries). People in high power distance cultures experience greater uncertainty and anxiety when communicating with people higher in status than do members of low power distance cultures. The Japanese, for example, with a relatively recent feudal background built on hereditary power and aristocratic rule, accept status differentials as natural, and interpersonal relationships and groups are highly structured to reflect these (Reischauer, 1988). This is *not* the same as social class distinction and does not necessitate autocratic rule – in democratic Japan, sense of class is very weak and the spread of income is relatively flat compared to other cultures, such as that of the US (Reischauer, 1988).

Hofstede's third dimension, masculinity versus femininity, reflects 'a preference for achievement, heroism, assertiveness, and material success as opposed to … a preference for relationships, modesty, caring for the weak, and the quality of life' (Hofstede, 1983: 337). Masculinity/femininity concerns the relative emphasis on achievement and interpersonal harmony, and is concerned with the social implications of being male or female (Hofstede, 1994b: 14). Feminine cultures stress quality of life, nurturance, warm personal relationships and fluid sex roles. In 'masculine' cultures competition, success and performance are more prevalent values, and there is a greater emphasis on sex-role differentiation.

Hofstede's fourth dimension, uncertainty avoidance, reflects 'the extent to which members of a culture feel threatened by uncertain or unknown situations' (1994b: 113.) Hofstede (1994b) puts this pithily: in high uncertainty avoidance cultures, 'what is different is dangerous': in low uncertainty avoidance cultures, 'what is different is curious'. Uncertainty avoidance concerns planning and stability as a way of dealing with life's uncertainties: those high on uncertainty avoidance have a strong desire for consensus, and deviant behaviour is unacceptable. Because high uncertainty avoidance cultures provide rules for dealing with other group members, individuals in high uncertainty avoidance cultures do not judge inter-group interactions to be as difficult as those in low uncertainty avoidance cultures. High uncertainty avoidance cultures are evident in Latin America, Latin Europe and the Mediterranean, whereas Denmark, Jamaica and Singapore score low on this dimension.

One frequent criticism of Hofstede's work has been that it was based on concepts derived from Western research. Bond and his colleagues recognised this and attempted to look at values from a Chinese perspective by asking Chinese social scientists to list at least ten fundamental Chinese values. These were then used to construct a forty-item scale administered to students in twenty-three countries.

In Bond's analysis, a main factor for individualism emerged, while a secondary analysis of the data revealed four factors. While three of these overlapped with Hofstede's conceptions (individualism–collectivism, power distance and masculinity/femininity), a new dimension for comparison across cultures emerged, which Bond termed Confucian dynamism (Bond, 1988a; Chinese Culture Connection, 1987). This long-term orientation is characterised by persistence, the ordering of relationships by status, thrift and having a sense of shame. It was positively correlated with national *growth* (Bond, 1988b; Hofstede, 1994b), and has thus been of particular interest in explaining the rise of the 'tiger economies' of the Far East, who typically score highly on this variable.

Trompenaars' study

Like Hofstede, Trompenaars was also interested in the relationship between cultural values and the world of work. He assessed some 15,000 employees from a total of forty-seven wide-ranging cultures, presenting them with dilemmas aimed at tapping core cultural values. Trompenaars describes seven dimensions of cultural values, five of which concern the ways in which we relate to one another. *Individualism–collectivism* was discussed above. *Universalism–particularism* compares generalist rules about what is right with more situation-specific relationship obligations and unique circumstances. A *particularist* might feel they should 'bend' official rules for a friend, a deviation which might be abhorred by a universalist. For example, the Japanese are often characterised as being highly particularistic in their relationships (Reischauer, 1988). This arises, according to some (e.g. De Vos, 1960), from a morality based on a high degree of family orientation. Although there are clear concepts of universal right and wrong in this as well as in all other societies (Reischauer, 1988), there may be little discomfort for the Japanese where there is an apparent dichotomy between universal principles and those actions which fit in with particular group relations.

 Neutral versus emotional relationship orientations compare 'objective' and 'detached' interactions with interactions where emotion is more readily expressed. For example, people in a neutral culture would keep emotions closely under control in many settings, while in a highly emotional culture (such as that of Italy) people will willingly show their feelings. The dimension of *specific versus diffuse orientations* builds on Lewin's (1936) notion of 'life space' and compares those diffuse situations in which a 'whole person' is involved in a business relationship (including those areas of life little related to business connections) with those in which private and work encounters are demarcated and 'segregated-out'. Finally, *achievement versus ascription* compares cultural groups which make their judgements of others on actual individual accomplishments (achievement oriented societies) with those where a person is ascribed status on grounds of birth, group membership or similar criteria. For example, while some 77 per cent of North Americans disagreed that a person's status depends on their family background, such disagreement was expressed by only 23 per cent of those in Nepal (Trompenaars, 1993). Trompenaars' groupings of cultural values have particular relevance for work relationships in the workplace. I therefore make detailed reference to these values again in Chapter 7.

Schwartz's value dimensions

One further set of studies on cultural values has been conducted by the Israeli social scientist Shalom Schwartz. He is critical of the simple individualism–collectivism divide, seeing culture as complex and multidimensional (Schwartz and Bilsky, 1990). Schwartz has now gathered a large data base comprising data from more than fifty countries (Schwartz, 1997). In most cases, data has been collected from two samples in each country – school teachers and university students, although in seven nations this data was complemented with data from nationally representative samples.

As is the case with most of the research on cultural values, Schwartz focuses on values well-established in Western research for his work, although he does conduct extensive analysis of the suitability of the items in each country, and researchers were permitted to add additional items where appropriate. Schwartz and his colleagues (e.g. Schwartz, 1992; Sagiv and Schwartz, 1995) demonstrated that forty-five of his original fifty-six values have similar meanings across cultures, and can be mapped into ten value types. These value types are organised along the dimensions of openness to change versus conservation, and self-transcendence (universalism and benevolence) versus self-enhancement (achievement and power). These ten value types have then been used in a number of settings – for example, Sagiv and Schwartz (1995: study 1) found that Israeli Jews who held strong universalism values were more willing to make out-group contact, while those with strongly traditional or conformist values were more hostile to such contacts.

Schwartz then goes on to average the value scores across the individuals in each country to provide a country-level analysis which allows us to compare nations on their values (Schwartz, 1994). This is different from an individual-level value analysis because, while individual values concern how differences between individual beliefs or behaviour relate to individual differences in value priorities, a cultural analysis is concerned with differences in cultural symbol systems and institutions. Schwartz's 'cultural-level' analysis focuses on seven value types falling along three dimensions. These he characterises as *conservatism versus affective/intellectual autonomy*; *hierarchy versus egalitarianism* and *harmony versus mastery*. *Conservatism* emphasises maintenance of the status quo, while *intellectual autonomy* emphasises creativity and *affective autonomy* emphasises the desire for pleasure and an exciting life. *Egalitarian commitment* reflects a belief in freedom and equality and a concern for others, while *hierarchy* emphasises the legitimacy of fixed roles and resources. *Mastery* is concerned with overcoming obstacles in the social environment – getting on through active self-assertion – while *harmony* concerns beliefs about unity with nature and fitting harmoniously into the environment.

Schwartz's data is complex, and the relationship between his dimensions and those of other researchers is not always what we might predict. Thus, while Schwartz (1994) does find that *individualism* is positively correlated with *autonomy* and negatively correlated with *conservatism* (as we would expect), he unexpectedly finds individualism to be positively correlated with egalitarian commitment (indeed the very notion of voluntary action seems to be an important part of an autonomous, individualistic, society). Furthermore, hierarchy and power distance do not overlap in the way we would predict, reflecting perhaps the different focus of the researchers who use these terms. Thus Schwartz argues that hierarchy is about power in general, while Hofstede's dimension focuses on employees' relationships with their employers.

When we look at the culture-level scores, the data produced by Schwartz is also somewhat surprising. First, if we consider *autonomy* to indicate individualism, the United States is not as individualistic as we might expect. Instead, the most individualistic nations are Western European, where people also believe in egalitarian commitment (i.e. the voluntarily helping of others). The US, however, places great value on *mastery*: mastering the environment is very significant for an entrepreneurial culture. China is often taken as one of the clearest examples of collectivism (Triandis, 1995), However, while China does score highly on hierarchical distinctions (usually correlated with collectivism), Chinese subjects also scored high on mastery, which can be interpreted as one reason for the strong entrepreneurial spirit in this country. The most 'collectivist' country is Singapore, which scores high on conservatism and hierarchy, but low on autonomy and mastery of the social environment.

The four elementary forms of sociality

One final scheme for categorising cultures is presented by Alan Fiske (e.g. Fiske, 1992), and is particularly concerned with relationship behaviour. Fiske suggests that there are four relational models or mental schemes which people use to construct and interpret the many different aspects of their social life. These models he terms communal sharing, authority ranking, equality matching and market pricing.

Communal sharing relationships (CS) see the members of a particular group as equivalent and undifferentiated. Group members favour their own group, and can be highly hostile to those outside that group. People pool their resources and work collectively, and desire to be like others in their group and to conform. They desire to be physically close to one another and are strongly traditional in their customs. Community sharing can be seen as the predominant approach to personal relationships in countries such as Japan. The reader will probably already be aware that this concept is very close to that of collectivism described above.

Authority ranking relationships (AR) involve a linear ordering of relations, with people high in rank having not only prestige, privileges and decision-making rights, but also possibly some responsibility for those lower down the hierarchy. Again, this concept has considerable conceptual overlap with Hofstede's notion of power distance. At the individual level, this is about 'knowing one's place'; at the cultural level, an individual is defined in terms of the authority they have. Examples would be filial piety, devotion to the emperor and the worship of ancestors, as found in China.

Equality matching relationships (EM) stress equality in social relations. These relations are manifested by turn-taking, equal contributions, an egalitarian distribution and balanced reciprocity. People in EM relationships are aware of where imbalances occur and, operating under the 'norm of reciprocity' (Gouldner, 1960), such people are keen to make amends.

Finally, market pricing relationships (MP) involve a rational cost–benefit analysis. While EM is about social exchange and the implicit sense of obligation, MP is more distrusting and concerns strictly economic exchanges. People think in terms of prices or investment returns. Such an orientation is likely to be more central in Western societies, although it appears to be present to some degree in most societies.

These four types of relationship models are rarely used alone, but are likely to be combined across different situations. They form the 'building blocks' of social interactions, and can be nested together in different interactions and at different stages of an interaction. Fiske (1992: 690) claims: 'the same four structures appear at all levels of social intercourse in diverse types of societies around the world'. Furthermore, there are likely to be common denominators in the operation of these relationship modes: for example, CS relationships are likely to occur between young children in most cultures, while EM is likely to occur between peers. However, this does not mean that these forms of sociality are 'culture free'; different cultures have rules as to when a particular model can be applied in practice, how to execute each model, and different levels of sanctions for violation of these rules. Fiske (1992) gives the example of how the authoritarian action of a brother towards his sister may be seen as unjust in an EM culture but perfectly just in a culture which stresses authority ranking for opposite-sex siblings. Similarly, communal sharing practices may contribute to living conditions that, in another culture, would be seen insufferable.

Overlap between schemas

As the reader may have noted, there is some considerable overlap between the four forms of social relations and the work of the Chinese Culture Connection, Trompenaars, Schwartz and Hofstede. Other sets of similar cultural dimensions also show considerable overlap but are not considered here. For example, Mary Douglas's classification of cultures (e.g. Douglas, 1970, 1982) also embodies concepts of individualism–collectivism, hierarchy, mastery and egalitarianism. In this book we will be drawing most heavily on Hofstede's dimensions, in particular that of individualism–collectivism, not only because of its conceptual overlap with the other dimensions discussed but because it is this dimension that has received the most attention in the relationships field. The studies carried out by Schwartz, Trompenaars and Fiske do, however, alert us to other aspects of cultural relations which should not be neglected, and in particular may help us identify where conflicts may occur in the value systems of a particular culture.

Smith and Schwartz (1997), Singelis *et al.* (1995) and Triandis (1995) posit two dimensions that appear to be consistent across different studies. The first dimension deals with the preferred cultural view of individual–group relations and the second one concerns perceptions of hierarchy. While these may seem to be simple reflections of our old friends individualism–collectivism and power distance, by treating these as separate dimensions we can obtain a four-way classification of cultures which embraces Schwartz's (1994) earlier findings that collectivism can occur in either a hierarchical or an egalitarian context. This also overlaps with cultural dimensions of grid ('the extent of regulation sought in any social setting': Douglas, 1982: 3) and group ('the degree to which a person is incorporated into and surrounded and dominated by a cohesive social group': Bloor and Bloor, 1976: 1). Table 2.2 outlines this classification.

In vertical collectivist cultures, such as the Pacific Asian nations, there is hierarchy in a collectivist context and an acceptance of inequality. In such societies members of the in-group are different from each other, some having more status than others. This overlaps with Fiske's (1992) communal sharing and authority ranking, Douglas's (1970) hierarchical culture and Schwartz's collectivism and hierarchy. Singelis *et al.* (1995) argue that this may be the most *essential* aspect of collectivism as represented in the existing literature. Singapore is an example of such a culture (Triandis, 1995).

Horizontal collectivist cultures, such as some those found in both Southern European nations and Israeli Kibbutzim, view equality in a collectivist context, with all members of the collective treated in a similar manner (Smith and Bond, 1998). Here we have Fiske's (1992) communal sharing and equality matching and Schwartz's (1994) collectivism and harmony. Slovakia is a further good example of such a country (Triandis, 1995).

'Particularist' or 'vertical individualist' cultures represents individualism within an unequal society, a combination of autonomy–individualism and a hierarchical culture. Here individuals see each other as different, and inequality is expected. Competition is important here. This is particularly

Table 2.2   Examples from the four dimensions of culture

	Collectivist cultures	*Individualist cultures*
Vertical cultures	Hierarchical and collectivist e.g. Pacific Asia	Hierarchical and individualist e.g. Modern Russia
Horizontal cultures	Egalitarian and collectivist e.g. Israeli Kibbutz	Egalitarian and individualist e.g. Sweden

Source: Derived from Smith and Schwartz (1997), Singelis *et al.* (1995) and Triandis (1995).

characteristic of Central and Eastern European states, which also exhibit the fatalism that Douglas (1982) sees as characteristic of low group membership in a situation where strong social rules operate. This overlaps with Fiske's (1992) market pricing and authority ranking. Using Schwartz's (1994) data, Triandis (1995) sees former Eastern Germany as a further good example of a vertical individualist society.

Finally, we have 'universalist'–'horizontal individualist' cultures. In these societies, individualism occurs in a lower power distance context, helping explain the universalist generosity of the church jumble sale in individualist cultures, and the horizontal individualist cultures of Australia and Denmark, where 'tall poppies' are gleefully brought down in status (Singelis *et al.*, 1995). This is also reminiscent of Fiske's market pricing and equality matching, Douglas's (1982) individualists, and Schwartz's (1994) individualism and harmony. Triandis (1995) sees Italy as a good example of such a society.

Some important caveats in dimensionalising cultural values

In this book we will be making great use of this concept of cultural dimensions, and in particular the dimensions of individualism–collectivism. These are the best tools we have available for summarising a great deal of work, but it should be noted that a large number of questions remain as to how exactly these concepts 'work' in real-life relationships. As one leading commentator notes in her discussions of individualism–collectivism, these concepts often suffer from the same weaknesses as the concept of 'culture' in that they are too readily used to explain everything that occurs in a society (Kagitcibasi, 1990, 1994).

Probably the most frequently discussed problem is the multidimensional nature of individualism and collectivism (Kim *et al.*, 1994; Schwartz and Bilsky, 1990). We can be both individualist in some situations and collectivist in others (Schneider *et al.*, 1997). Sinha and Tripathi (1994) and Mishra (1994) demonstrate how, in Indian cultures, the boundary of the self may shift constantly with the context, leading to an apparent coexistence of opposites. For example, collectivist values may be important in family settings but self-control and meditation are an important feature of religious practices. Their coexistence model suggests that, while individualists may have 'one' self, in some collectivist cultures individuals may have two, the private and the public (Kim, 1994). Thus the relational mode for close relationships can stress 'oneness' while the coexistence mode for public performances can emphasise 'sameness'. This 'oneness' of relationships does not, however, mean sacrificing all to the group; instead, individuals are taught to align their own self-fulfilment goals with those of the group (Kim, 1994). An example of the limits of a simple individualism–collectivism divide can be found in Japan. Japan is a culture often viewed as highly collectivist (although, interestingly, it is only mid-table on individualism–collectivism in Hofstede's 1980 listing of cultures). In Japan there appears to be a great deal of conformity in style of dress and conduct within the in-group, and although there is evidence of a search for individual self-expression, particularly among the young, the concept of 'individualism' (*kojin-shugi*) may be seen as expressing selfishness (Reischauer, 1988). However, perhaps reflecting Japan's positioning in Hofstede's list, a Western view of the Japanese as obedient robots simply obeying rigid rules is erroneous, ignoring the dynamism and rapid change evident in this culture (Reischauer, 1988). There is also a strong individuality expressed through the taking of classes and the adoption of specific interests, reflecting 'tastes' which should not be seen as simple hobbies but reflecting the multiple groups to which a Japanese person might belong (Reischauer, 1988). Furthermore, the cooperation and group orientation of the Japanese should not be seen as an example of blandness and simple conformity, but as an example of strong inner control and control over their less rational instincts (Reischauer, 1988). The self is probably therefore multiple in all cultures, and simple dichotomies which compare the collectivist inter-connected self with the American individualised self are too simplistic (Rosenberger, 1992b).

Different societies also have different 'group' identifications. In France, identification might be with the country or the family; in Japan with the corporation (Trompenaars, 1993). Collectivism is largely defined by context, group or relationship-specific attitudes, beliefs or behaviours, thus making group variability essential for an understanding of individualism–collectivism (Matsumoto *et al.*, 1997). Unfortunately, the range of social relationships which should therefore be separately studied is rarely assessed in individualism–collectivism measures (although see Matsumoto *et al.*, 1997, for a new measure). Often the concepts used are very loosely defined, and as a consequence it is hard to be sure that they mean the same in each cultural sample and to control for confounding variables (Fijneman *et al.* 1996; Schwartz, 1994). Perhaps unsurprisingly, therefore, problems with the statistical reliability of the measures of individualism–collectivism are widespread, with the most widely used measures of individualism–collectivism being low in *internal reliability* (i.e. the various questions asked do not correlate together in the way one would expect a set of items to inter-relate) (Singelis *et al.*, 1995; Smith, 1993).

When we turn to the actual use of data based on cultural dimensions, one frequent error is to use single cultural scores to interpret individuals' behaviour, an error often referred to as the *ecological fallacy* (Kim *et al.*, 1994). Most of the cultural dimensions discussed reflect *central tendencies* in cultural values, rather than the scores of individuals within those cultures. As a result, data has been analysed on a *cultural level*, with scores being the average for those cultures. However, the culture of a country is not a simple aggregate of 'average citizens' but a set of likely reactions of people who share a common mental programming, and it reflects a statistical tendency within a society (Hofstede, 1994b). There is considerable room for individual variation, particularly given the selective samples from which the data is usually derived (Cha, 1994; Hofstede, 1994b).

Because of *within-cultural* variations, Triandis *et al.* (1985) refer to the personality dimensions of idiocentrism and allocentrism, concepts which can be paired with the culture-wide concepts of individualism–collectivism. Markus and Kitayama (1991) similarly talk of the independent self and the interdependent self to reflect these cultural dimensions, while Kagitcibasi (1996) refers to separateness versus relatedness of self. Unfortunately, these *individual*-level concepts, most appropriate for measuring *individuals*, have as yet only been occasionally applied to the study of personal relationships. Furthermore, as yet we do not know what encourages an individual to be idiocentric or allocentric, how fluid this individual variability is likely to be across domains, and the consequences of this 'deviancy' for the individual concerned. Finally, expressed cultural values are not necessarily the same as behaviours (Han and Choe, 1994). Thus, while people may have become more individualistic in their attitudes in many collectivist societies, most people in these societies, even if idiocentric in their individual attitudes, show *behaviours* that comply with the norms. The disparity between cultural rules and individual behaviours may be particularly large in autocratic societies where what one does might be very different from one's actual beliefs (Alechina *et al.*, 1997).

Much of the work that uses cultural dimensions must be firmly located within the confines of the values tested and the samples used. Hofstede's classic work on cultural values has often been criticised for reflecting his own beliefs about what is and is not an appropriate measure of a value, and certainly many of his items had significant loadings on more than one factor (Fernandez *et al.*, 1997). For obvious reasons of practicality, most of the data collected in the large-scale studies discussed above has been collected primarily from middle-class professional employees (Hofstede and Trompenaars) or students and teachers (Chinese Culture Connection and Schwartz). While Hofstede (1994b) argues that matching workers in different countries is a strength of his analysis, there may be considerable divergence between these groups and other members of their countries' populations (a point Hofstede (1994b) recognises himself). Indeed, the very *meaning* and *actual practice* of doing the same jobs in different countries may be quite different. Relatively little data has been gathered in Africa or in Communist societies, despite the apparently unique clustering of values of the latter societies (Bardi and Schwartz, 1996; Smith *et al.*, 1996). There is also evidence of important cultural changes in values since the collection of the most influential data set, that of Hofstede. Using new scales, Fernandez *et al.* (1997) examined time differences over the twenty-five years since Hofstede's study. During this period, they argue, Japan has become less uncertainty avoidance oriented, Mexico has become more individually oriented, and Germany and the US have become more feminine. This alerts us to the importance of attending carefully to the groups sampled and the date of the study when considering cross-cultural variations in personal relationships.

Finally, writing from Turkey, Kagitcibasi also notes how the concept of individualism–collectivism is value-laden (Kagitcibasi, 1994, 1996), with collectivism in particular suggesting a blind conformity to the group and lack of individuation. Westerners living in 'developed' and 'modern' societies see themselves as rational, logical creatures, unmarred by the collective's cohesion which smacks of patronage, emotionality and superstition. Consequently, groups such as the Japanese are seen either as simple, disciplined and submissive with little internal autonomy, or suppressed and resentful, so 'bottled up' by society that they are always prone to violence against others from the out-group (Rosenberger, 1992a). Kagitcibasi goes on to remark that the assumed movement from collectivism towards individualism is similar to earlier debates about modernisation which made little progress. Instead, it is probably more accurate to see certain aspects of individualism–collectivism as changing as a result of changing lifestyles (such as group memberships), but at the same time to recognise that the way in which an individual relates to these groups may stay the same. We discuss this in more detail in the final section of this chapter and again in Chapter 6.

Ecological explanations of behaviour

For some, broad patterns in social behaviour may be attributed less to variations along cultural dimensions and more to socio-cultural or physical environmental influences, with differences in behavioural repertoires a direct function of such differences (Fijneman *et al.*, 1996). Theorists interested in an ecological perspective, such as John Berry (e.g. Berry, 1994), are interested in how factors such as climate and socio-political factors affect our behaviours. They are particularly concerned with the natural conditions affecting food production, and the implications this has for societal functioning. From this perspective, ecological forces are the main shapers of culture and behaviour, constraining, pressurising and nurturing cultural norms which in turn shape behaviour. Influences on individual development are both direct from the ecological surroundings, and indirect (mediated by culture and biology). Humans are seen as adapting to their ecological contexts, with individual psychological characteristics developing out of these contexts (Segall *et al.*, 1990). Most complex behaviours, and the cultural recipes for them, are selected for their adaptive character and transmitted intergenerationally through the socialisation of the young (Segall *et al.*, 1990).

This work has been particularly influential in explaining adaptations in family patterns (Lee, 1987). Historically, the extended family has tended to coincide with agricultural economies as agriculture requires large numbers of people for it to be maximally efficient. Agriculture offers the advantage to the younger generation of inherited property, which can provide an important source of future income. In contrast, hunter-gatherer societies, and more recently industrial societies, require mobility and promote nuclear family formations. Furthermore, in industrial societies the greater premium on individual achievement may weaken the traditional authority structures associated with the extended family (Lee, 1987).

From Cole's ecological perspective (e.g. Cole, 1990), culture itself represents a group's response to the physical ecology. In Cole's framework, this group response first leads to the evolution of technology, which then frames future economic activity, which in turn shapes social organisation, the division of labour, and then child-rearing habits and mental characteristics (Cole, 1990). Cole's own call for 'cultural psychology' is echoed in the present book, encouraging a movement away from simple universal laws towards the embracing of cultural diversity. This should not mean that we should reject any regularities in personal relationships (Jahoda, 1990), but it does alert us to simplistic statements about universal processes and makes us challenge why particular behaviours and attitudes have evolved.

Although ecological accounts of the family have been primarily applied to the study of pre-industrial societies, some of the debates concerning the adoption of 'modern' values in industrial settings can be interpreted within a 'speeded-up' ecological theory that involves the study of change within a short-time framework. Thus, from Inkeles' (1977) Marxist perspective, particular institutional environments encourage personal efficacy, openness to experience and other characteristics central to the modernisation process. In a more complex analysis of socialisation and educational values, Tudge *et al.* (1997) combined Vygotsky's cultural–historical theory with Bronfenbrenner's ecological systems theory to demonstrate the way in which human activity is both individually and socially located. Tudge and his colleagues show that education and social class are important in the way in which parents encourage self-direction in a child. At the same time, physical conditions dictate variability in this process, as his analysis of four very different environments demonstrates (this work was conducted in Russia, Estonia, South Korea and the United States). Furthermore, different children interpret the cultural messages being provided by both their society and their parents in a different manner, transforming the message themselves in subtle and novel ways.

The ecological perspective offers a powerful approach to understanding many aspects of relationships across the world. By recognising the importance of the 'material realities' of many aspects of relational life, it can incorporate observations from a number of different theoretical perspectives (forming an unlikely liaison between Marxist and Functionalist perspectives). It also provides an important challenge to researchers to develop theories for the evolution of cultural values, and raises important questions about the ways in which cultural values may change. However, as is the case with broad biological theories of evolution, there have been few examinations of directly testable hypotheses from an ecological viewpoint, and thus little opportunity to directly define what is, and is not, adaptive behaviour in the personal relationship field. Thus, while I will often refer to adaptations in the later chapters of this book, it should be acknowledged that there still remain important questions about whether the behaviour that emerges was the 'most' adaptive/suitable behaviour in that ecological context.

Personal relationships in a changing world

There can be little doubt that the last four decades have seen huge demographic changes across the world. The 1950s witnessed a great movement of peoples from isolated and tradition-oriented societies to urban areas, and the period since then has witnessed large-scale ecological change (e.g. deforestation), large increases in population in most societies, as well as new educational opportunities for hundreds of millions of people (Stanton, 1995). The lifestyle impact of these changes has undoubtedly been profound (Stanton, 1995). Stanton uses the example of the inhabitants of Polynesia over the last four decades to underline this point. In 1950, only a handful of Polynesians had ever left their home villages. Within just one generation, more than half of all Cook Islanders moved to New Zealand, and one-third of all Tongans now live in Australia, New Zealand or the United States. This has had a dramatic impact on the family living arrangements of these islanders, the nature of the work pursued by these migrants, and the languages spoken – and values adopted – by the new generations.

One constant theme of this book is an emphasis on *social change*, and in particular the way in which large-scale changes in societies may influence the ways in which people relate to one other. While we can never be completely sure how changes in economic/political reality impact on people's relationships with one another (Schneider *et al.*, 1997), I now go on to review three important issues that have greatly occupied social scientists interested in relationships and relational change. First, I consider the effects of 'modernisation' on the nature of personal relationships. I then discuss the way in which attitudes about relationships and appropriate relationship behaviour may be transmitted between groups and across generations. Finally, I consider the way in which a change in cultural locality may influence the relationships of acculturating individuals and groups.

The modernisation hypothesis

'Modernisation' is a much-discussed but little-understood process. As a concept, it is often linked, albeit contentiously, to concepts such as 'civilisation', 'Europeanisation', 'economic development', 'Westernisation' and 'individualism', among others (Segall *et al.*, 1990). Although modernisation can be seen as operating at both the national or the regional levels and the more individual level, it is usually discussed in relation to the national level. Modernisation is associated with a number of inter-related variables, including the movement of large populations from the town to the country, industrialisation, the development of mass communications, a widening of political involvement and the introduction of formal education (Segall *et al.*, 1990; K. S. Yang, 1988, 1996). In some areas, such as parts of Africa, the concept (if not the reality) of modernisation also includes an increase in water supplies, health improvements, and the development of a cash economy (Super and Harkness, 1997). Some theorists (such as McClelland, 1961) have argued that certain individual values are necessary prior to modernisation (in his case, the emphasis was on a need for achievement), while others have focused on the influence of structural and cultural changes on the rise of 'modern' attitudes (Segall *et al.*, 1990).

The 'modern' person is viewed as having a number of characteristics, usually seen as a constellation of attitudes, values, needs and 'modes of acting' (Inkeles, 1977). For the 'modern' person, personal relationships, and in particular kin networks, are seen to be of lesser importance than they are in 'traditional' societies. 'Modern' behaviour is 'rational' rather than 'traditional', and change is seen as both normal and desirable (Boudon, 1986). Some of the characteristics associated with modernisation seem highly admirable (examples include an openness to change, tolerance and respect of others, egalitarian family role structure (e.g. Inkeles, 1977)). Other effects of modernisation are arguably far less positive. According to Parsons (1943) and Goode (1963), the modernisation of socio-professional structures is destructive of the traditional type of family. Others have pointed to the alienation and anomie associated with modernisation, as a range of friendships and work relationships are undermined (Rosenberger, 1992a; Yang, 1986, 1996). Modernisation often presents individuals and families with critical choices which may have long-term impacts. Super and Harkness (1997), in their analysis of Kenyan families, claim that the choices made by members of one generation with regard to agricultural methods, schooling and marital relations can have a dramatic impact on the development of future generations.

Ritzer (1993) offers a similar notion of modernisation, one that he terms 'McDonaldization', which he sees as an updated version of Weber's concept of rationalisation (Weber, 1921/1968). According to Ritzer, McDonaldization affects not only the fast-food business but also education, work, travel, leisure-time activities, dieting, politics, the family 'and virtually every other sector of society' (Ritzer 1993: 1). It is also 'engulfing more and more sectors of society and areas of the world' (Ritzer 1993: 16). This rationalisation process helps explain the 'generally false and insincere camaraderie' characteristic of fast-food restaurants and 'all other elements of our McDonaldized society' (Ritzer 1993: 85). In addition it leads to a sense of job dissatisfaction and alienation among those who work in these restaurants, and the decline of relationships between members of staff, between customers and staff, and even between customers and customers (Ritzer claims it is practically impossible to hold a meaningful conversation in a McDonald's). Ritzer sums this up nicely in his discussion of those fast-food workers who say 'nice day' as the customer is leaving:

> In fact, of course, they have no real interest in, or concern for, how the rest of one's day goes. Again, in a polite and ritualized way, they are really telling us to 'get lost', to move on so someone else can be served.
>
> (Ritzer, 1993: 134f)

Ritzer further relates this McDonaldization to the 'disintegration of the family', where TV dinners have lost their socially binding roles and provide minimal opportunity for meaningful interaction.

Such concepts of modernisation, however, have recently attracted much criticism. Some have simply argued that there has in fact been little systematic convergence of values across the globe (Hofstede, 1994b). The assumption that modernisation and individualism follow industrialisation (see, for example, the link between individualism and Gross National Product noted by Hofstede, 1980) can also be challenged by historical data, notably from Britain where the nuclear family long preceded industrialisation (Kagitcibasi, 1996; Wagels and Roemhild, 1998). Indeed, even the notion that there was a simple 'English Industrial Revolution' can be questioned, as the 'event' in question took place over a period extending from the thirteenth to the nineteenth century (Schumpeter, 1954).

Many commentators have noted that modernisation is not a uniform phenomenon but has a number of different components (e.g. K. S. Yang, 1988), with people who are going through a process of modernisation also retaining many of their traditional beliefs (Lee, 1987; Yang, 1986). Here the objections frequently mirror those levelled at a simple individualism–collectivism divide, discussed above. Kagitcibasi (1994, 1996) suggests that the notion that 'developing' societies are 'evolving' towards the Western pattern can be severely challenged in the area of personal relations. Consider the example of nations such as Japan and the new 'dragons' of the Far East. Although there has been rapid industrialisation and urbanisation in these countries, there is little evidence of the decline in personal relatedness between individuals in these societies. Indeed, it is the very collectivist–interdependent family pattern that has helped stimulate successes in the workplace (Kagitcibasi, 1996). The Japanese may have taken on some concepts and accompaniments of the 'modern' world on the 'outside' (such as Western clothes), but these are integrated with other, more traditional, behaviours (Rosenberger, 1992a). In South Korea, friends visiting a McDonald's will act in a 'collectivist' manner, pouring the contents of their packets of chips onto a tray and eating together from the pile (Watson, 1998). Thus modernisation operates within the unique cultural 'equipment' of a society (Befu, 1968), building on the foundations of a traditional culture (Reischauer, 1988: 172).

Overall, the notion that human history is moving towards a simple point of progress can be seen as highly problematic (Wagels and Roemhild, 1998). Instead of a coherent pattern of 'modernity', those characteristics that meet the demands of urban living are more likely to be accepted while those that do not have largely failed to survive. An example of the complex ways in which traditional practices can exist even in 'modern' societies such as Germany is provided by Bruno Hildenbrand in his examination of the family farm in West Germany (Hildenbrand, 1989). Here the situation seemed ripe for conflict: traditional models of orientation towards the farm and its continuity were echoed in traditional patriarchal family lifestyles, and the modernisation of labour threatened to introduce new lifestyles and attitudes which seemed to endanger the 'traditional' family structure. However, the individual parties concerned seemed able to maintain two apparently opposing orientations: on the one hand, they embraced modernisation, learning the new skills necessary to ensure the farm survived; and on the other hand they maintained traditions such as the communal sharing of income from any work outside the farm as well as important family rituals such as the common midday meal. Thus the older patriarchal and authoritarian family format disappeared but was replaced by a strong core family, apparently well suited to modern agricultural demands.

The transmission of ideas: the theory of social representations

How do cultural values spread within a society? How, in Inkeles' words, do people 'become modern?' (Inkeles, 1977). While it is common to see values such as 'modernity' as a product of the early family environment (e.g. Klineberg, 1973), it is often far from clear how such values may be transmitted, as broad notions of 'socialisation' are rarely defined. Furthermore, as noted above, linking concepts such as liberalism with the growth of individualism (Kim *et al.*, 1994) fails to address how the transmission from a cultural norm to an individual behaviour or belief takes place.

Every society is full of artefacts and norms or rules that help maintain and bolster cultural values (Kitayama, 1992). These ideas become shared among members of a society who take them for granted. Adapting Durkheim's notion of representation collective (1898), Moscovici examines what he terms 'social representations', which he defines as 'sets of concepts, statements, and explanations originating in daily life in the course of interindividual communications' (Moscovici, 1981: 181). These social representations are created and shaped by individuals through everyday interactions and conversations. Social representations are the equivalent in our society of the myths and belief systems of traditional societies – a kind of modern 'common sense'. They can be seen as the contents of everyday thinking, the stock of ideas that gives coherence to our beliefs, guiding (or misguiding) perceptions and providing a backdrop for social exchange (Moscovici, 1981). Such representations explain how the strange becomes familiar, providing a sense of historical continuity within a group's cultural background and providing a framework within which children are socialised. They are particularly concerned with how individuals and groups can 'make sense' of an unpredictable and diverse world, and may be of greatest relevance and force during times of crisis and upheaval (Moscovici, 1984).

Two cognitive mechanisms, anchoring and objectification, are critical to an understanding of these representations. To cope with a strange idea, we 'anchor' it to an existing representation, giving it an appropriate name and classifying it in terms of something we already know. For example, the unfamiliar phenomena that occurred following the Chernobyl disaster (explosion, food contamination, etc.) were absorbed with the help of religion, science-fiction and medical imagery (Moscovici, 1988). As we shall see in Chapter 5, the new scientific work on HIV/AIDS became absorbed into existing concepts of illness and prevailing prejudices and stereotypes. Eventually the familiar becomes assimilated and unified into a representation of the new object: objectification. By naming an abstract idea and matching it up with a known image, the idea becomes a 'real thing'. In Moscovici's classic study of the dissemination of the ideas of psychoanalysis (Moscovici, 1961), unfamiliar scientific and academic ideas became objectified into clichés, accessible and used by everyone. Sperber (1985: 74) has used the analogy of diseases to illustrate how cultural representations may influence different people and groups in varying ways. In his analogy, 'the human mind is susceptible to cultural representations, in the way the human organism is susceptible to diseases'. Representations can be 'cultural' in different ways: cultural traditions may be transmitted slowly over generations while other representations may have a short lifespan.

The study of social representations now forms a major part of British and Western European (particularly French) social psychology. Studies have been conducted on a wide range of representations, including representations of health and illness (Herzlich, 1973), mental illness (Jodelet, 1989), and aggression (Campbell and Muncer, 1993). Although much of the earlier work used qualitative methods, research now uses a healthy diversity of methodologies (e.g. Doise *et al.*, 1993) and data is increasingly being gathered from a range of cultures (e.g. Doise *et al.*, 1995). The theory of social representations can make a number of useful contributions to cross-cultural relationships research. By linking personal relationships with wider societal concepts, social representations theory can be particularly useful when tackling relationships issues already heavily influenced by prevailing prejudices – for example, in understanding the difficulties surrounding the formation of inter-ethnic relationships, and in comprehending the spread of some sexual diseases. Studies of social representations can also offer important guidance on the way in which values may persist or evolve and are generated between groups and generations. Finally, social representations research has illustrated the important manner in which representations may operate on a number of levels of consensus. While some aspects of a broad representation may form relatively rigid norms, others may emerge through social interactions and particular experiences. Thus, for example, in Jodelet's classic work on madness (Jodelet, 1989) there was considerable consensus about not sharing eating utensils with the lodgers (who were considered to be 'mad') but far less consensus about who was or was not dangerous. Similarly, in many cultures there are shared rules about some aspects of family management but greater flexibility in other aspects of the familial relationship. By allowing for the interplay between individual practices and social structure, social representations theory also allows us to move between the 'individual level' obsession of most North American research on social cognition and the sociological emphasis on societal structure, without necessarily rejecting the work of either tradition (Morgan and Schwalbe, 1990).

As yet, there is practically no dedicated work on the social representations of personal relationships. There is also a persisting uncertainty about the relationship between culture and social representations. In this book I will therefore only be suggesting possible routes through which relationship values may emerge in different cultures. I will interpret social representations as a form of social 'glue' that can help explain why some practices persist and spread between group members and across generations. Future work in the burgeoning social representations field will hopefully help clarify some of these processes.

Acculturation

Acculturation is traditionally defined as 'the cultural change that is initiated by the conjunction of two or more autonomous cultural systems' (Social Science Research Council, 1954: 974). When individuals move to a new society, they adopt a complex pattern of continuity with their old culture, and new behaviours appropriate to their new setting (Berry, 1997). A distinction can be made between two types of acculturation: broad *population level acculturation* (which concerns changes in the cultural and social system) and *individual* (or *psychological*) *acculturation*, which reflects how an individual's behaviours, values, identity and attitudes change. Most theorists assume that changes at the individual level result from earlier changes in the broader population (Berry, 1990).

Most researchers focused on the negative impacts of acculturation, pointing to the high rates of suicide and drug abuse among many migrant communities (Schneider *et al.*, 1997). However, changes in the acculturating individual are likely to affect his or her relationships in a complex manner, reflecting the adaptive demands of the situation (Trickett and Buchanan, 1997). Acculturation is thus best seen as a set of alternatives rather than a simple process of assimilation or absorption (Liebkind, 1996). Migration can lead to a range of changes in attitudes, from assimilation into the new community and losing contact with the old culture, to rejecting the new community outright. Acculturation can also lead to a range of behaviours, from complete behavioural assimilation to violent protests. For example, just as family arrangements may be disrupted by migration, close family ties can also provide powerful social support following movements between cultures, with the family acting as a critical coping resource (Gil and Vega, 1996). Indeed, family ties may actually be strengthened by the migration process. Ethnic revitalisation can also occur where a sense of continuity with the past can play an important part in the formation of new social groupings (Eriksen, 1995).

Berry (1994) lists three strategies of adaptation which have different outcomes. *Adjustment* brings the individual into harmony with the new environment, allowing them to become part of the dominant society. *Reaction* involves trying to 'fit in', by organising culturally-based groups and trying to get the dominant group to accept the new group's needs. This strategy is often unsuccessful if political power is absent. Finally, *withdrawal* involves a reduction of contact with the environment (e.g. by returning home or establishing an enclave). In many cases, such 'withdrawals' might be encouraged (or enforced) by the outside political system.

Several critical factors influence the strategy chosen and the success with which groups deal with their acculturation experience. These include the reasons for migration, the length and anticipated permanence of the move, the size of the acculturating group and the values of the new society. Also of importance are the 'acculturation messages' of a society – the national policies and attitudes of the host population (Basic Behavioral Science Research for Mental Health, 1996; Berry, 1990). Men and women and individuals from different generations are likely to acculturate at different rates, and individual factors influencing acculturation include education, type of wage employment, urbanisation, media contact, political participation, religion, language and degree of social interactions in the new culture (Berry, 1990; Trickett and Buchanan, 1997). Acculturation styles are also related to basic personality variables. Such personality variables may be important mediators in the kind of coping style adapted by migrants (Schmitz, 1994).

One area of acculturation research with particular relevance to the present book concerns the relationship between adolescents and their families in acculturating groups. Adolescents of immigrant status, or those whose parents were immigrants, often face the problem of dealing with two cultures at the same time, with the old culture represented by the family and the new one by their peers and their school environment. This often leads to adolescents receiving conflicting messages, which can in turn lead to complex behavioural outcomes.

Rosenthal *et al.* (1989) examined the congruence of values held by parents and children among Greek immigrants to Australia. They sampled mothers, fathers and adolescents from forty working-class families in Melbourne (half of them Anglo–Australian and half Greek–Australian) as well as an additional twenty working class families resident in Greece.

Respondents were asked to list the values they wished to develop in their children, and the values most respected by Australians or Greeks. Parents were also asked what they thought was expected of a good Australian/Greek mother/father, while adolescents were asked about appropriate parental behaviours and appropriate adolescent behaviour towards parents.

Rosenthal *et al.* found that the Australian and Greek cultures emphasised very different child-rearing values, and that these values persisted for the Greek sample even after immigration. Greek respondents focused more on the family, and emphasised the importance of respected members of their community. Greek parents were likely to act as 'moral guardians', concerned with the 'proper' upraising of their children. This was in contrast to the more individualistic values of Anglo–Australian culture, which emphasised independence, material security and individual happiness. However, the Greek father's role in Australia seemed less authoritarian and more loving than in Greece. There was more evidence of shifting towards Anglo–Australian norms in behaviour rather than values, suggesting that new cultural norms are more likely to be reflected in behaviour than in core values. This echoes the findings of Horenczyk and Bekerman (1993), who studied Russian emigrants to Israel. They argued that 'bodies' migrate much faster than 'selves', and that core self-identities are difficult to change over a short period of time. Horenczyk and Bekerman's findings also reinforce the message that changes in ethnic and cultural identity are rarely uniform or sudden, but involve a continuous reorganisation of sub-identities.

Feldman and Rosenthal (1990) examined autonomy values among Chinese adolescents in the United States and in Australia. They questioned more than three hundred US high school students (Euro–Americans and first and second generation Chinese–Americans), as well as Hong Kong Chinese in Hong Kong and Anglo– and Chinese–Australians in Australia. Respondents were given a 'teen timetable', measuring their degree of behavioural autonomy across a range of everyday life activities. Examples included going to girl/boy parties at night, going out on dates, doing things with friends rather than family, and no longer having to tell parents where they were going. Feldman and Rosenthal concluded that changes in autonomy expectations are likely to take place slowly, especially in the United States, and do not proceed evenly across all behavioural domains. Overall, the host culture exhibited only a modest influence on the behaviours of the young: early dating behaviours and going on overnight trips with mixed-sex groups of friends, for example, were far less frequent among the Chinese youth of migrant families. Feldman and Rosenthal argue that the Chinese family structure may be particularly resilient to change because of its strong emphasis on generational transmission, no doubt enhanced overseas by an eagerness to maintain cultural integrity.

A final example is the work of Hanassab and Tidwell (1989), who conducted in-depth interviews with young Iranian women in the United States. Hanassab and Tidwell note that, although a generation gap between parents and children has been observed in the white US culture, this gap is probably exacerbated for those coming from a culture as different as that of Iran. They note that, while simple assimilation to the larger culture can appear disloyal and lead to fear of abandonment by the family, a 'simple' reaffirmation of cultural identity is rarely a simple resolution in a country where assimilation pressures are considerable. These findings may, of course, reflect the relatively small size of the American–Iranian community in comparison with the larger, and more confident, Chinese–American population.

In considering personal relationships in a changing world, the impacts of modernisation and migration are often cited as important factors contributing to the breakdown of 'traditional' (and usually desirable) personal relationships. Those who live in modernising societies, or who move cultures (usually from a rural/traditional/'undeveloped' culture to an urban/'modern'/'developed' society), are frequently described as living in an 'anomic' state (Merton, 1968), characterised by alienation and separated relationships. Yet, as should be clear from what has been said here, modernisation and changes in geographical location can have many different effects on individuals and their friends, families and wider communities. Individuals and groups are likely to appraise the consequences of changes in their society and location in different ways: some may view these changes as a threat, others as a benefit, and others still as a challenge (a challenge which may be stressful but may also offer new opportunities (Lazarus, 1991; Schwarzer and Chung, 1996)). As yet, however, we are only just beginning to recognise such important cognitive/emotional considerations when examining personal relationships in a changing society.

Summary

Recent years have seen a growing interest in evolutionary theories of social behaviour, which stress the universality of certain relationship behaviours. Much of this work, however, must be seen as highly speculative. More productive has been research which has attempted to dimensionalise cultures, with the value dimensions of individualism–collectivism and power distance being the most powerful divisions for conceptualising cultural variations in relationship behaviours and beliefs. Such cultural values are likely to be strongly rooted in the ecological environment in which cultures are located. Personal relationships across cultures are changing in a number of ways, with modernisation and mass migrations producing a complex cocktail of relationship adaptation and conflicts. Social representations theory helps us understand how cultural myths and stereotypes about relationships are spread and maintained, and how new, often threatening, relationship challenges are processed and integrated within existing cognitive precepts.

3   Relationship formation

Introduction

How we choose a partner, or the way in which other people select a partner for us, forms one of the most enduring questions in the study of personal relationships, and one of the most fascinating for the cross-cultural researcher. Partner formation and marriage in some form takes place in the majority of world cultures (Rosenblatt and Anderson, 1981), However, the apparently 'free' mate choice commonly practised in modern Western societies is not the way in which people in most societies choose a mate (Ingoldsby, 1995b; Stephens, 1963). The next two chapters will discuss the cultural bases for the formation of long-term relationships and the dynamics that might underlie the relationship formation process. Because of the overwhelming emphasis of the cross-cultural literature on heterosexual pairings, I will focus on opposite sex couples in this review. In the following pages I consider the role of the arranged marriage in many societies, and the kinship rules practised in many cultures, before moving on to consider preferences for a partner, and the roles and meanings of love in different cultures.

The arranged marriage

Throughout the world, marriage can be divided along a continuum ranging from those societies where marriage is totally arranged to those where individuals have complete freedom in mate choice, although there are relatively few societies at either extremes of this division (Rosenblatt and Anderson, 1981). People in almost all cultures have some general limitations as to whom they can marry and share sexual relationships with (Eriksen, 1995; Rosenblatt and Anderson, 1981; Schlegel, 1995), and rules of exogamy and incest are evident across cultures (Parker, 1976). Indeed, the nervous anticipation associated with the first meeting of future parents-in-law suggests that 'outside' forces are likely to be significant in even the 'freest' of 'free choice' societies (Denmark *et al.*, 1991; Sprecher and Chandak, 1992). Nevertheless, it is wrong to equate the influence of such external forces in

Western societies with the degree of restraint imposed in many of the non-Western societies, where the arranged marriage is primary.

Worldwide, the most common method of mate selection is by arrangement, usually by parents with the aid of relatives or matchmakers (Ingoldsby, 1995b). In the arranged marriage, marriage is perceived primarily as a relationship between groups rather than individuals (Eriksen, 1995), and the idea that 'we fell in love' may be better replaced by the concept of 'it is a good match for our families' (Duck *et al.*, 1997: 15; see also, for example, Nassehi-Behman, 1985, on Iran, and Sow, 1985, on Africa). Arranged marriages can be seen as having a number of potential benefits for a society: they foster the preservation of the social structure of a society, enable elders to maintain family control, allow for the furtherance of political and economic linkages between families, and help preserve families over generations and family property within the larger kin unit (Fox, 1975). Alliances between families can often provide the only form of social and economic protection in a poor society.

In the arranged marriage the couple will often have met each other only infrequently prior to marriage (Rosenblatt and Anderson, 1981). Women in particular may marry at an early age (most brides worldwide are in their mid-to-late teens (Schlegel, 1995)). If women marry later, they are likely to be chaperoned in public. For example, in Iran the choice of spouse is supervised by family members, with dating and the free choice of a partner being very rare (Hanassab and Tidwell, 1989; Nassehi-Behnam, 1985). In some societies, however, the opportunity is given for an 'escape' through a tradition of accepted elopement (Ingoldsby, 1995b). Stephens (1963) describes the custom of *nunghop bui*, practised by the Iban of Borneo. Here a man can carry his beloved back to his village, leaving gifts for the pursuing family along the way. These serve to placate the girl's family, and he is left in peace with his new wife.

In the arranged marriage, partner matching will often be determined by *price* (Ingoldsby, 1995b: Stephens, 1963), with the groom's family paying for the bride (bride-price) or the bride's family paying a dowry to the husband. Bride-price compensates the family of the bride for the loss of her services (Ingoldsby, 1995b), and Stephens (1963) estimated that in nearly two-thirds of the world's societies a man must pay to marry a woman. 'Bride-price' is common in Africa, and here the groom's kin transfers resources to the bride's kin in return for her labour and reproductive powers. If this is not paid, the marriage might be considered void, and often there are disagreements about such payments (Eriksen, 1995). This establishes two kinds of moral bonds between people: first, it creates a contractual tie, a link which symbolises trust; second, it solidifies the paying group, as often the groom must borrow from relatives to pay this price (Eriksen, 1995). Mwamwenda and Monyooe (1997) found considerable evidence of support for bride-price among Xhosa-speaking graduate students in South African universities, with 88 per cent of their sample supporting the practice of bride-price payment (84 per cent of the men and 90 per cent of the women). Bride-price was seen as heightening the husband's gratitude for a good wife, making him appreciate her dignity and worth and assuring that he receives continuing recognition and respect from his wife.

Less common is the dowry, where a man is paying a family to relieve them of the burden of the daughter (Ingoldsby, 1995b). The dowry has been traditionally an important institution in Europe and some Asian societies (Eriksen, 1995). Here the bride brings in gifts from her family, often consisting of items for the home, which can be seen as a compensation for the man's economic support of his wife. This may be more likely in a culture which places a low value on women (Ingoldsby, 1995b). A dowry can serve to exchange wealth for a higher social position, to marry a social equal, or to bring in a loyal son-in-law who will serve the family that brought him these goods. Virginity is a valued asset in such societies, as the son-in-law is being 'bought' (Schlegel, 1995). In India, the 1961 Dowry Prohibition Act supposedly made the giving of a dowry illegal, but the custom persisted (Teays, 1991), often being used as an opportunity for the obtaining of consumer goods in a society where such goods are still difficult to obtain for large portions of the population (Ramu, 1991).

Even where there is no tradition of giving dowries (for example, among some lower-caste Hindu groups in India) there can still be a considerable pressure for a father to provide for his daughter properly, to show *izzat* (self-respect). This list of expected marriage gifts was produced by Chander, a low caste ('sweeper') servant who is the central character in Mark Tully's *Ram Chander's Story* (1995: 23f)

* one television set
* one scooter
* thirty-one degchis (handleless saucepans) and other cooking pots and pans
* thirty-one saris for the women and seven kurta pyjamas for men of the boy's family
* five saris and five silver ornaments for Rani
* one tin trunk
* one wall clock
* one wristwatch for the boy
* two chairs
* one table
* one sofa
* one bed with bedding
* 2,500 rupees cash
* Total value: 80,000 rupees

... a considerable sum!

This high cost of a woman's dowry can be seen as a contributing factor towards the high rates of female infanticide in India (Eriksen, 1995). However, the importance of such economic factors to the institution of marriage is evident across a number of cultures. For example, among the Afro-American population in the US, marriage rates are often lower because of the difficult economic circumstances that confront so many members of this population (Tucker and Taylor, 1989). While being on low income may not prevent the *formation* of a romantic relationship, it is a deterrent to the establishment of a formal marital relationship in which the man plays the role of provider.

The *social status* and reputation of the family from which the spouse will come is also an important consideration for partner matching. A further consideration in some societies is the existence of traditional marriage patterns held across generations, such as marriage between cousins (Ingoldsby, 1995b: Stephens, 1963). Marriage in Iran is usually within social class, and is often endogamous (between parallel cousins or cross-cousins) (Hanassab and Tidwell, 1989). Similar marriages arranged within the extended family can be found in traditional African societies, where unions between nephews and nieces may be encouraged (Sow, 1985). In Kuwait (Al-Thakeb, 1985) a study of 526 heads of households showed that almost half were married to relatives, more than three-quarters of these being first cousins, although this marriage pattern among relatives was less common in the educated and upper classes. In other societies, complex kinship categorisation rules may operate, although these are not necessarily based on simple biological distinctions but may be determined by the convenience of allegiances (Eriksen, 1995). Thus biological kin relations may be less important than the 'appropriate' genealogy a group may wish to present, in order, for example, to claim land rights (Eriksen, 1995). Marriage within the group may be particularly significant when considerable resources are to be transmitted through marriages (as in the British royal family) (Eriksen, 1995).

One final practice of marital arrangement deals with remarriage patterns after the death of the first spouse. In sororate cultures, a sister replaces a deceased wife. In contrast, under the levirate system, the death of a husband leads to the marriage of his wife to his brother (Ingoldsby, 1995b).

Gupta (1976) reports a number of religious rituals and beliefs associated with partner selection, claiming that India is arguably the only part of the world where a wide variety of mate selection processes exist. For example, in the Indian Gandharva marriage there is marriage by mutual choice, whereas in Hindu communities the boy's family begins a marriage proposal and the girl's parents give away their daughter to a suitable partner. However, partners in love can also marry provided they are not considered unsuitable. In modern India, most younger people may know their partners 'fairly well' prior to marriage. Sprecher and Chandak (1992) examined attitudes towards the arranged marriage system amongst sixty-six young Indians. Participants in this study were generally positive towards *both* arranged marriages and the dating system. Respondents strongly believed that a young couple should have some say in an arranged marriage. While arranged marriages were perceived as having the advantage of obtaining support from the families and allowed individuals to meet partners with similar backgrounds, respondents also noted the disadvantages inherent in not knowing each other well and the financial implications of the dowry for the woman's family. In contrast, while the dating system had the advantages of getting to know the partner and 'having fun', the principal disadvantages were the risk of pregnancy and concerns that such relationships may be only temporary.

The role of individual choice can often be heavily influenced by wider political and social factors. In China, the roles of state regulation and modernising forces provide a fascinating insight into the impact of macro-level factors on partner choice. In feudal times, the economic background of the family was of primary significance in mate selection. As a reaction to this, the right to choose one's own spouse was guaranteed by the 1950 Marriage Law (and reinforced by the 1980 Marriage Law). Nevertheless, parental influence and participation in the process continued, and during the Cultural Revolution the political background of the couple's family became an important consideration. Even in the 1980s, 'informal' matchmaking between Communist Party members was actively promoted by the state, with couples often matched on the basis of their 'moral character' (Honig and Hershatter, 1988).

Harrell (1992) examined the effect of China's post-1978 decollectivisation reforms on rural marriage practices. He studied three different villages of varying wealth on the Sichuan–Yunnan border, and demonstrated how the return to bride-price and dowry payments had considerable economic consequences. He recalls attending weddings at which both the bride's and the groom's families fed two meals a day to as many as forty tables of guests for three or four days. Harrell argues that much previous Western research, based on 'officially representative' regions (i.e. those accessible to outsiders during stricter times), was probably less representative than the researchers realised, with many pre-revolutionary practices (such as marriage at an early age) continuing even at the height of Maoist rule.

During the 1980s in China, rural economic reforms meant that the heads of households now had greater control over the labour of family members. This then increased the economic power of the family unit. Rather ironically, such 'modernisation' increased the traditional demand for large families and the pre-revolutionary practices of childhood engagement, early marriage, and the marital 'exchange' of relatives (Honig and Hershatter, 1988). Thus a 1986 sociological survey showed that less than a third of marriages were free of family influence, and in many rural areas, four- and five-year-old girls were sent to live with a boy's family with the intention of marrying as early as possible (Honig and Hershatter, 1988). This demonstrates that economic changes can have far-reaching, and often unexpected, implications for family practices and partner selection.

Partner preferences

For more than fifty years, family researchers and experimental psychologists have listed the attributes that individuals desire in their partners in romantic relationships (Goodwin, 1990). The largest study of partner preferences to date was described in Chapter 2 (Buss, 1989; Buss *et al.*, 1990). Western research has emphasised the primacy of 'abstract' qualities of honesty and kindness as desirable traits in a partner, desires seen as characteristic of an 'individualist' society (Goodwin, 1990; Woll, 1987). These relatively 'abstract' desires may be contrasted with the more pragmatic attributes (such as income and kinship obligations) stressed in societies such as rural China (Dion and Dion, 1988). Thus, for example, Goodwin and Tang (1991) tested British and Hong Kong Chinese university students using a modified version of Buss's partner preference questionnaire. They found that while British respondents stressed sensitivity and humour in romantic partners, Chinese respondents stressed a more pragmatic money-mindedness.

Hatfield and Sprecher (1995) examined partner preferences in the US, Russia and Japan, chosen to represent a Western individualist culture, a 'mixed' culture influenced by both individualism and collectivism, and an Eastern collectivist culture. More than 1,500 university students in the three countries indicated their partner preferences using similar items to those used by Buss. Generally, kindness and understanding, a sense of humour, and expressiveness and openness were the most desired characteristics, although US students considered more traits to be indispensable and expected more from their relationships than those in Japan.

In a study of young Indians, Sprecher and Chandak (1992) found that kindness, sense of humour and an expressive and open personality were the characteristics most desired in a marriage partner. These are very similar preferences to those that emerge from the Western literature, although, in a comparative sample, there was a slight preference for non-Indian Americans to prefer the physically attractive, athletic and outgoing partner (Sprecher and Chandak, 1992). Although this was a small-scale study, primarily of a student population, the results suggest that when presented with a *free choice*, particular psychological characteristics may be universally valued.

The values of masculinity/femininity may also be significant in partner choice. Hofstede (1996) asked 400 women in their twenties, taken from eight Asian cities, to rate fifteen traits they would seek in a steady boyfriend and a husband. Across these eight cities, boyfriends (more than husbands) were sought with a sense of humour, while husbands were sought who had health, wealth, understanding ('the ability to understand me') and social status. In countries high on Hofstede's concept of 'masculinity' (such as Japan), health, wealth and understanding were sought in husbands but less in boyfriends, while personality and affection were sought more in boyfriends than in husbands. In 'feminine' countries, such as Thailand, these latter traits were considered equally desirable. Hofstede (1996) suggests that this indicates that, while the boyfriend may be seen as the symbol of love and the husband as the symbol of family life across cultures, in 'masculine' countries people differentiated more between preferred boyfriends and husbands than in 'feminine' countries. Note, however, that this differentiation in preferences for the husband versus the boyfriend did not correlate with individualism–collectivism scores.

In another study which indirectly incorporated notions of masculinity and femininity, Murstein (1976) compared the qualities of a desired spouse between French and US students. Murstein hypothesised that French college students would be more traditional and less egalitarian in their desired spouse than US students, as sex role equality is more pronounced in the US than in France. An interesting feature of Murstein's method is that he asked respondents to indicate their 'realistic' expectations for a partner, rather than just to express socially desirable partner characteristics. A comparison of these expectations demonstrated, contrary to Murstein's expectations, that French men wanted a wife who is 'aggressive, sexy, unidealized, egalitarian, unconventional, but socially popular' (1976: 466), while the ideal French husband differed from the American one by being 'more egalitarian, pragmatic, and less idealized, more aggressive, less conventional on sex matters, and more popular socially' (1976: 467). Although these findings contradict Murstein's own hypothesis, they are in line with the greater femininity in France, evident in Hofstede's (1980, 1983) value scores (the US ranked fifteenth out of fifty-three countries/regions in masculinity, while France ranked thirty-fifth). They are also consistent with other studies on sex roles across cultures in finding that women in both cultures focus more on expressive concerns in relationships (Williams and Best, 1982, 1990).

One interesting source of data that has been used by a number of researchers is the 'personal advertisement'. While we cannot be sure about the social pressures that underlie the placement of these advertisements, the characteristics desired in a spouse may reflect at least some of those characteristics also sought in a more traditional arranged marriage (Fox, 1975). Ethnic Indians in Britain or Pakistan, who return to the Indian subcontinent to find a spouse, may place personal advertisements in newspapers which stipulate desired background characteristics (such as education and religion) (Ingoldsby, 1995b). Both Camilleri (1967) in Tunisia and Abu-Loghod and Amin (1961) in Egypt found that status characteristics such as education and income were frequently cited in these advertisements. Despite the officially equal status of the sexes in China, Honig and Hershatter (1988) noted how Chinese women were more likely to stress their desire for particular occupations and education in men, while Chinese men seldom mentioned education or occupation in their list of partner preferences but sought women with beauty, gentleness, poise and the ability to run a household. While men in China often failed to find partners because they had low salaries or were from poor districts, women often had difficulty because they were highly educated, or held demanding posts. Indeed, some Chinese marriage bureaux refused to allow women to register who had university degrees, and many men seemed to fear that a well-educated women would be too domineering and a poor mother to their children.

Attitude similarity seems to be important in partner choice – when, of course, individual partner choice is permitted. Byrne (1971) found students were attracted to those with similar attitudes, a pattern found among different ethnic subgroups in the United States as well as respondents in India, Japan and Mexico. Similar attitudinal similarity effects were reported by Shaikh and Kanekar in India (1994), and by Chang (1976) in Taipei. Chiasson *et al.* (1996) found French Canadian participants were more attracted to similar ethnic group members than to dissimilar out-group members. However, we must remember that the notion of 'attraction', with its metaphor of magnetism, assumes that we have a list of characteristics that we find desirable in a partner and that individuals are 'drawn' to one another by primarily personal characteristics. Such a metaphor largely ignores the outside world (Duck *et al.*, 1997). Religion, race and class may be far more significant for partnership formation in many societies, and social stratification of suitable others is itself constrained by the social context (Duck *et al.*, 1997; Pepitone and Triandis, 1987). In fact, this simple image of attraction may be misleading even in the West, with different psychological or material aspects of a partner becoming important at different stages in a relationship (Duck *et al.*, 1997; Murstein, 1986).

Physical attractiveness

People have tried to manipulate their own attractiveness in every country and culture throughout history (Liggett, 1974). The study of physical attractiveness forms a large part of the research in the personal relationships area (see, for example, Patzer, 1985). Thakerar and Iwawaki (1979) asked English, Chinese and Indian female judges to rate the physical attractiveness of Greek males, and found significant agreement in the subjects' ratings of physical attractiveness. In Germany, Bosse (1976) manipulated physical attractiveness by varying the appearance of health in facial skin by 'touching up' photographs. Stimulus photographs made to be more physically attractive were seen as more appealing and led to respondents preferring closer social interactions with the target represented.

A large amount of Western research suggests that we make inferences about personal attributes on the basis of attractiveness. The 'what is beautiful is good' hypothesis (Dion *et al.*, 1972) assumes that physical attractiveness is a central part of the cognitive structure which processes information about people, and that any cultural differences in the content of the person's attractiveness does not affect this basic processing (Pepitone and Triandis, 1987). In Dion *et al.*'s (1972) classic study, subjects ascribed more favourable personality traits and life outcomes to physically attractive individuals. However, in Eagly *et al.*'s (1991) meta-analysis the overall magnitude of this stereotyping effect was found to be only moderate, and varied greatly from study to study. Eagly *et al.* found that much depended on the type of inference the judge was asked to make. Thus, while physical attractiveness had a strong impact on perceptions of social competence, it had a less positive influence on perceptions of integrity or concern for others, with attractive people less likely to be rated as modest. Very similar findings were reported by Feingold (1992b) in a second meta-analytic study of this literature.

Dion (1986) has suggested that this tendency to stereotype is dependent on socio-cultural context, with the emphasis on personal attributes in individualistic societies likely to encourage greater stereotyping on the basis of attractiveness. Dion *et al.* (1990) examined students of Chinese ethnicity in Canada, comparing those who were highly involved in the Chinese community to those less involved. They found that those most involved in the Chinese community were less likely to stereotype a target's personality on the basis of their appearance, although involvement in this community did not affect respondents' assessments of the life chances of those they judged attractive. It should be appreciated that this was, however, an indirect test of Dion *et al.*'s cultural stereotyping hypothesis, with no direct assessment as to the individualist or collectivist beliefs of their respondents.

In contrast to Dion *et al.* (1990), Wheeler and Kim (1997) examined the content of the physical attractiveness stereotype in a collectivist culture (Korea) and in an individualist culture (North America). They found that the physical attractiveness stereotype was quite strong in both cultures, but that the content of the stereotypes varied with cultural values. On the basis of previous research on collectivism–individualism, they predicted and found that integrity and concern for others was part of the collectivist physical attractiveness stereotype, but not of the individualist stereotype. 'Potency' was part of the individualist stereotype but not part of the collectivist stereotype. In both cultures, modesty was seen as negatively related to physical attractiveness. In a conceptually similar study, Chen *et al.* (1997) offered a modified socio-cultural hypothesis, arguing that Dion *et al.* (1990) may have failed to observe physical attractiveness stereotyping because the dimensions on which the assessments were based ignored the contents of these stereotypes. In an investigation of Taiwanese students, they found that physical attractiveness stereotyping was only obvious for attributes that reflected important cultural beliefs of the participants.

Socio-biological research in a wide range of cultures has found that the 'attractive' face is unlikely to have highly distinctive features, such as crooked teeth (Gangestad *et al.*, 1994; Thornhill and Gangestad, 1993). Thornhill and Gangestad (1993) argue that this is because average features suggest a high level of heterozygosity, an attribute positively related to pathogen resistance. Symons (1995) elaborates on this hypothesis, suggesting that in any given human population the composite of faces of each age or sex constitutes a template of attractiveness. This composite represents a desirable 'default' position, unless other psychological mechanisms suggest that a particular deviation from the composite is valued.

Some socio-biological research has suggested that neonate features are likely to be highly desirable across cultures (e.g. Cunningham, 1986). Faces which suggest both innocence and maturity are likely to be considered attractive (e.g. women with big eyes and small noses, and men with prominent cheekbones, strong jaws and chins (Cunningham *et al.*, 1990)). However, this assertion is controversial even among socio-biologists. Symons (1995) has argued that there is no reason why selection should have favoured male sexual attraction to neonatal features. Cultural variation in preferences for feminine facial beauty have also been noted. Daibo *et al.* (1994) compared judgements of female attractiveness by Japanese and Korean students. Large eyes, a small mouth and a small chin were positively correlated with beauty in Japan, whereas large eyes, small and high nose and a thin and small face were highly rated in Korea. Korean respondents also attached more emphasis to multiple affective dimensions, stressing a combination of beauty, maturity and 'like-ability' in a partner.

Cunningham *et al.* (1995) provide a more ambitious account of the factors involved in assessing physical attractiveness, which they term the 'Multiple Fitness' model. They argue that biological evolution, socio-cultural forces and individual personality and motivation all influence perception. Thus, evolutionary variables are important because physical attractiveness responses are related to sexuality and reproduction (see Chapter 2 for a recounting of this argument). Large eyes as neonate features are recognised in both the US and Korea (McArthur and Berry, 1987) and such neonate features may suggest vitality and youthfulness and are attractive particularly when combined with sexual maturity features, such as high cheekbones in women and large chins in men (Cunningham *et al.*, 1995). These are likely to combine with features of expressiveness such as smiling, which are universally recognised (Scherer and Wallbott, 1994). However, features such as grooming (e.g. having shiny and well-kept hair) may vary across time, individuals and cultures (Cunningham *et al.*, 1995). Similarly, the ratings of other people may influence our attractiveness to another (Graziano *et al.*, 1993).

Cunningham *et al.*'s (1995) own research examined the responses of students from four ethno-cultural groups (Asians, Hispanics, Black and White Americans) to female target faces. They found high correlations between groups in facial attractiveness ratings, but greater variability in ratings of sexual maturity and expressiveness features. Asian respondents were less positively influenced by some sexual maturity and expressiveness features, and Black and White Americans differed in their preferred body shape and weight. However, Cunningham *et al.*'s interpretation of these findings, couched primarily in socio-biological terms, remains largely speculative, especially as their sample sizes for participants are small and respondents were highly selective in each of their studies – their first study had only thirteen Hispanic participants, spread across seven countries as diverse as Spain and El Salvador. Multiple Fitness models which recognise the interplay of individual psychological, cultural and biological factors are likely to be important in the development of this field, but future work must aim to measure directly the various cultural variables involved in a more systematic manner.

Ethnocentrism in dating

There is a growing literature on inter-ethnic dating, although, as with most personal relationships research, nearly all this work has been conducted in the US. Although only a small proportion of married couples is comprised of individuals from different ethnic groups, the rate of intermarriage has increased greatly in the last two decades: in 1970 there were just over 300,000 intermarriages in the US; by 1994 there were 1.3 million (Saluter, 1996). Inter-racial marriages are susceptible to relatively rapid changes in the external social and political environment: Wilkinson (1987) suggests that the civil rights movements of 1960s America led to a marked rise in inter-racial marriage during this single decade.

Taylor and Tucker (1997) examined inter-ethnic dating and marriage attitudes among more than 3,000 telephone respondents across twenty-one large cities throughout the US. They found that inter-ethnic dating and a willingness to marry outside the ethnic group was becoming widely accepted, with only Mexican-American women expressing severe reservations about inter-ethnic marriage. The two factors most likely to determine willingness to marry outside one's ethnic group were a belief that similarity in background characteristics is less important for a successful marriage, and previous experience with inter-ethnic dating. Taylor and Tucker (1997) claimed that willingness to 'outmarry' was based more on instrumental concerns on the part of women than men – women who felt lonely and poor were more willing to consider intermarriage. Other important socio-structural influences on inter-ethnic marriage were education and religion, with religious Whites more willing to marry Blacks and Latinos.

Similar findings were reported by Liu *et al.* (1995), who questioned US Asian-American, African-American, Latino-American and Euro-American students. Their respondents also showed a high tolerance of inter-ethnic dating, with two-thirds of the sample having experienced a previous inter-ethnic dating relationship. While there was some evidence of in-group favouritism (members of all four groups rated opposite-sex members of their own group higher than did out-group members), Asians and Latinos rated opposite-sex Whites as more physically attractive than average members of their own group. Although based on an actively-dating student population and involving relatively small group numbers, this research is important in highlighting the way in which group status may also play a crucial part in the mating choice scenario.

Shibazaki and Brennan (1997), in another student study, found that individuals in inter-ethnic relationships identified less with others of their own ethnic group than did individuals in in-group relationships. Individuals in inter-ethnic relationships also perceived a greater availability of partners outside their ethnic group and were less prejudiced about other kinds of inter-ethnic social contact.

Finally, McLaughlin-Volpe *et al.* (1997) used a diary method to examine interactions with members of ethnic groups. They found a higher rating of closeness of interaction with romantic partners from the out-group than those found for in-group romantic partners, possibly reflecting the different boundaries such relationships had to encounter (what Driscoll *et al.* (1972) have termed the 'Romeo and Juliet effect'). The success of such inter-ethnic relationships may be heavily dependent on the degree of consequential stigma. Using Goffman's (1963) concept of 'stigma', Gaines (1997) argues that, if at least one romantic partner is marked by stigma (for example, an African-American married to an Anglo-American), both partners may be rejected by members of the majority society.

Marital choice in British Asian populations

Within British immigrant communities, there is considerable diversity in the level of partner choice, with different ethnic groups adapting to the issues surrounding marital choice in a new society in different ways (Ghuman, 1994). In a study of Sikhs, Hindus and Muslims living in Britain and Canada, Ghuman (1994) found arranged marriages to be widely spread. Marriages were arranged by parents and go-betweens, mainly on caste, religious and social class lines. Individual wishes and feelings were generally considered secondary to family interests, reflecting a belief that 'love follows after marriage'. Asian parents were likely to be particularly protective towards their daughters, allowing them less freedom in their dating activities than their sons. This was causing considerable inter-generational problems, as young people in these 'Westernised' countries considered individual choice in partner selection to be important.

In Ghuman's (1994) study, Hindus and Sikhs were more willing to accept arranged marriages than were Muslims, but this may be partly because the arranged marriage customs in Hindu and Sikh communities were more likely to be modified by parents. Thus, among Hindus and Sikhs there was a willingness to allow girls and boys to meet in a family situation prior to their betrothal, and potential mates were given a limited degree of veto in partner choice (see also Stopes-Roe and Cochrane, 1990a). In contrast, Muslim parents preferred to maintain firmer control over the choice of marriage partners.

In a more detailed study of seventy Hindu Gujarati couples living in Leicester, England (Goodwin, Adatia *et al.*, 1997), it was found that only 9 per cent of respondents had 'completely arranged' marriages, in which parents were sole selectors of the spouse. Three-quarters of the respondents were introduced by a third party (usually a family member or a respected member of the community) and were given some choice as to whether or not to accept their partner. Often they had seen each other several times beforehand at large social events, although they would have had little close interaction. They were also given considerable choice as to how long they waited before being married. In contrast, the 'self-introduced' couples, who had sought only minimal parental consent, were more likely to have known each other for a longer time prior to marriage, with many delaying marriage in order to forge a stronger relationship with their spouse or to develop work opportunities. As I shall discuss again in Chapter 8, this group often lacked social support from their family members when the relationship went wrong: from the wider family's perspective, this partnership was the couple's choice, and the couple had to deal with its negative consequences themselves.

In talking about marriage, nearly all Goodwin, Adatia *et al.*'s (1997) respondents claimed that the general purpose of marriage was the 'union of two families'. Yet when asked to describe *their* marriages, this description was couched in more individualistic terms, with the majority of the respondents emphasising the 'like-mindedness' of their partners. This suggests that, while the *event* of marriage was largely a family affair, there are deeper individualistic motivations which underpin its functioning in practice. This echoes the findings of Bhachu (1985) in her description of Sikhs from East Africa who have settled in Britain. In her words:

> ... marriage is not seen so much as an alliance between families as a union between two people: an adoption of the indigenous British society's focus on the individual. This feature, combined with others such as the increased earning powers and independence of the women, the predominance of nuclear households which tend to loosen kinship obligations, and modifications of traditional criteria of spouse selection, are all indicative of developing individualism.
>
> (Bhachu, 1985: 164)

The timing of marriage

Goodwin, Adatia *et al.*'s (1997) Hindu Gujarati respondents had a considerable choice about when they were to marry. The time at which an individual marries may depend heavily on their educational and working aspirations. In a study of the lifecycle of the Japanese family, Kumagai (1984) found that, while there was little evidence that the Japanese were rejecting the institution of marriage, there was a strong tendency for women to delay their marriages, primarily due to their enhanced educational aspirations and achievements. This had important consequences for child-rearing, with a fourteen-year reduction in the number of years spent childbearing the 1970s as compared to the 1930s. This delay was having a significant impact on the size and structure of the typical family, as well as on family roles within this society.

Love and love styles

The positive and negative sides of love

According to Burgess and Wallin (1953): 'The expected, approved, and sanctioned precondition to marriage in American society is falling in love. According to our mores, love is the only right basis for marriage' (cited in Berscheid and Walster, 1978: 148).

Hsu (1981: 50) observes: 'An American asks "How does my heart feel?" A Chinese asks "What will other people say?"'

Jankowiak and Fischer (1992) found romantic love to be present in nearly 90 per cent of the 166 samples they examined from the *Standard Cross-Cultural Sample*. Although *expectations* of love may be rare in many tribal cultures, this does not mean that there is no love, with passionate and sexual love often occurring against a backdrop of resistance from powerful religious and political authorities (Doherty *et al.*, 1994; Jankowiak and Fischer, 1992). However, as can be seen from the quotations above, love is a multi-dimensional phenomenon which has been viewed differently at different times and in different cultures (Hatfield and Rapson, 1987, 1996; Wu and Shaver, 1993). Despite the love sonnets and dramas of Shakespeare and his contemporaries, it was not until relatively recently (at least until 1700) that love was equated with marriage in Western literature, with the passionate love of secretive lovers often coming to a tragic end (Hatfield and Rapson, 1996; Ingoldsby, 1995a; Murstein, 1986). Furthermore, the degree to which love is expressed openly and forms the basis of marriage may vary substantially across cultures (Hatfield and Rapson, 1996; Rosenblatt and Anderson, 1981). There is strong evidence that Western beliefs in the significance of love for marriage may not be universal (e.g. Goode, 1959; Gupta, 1976; Levine *et al.*, 1995). Instead, as is the case in the arranged marriage, practical considerations are likely to be of greater importance in non-Western cultures (Gupta, 1976).

Some of the more disruptive effects of love for 'traditional' societies were noted by Goode (1959). He argued that stratification and lineage patterns are weakened if the potentially disruptive effects of love are not restrained. The bond of love between spouses can undermine traditional family alliances in the household and replace an individual's commitment to the family, with a transference of loyalty from the family to an 'outsider' (Gupta, 1976). Hence, in societies where the extended family is of importance for economic and socio-emotional reasons, love relationships must be kept to a minimum (Fox, 1975) or chaperoned, so that only approved linkages are achieved. Alternatively, love can be encouraged within sanctioned situations, allowing for the formation of an important 'social glue' between approved parties and their wider kin (Gupta, 1976). Love as a binding force for the family and community thus exists within set parameters, whether these be explicit rules (such as those governing incest) or rules concerning the 'suitability' of a mate. As a result, 'people seem to be attracted to the people they should be attracted to' (Rosenblatt and Anderson, 1981: 233).

The notion of love as a culturally approved binding force can be reflected in the cultural discourses that surround love within a society. Hatfield and Rapson (1996: 3) differentiate between passionate love ('a "hot" intense emotion ... A state of intense longing for union with another') and companionate love ('a "warm", far less intense emotion, [combining] feelings of deep attachment, commitment, and intimacy'). Fox (1975) examines these two types of love in the works of social scientists writing on love. 'Love as fission' is the metaphor which most clearly dominates the Western mate selection literature: here love is seen as explosive, romantic and illogical. In contrast, the 'love is fusion' metaphor is used primarily in the analysis of love in the extended family. Love is then seen as a strong binding force that brings individuals together.

Love and cultural values

The greatest debate concerning love and cultural values surrounds the extent to which individualistic values may promote or inhibit love (Sprecher *et al.*, 1994). For some analysts, the selfishness of individualism is incompatible with love (e.g. Beck and Beck-Gernsheim, 1995; Bellah *et al.*, 1985). Others assert that love is a good complement to individualism. In modern North America, argues Ting-Toomey (1991), romantic love acts as a solution to the 'disconnection' felt in this highly individualist society, replacing otherwise weak familial and other group ties. She questioned 781 university students in the US, Japan and France on their love commitment, using items which measured the respondents' feelings of attachment, belongingness and commitment towards their relational partner. As predicted, she found that respondents in the US reported the highest degree of love commitment, followed by the French. Both the Japanese and US female respondents were more 'love committed' than their male counterparts, but there were no significant differences between the sexes in the French sample. Ting-Toomey explained this in the context of the femininity of French culture, where the boundaries between the sexes are less clear (Hofstede, 1980).

K.K. Dion and K.L. Dion (1993) also contend that romantic love is more likely to be important in individualistic societies. They see romantic love as an opportunity for exploring the 'real' (and rather individual) self. In contrast, as we saw earlier in this chapter, love in collectivist societies is downplayed as the basis for marriage. Dion and Dion also contend that psychological intimacy in a marriage is less important for marital satisfaction in collectivist societies, as other commitments – such as family relationships with parents and siblings – may be more important players. In societies such as the Japanese, they claim that long-standing friendships and relationships with children form the central source of intimacy. This is consistent with the data of Lee and Stone (1980), who found, in a survey of more than a hundred non-industrial societies, that loved-based marriage was less present in extended family systems than in nuclear structures. However, the Dions (K.K. Dion and K.L. Dion, 1993) recognise that individualism can be a double-edged sword, as members of a couple attempt to retain personal control while reconciling the shared needs of others in the relationship. Thus Dion and Dion (1991) found that an extreme, 'self-contained' individualism was negatively related to caring, need and trust of one's partner. This ambiguity at the centre of individualism and love they cite as one possible contributor to the high divorce rate in the US and Canada.

A number of studies have attempted to assess the importance of love for choosing a marital partner. Kephart (1967) asked US college students about the importance of love for choosing a marital partner, asking 'If a boy/girl had all the other qualities you desired, would you marry this person if you were not in love with him/her?' Nearly two-thirds of the male respondents and a quarter of females answered 'no' to this question. Simpson *et al.* (1986) obtained similar responses when they repeated this question in 1976 and 1984. They also found that the absence of love was a strong reason for relationship dissolution.

To test the importance of love in marital choice across cultures, Levine *et al.* (1995) compared the responses to Simpson's (1986) question among 497 men and 673 English-speaking college students from eleven 'developed' and 'underdeveloped' countries (India, Pakistan, Thailand, Mexico, Brazil, Japan, Hong Kong, Philippines, Australia, England and the US). Table 3.1 summarises their findings.

As can be seen from Table 3.1, Levine *et al.* found considerable between-country differences on all three questions. The four 'Western' 'Westernising' nations (US, England, Australia and Brazil) were those most likely to see love as a prerequisite for marriage. Indian and Pakistani respondents were the most likely to say they would marry without love. Brazilians were most likely to believe absence of love was sufficient reason for ending a marriage; Filipinos were least likely to believe this. On the basis of the previous work of Goode (1959) (who had claimed that individual freedom is controlled in societies with a powerful extended family), Levine *et al.* (1995) predicted that collectivism would be negatively related to the importance of romantic love. Using data taken from Hofstede's national scores on this dimension, Levine *et al.* reported a significant correlation between collectivism–individualism and responses for Question 1, with the collectivist countries most likely to respond 'yes' to this question. Countries placing greater importance on the role of romantic love in marriage also had a greater gross domestic product, significantly higher marriage rates

Table 3.1 The importance of love in eleven cultures

Question: 'If a man (woman) had all the qualities you desired, would you marry this person if you were not in love with him (her)?'

Reply:	India	Pakistan	Thailand	US	England	Japan	Philippines	Mexico	Brazil	Hong Kong	Australia
YES	49.0	50.4	18.8	3.5	7.3	2.3	11.4	10.2	4.3	5.8	4.8
NO	24.0	39.1	33.8	85.9	83.6	62.0	63.6	80.5	85.7	77.6	80.0
UNSURE	26.9	10.4	47.5	10.6	9.1	35.7	25.0	9.3	10.0	16.7	15.2

Question: 'If love has completely disappeared from a marriage, is it best for the couple to make a clean break and start new lives?'

Reply:	India	Pakistan	Thailand	US	England	Japan	Philippines	Mexico	Brazil	Hong Kong	Australia
YES	46.2	33.0	46.9	35.4	44.6	41.1	45.5	51.7	77.5	47.1	29.3
NO	26.0	49.6	32.1	34.7	23.2	17.1	40.9	28.0	12.7	25.5	31.1
NEUTRAL	27.9	17.4	21.0	29.9	32.1	41.9	13.6	20.3	9.9	27.4	39.6

Question: 'Is the disappearance of love a sufficient reason for ending a marriage?'

Reply:	India	Pakistan	Thailand	US	England	Japan	Philippines	Mexico	Brazil	Hong Kong	Australia
YES	34.6	35.7	34.2	40.3	46.4	27.9	23.9	50.9	63.4	24.8	22.6
NO	47.1	54.8	50.6	36.8	26.8	26.4	71.6	34.8	26.8	51.6	39.6
NEUTRAL	18.3	9.6	15.2	22.9	26.8	45.7	4.6	14.4	9.9	23.6	37.7

Source: Freely adapted from Levine *et al.* (1995: 561–3).
Note: Figures are percentages.

and significantly lower fertility rates, while divorce rates were strongly correlated with a belief that it was better to end marriages when love had disappeared. Levine *et al.* (1995) summarised their findings by suggesting that economic prosperity influences individualism–collectivism, which then influences the importance of love in marriage choice and eventual divorce rates.

Levine *et al.*'s findings offer an attractive summary of a whole tradition of work comparing 'love-centred' Western relationships with other, less 'love-centred', non-Western cultures. Yet the results of Levine and his team beg as many questions as they answer. One puzzle is why cultural norms important for establishing a marriage do not correlate readily with those involving relationship dissolution. For example, US respondents gave the highest ratings for the importance of love in establishing a marriage, but only a third of them were certain that the absence of love should lead to a 'new start', with a similar proportion of respondents from seven very different cultural groups (from India, Thailand, England, Japan, the Philippines, Mexico and Hong Kong) answering 'yes' to this question. We must also question the methods used by Levine *et al.* All the respondents in this study were English-speaking college students, and therefore unlikely to be truly representative of these cultures. Question responses were not standardised, which means that response sets in each culture may have been a major determinant of the findings which emerged (Hui and Triandis, 1989). For their estimations of the relationship between economic variables and beliefs about love, Levine and his colleagues treat each country as an individual participant. This means that they had effective sample sizes of only eight for divorce rates and nine for marriage rates. Finally, of course, *wanting* to marry for love is not the same as doing so: particular preferences for a relationship partner may be widely held, but the link between preferences and actual partner choice may be more culturally variable (Brown, 1994).

A more in-depth analysis of love and culture, this time focusing on just three cultures (North America, Russia and Japan) was conducted by Sprecher and her associates (Sprecher *et al.*, 1994). This study examined a number of relationship beliefs and values, including beliefs in love as a basis of marriage, frequency of love experiences, attachment and love styles and romantic attitudes. Japanese (223), Russian (401) and North American (1,043) students were presented with a lengthy questionnaire in English (for the North American and Japanese samples) and Russian (for the Russian sample). Sprecher *et al.* noted a number of commonalities across the samples: most of the students studied believed love should be the basis for marriage and held at least moderately romantic views about love. Physical attractiveness, personality and reciprocal liking were major determinants of falling in love. However, some cross-cultural differences did emerge. Significantly more Russian students reported being in love, and Sprecher *et al.* speculated that the lower scores for romantic beliefs among the Japanese may reflect a Japanese collectivist orientation (although more than 80 per cent of Japanese respondents did link love with marriage). Once again, however, this study was limited to a student sample, the questions asked were based on 'imported' Western items, and there was no control for response sets in the data.

Romantic love has typically been viewed as playing only a small part in African societies (Oppong, 1980). Thus for example among the Masai, cattle nomads in East Africa, strong romantic love between spouses may be seen as disruptive, as it may contribute to jealousies that can disrupt business (Eriksen, 1995). A small set of studies have contrasted African with Western love attitudes using the Munro–Adams Love Attitude Scale (Munro and Adams, 1978). This scale assesses three aspects of love: Romantic Idealism (love as the essence of life), Romantic Power (love as a powerful force) and Conjugal Love (love as a more considered, calming influence). Philbrick and Opolot (1980) tested fifty Ugandan university students on this scale, finding a relatively strong endorsement of romantic love attitudes. In a second study, Vandewiele and Philbrick (1983) compared those scores obtained by Philbrick and Opolot (1980) and Munro and Adams (1978) with a further sample of Senegalese students. Their results showed that, while conjugal love was particularly important in America, it was less significant in Uganda. In Senegal, conjugal and romantic love were rated as being of similar importance. While this African endorsement of romantic love may seem surprising, Vandewiele and Philbrick (1983) contend that romantic love is very much part of the courting ritual through which young people are initiated in many African societies. In the case of Senegal, the long association between the Senegalese culture and other societies and ethnic groups is used to explain this country's blending of traditional concepts of love and Western ideals of romantic love.

In a third study, Stones (1986) used the Munro–Adams love scale to examine 375 black and white university students in South Africa. His results found that, although South African Romantic Power scores were similar to US and Ugandan scores, Romantic Idealism and Conjugal Power scores were much lower than in these other cultures. Finally, Payne and Vandewiele (1987) gave the Munro–Adams test to 369 students on the Caribbean islands of Barbados and St Lucia. Their results showed a strong endorsement for romantic and idealistic love and a downplaying of the conjugal aspects of adult relationships. This is interpreted in the light of the increasing gap between 'ideal' romantic and real-life conjugal experiences in a society where marriage is relatively rare (Cross, 1979) and where the main source of intimacy may lie in the mother–child relationship. Such studies, although clearly limited in size and scope, are important in showing that many aspects of 'Western' love *are* important in African and West Indian societies, but that the particular constellation of love beliefs and behaviours adopted is likely to be a complex synthesis of traditional beliefs, local conditions and outside influences.

Simmons and her colleagues (Simmons *et al.*, 1986, 1989) have also contrasted romantic love scores across cultures, using other scales measuring romantic love. Simmons *et al.* (1986) examined perspectives on romantic love among West German, Japanese and white US students using the Hobart Scale of Romanticism (Hobart, 1958) and the Knox–Sporakowski 'Attitudes towards love scale' (Knox and Sporakowski, 1968). Romantic love was less positively valued by the Japanese sample than by the West German or US samples, although there were significant culture cross-gender interactions, and there were no cultural differences on the Knox–Sporakowski sub-scales of 'traditional love' or 'power' (which assesses the belief that 'love overcomes all'). While American responses emphasised the notion that love has little relation to social position, the West Germans had the more passionate approach to romantic love. Although the Japanese saw love as a 'dazed state', they also believed that true love lasts forever. Simmons *et al.* (1989) also gave the Hobart and Knox–Sporakowski tests to French and North American students. French students more strongly endorsed beliefs about traditional, irrational romantic love, while the US students were more pragmatic and less likely to see romantic love as an ideal experience. Once again, there were no cultural differences on the 'traditional love' or 'romantic power' sub-scales of the Knox–Sporakowski scales.

A number of studies have compared Chinese and Western cultures. Several researchers have suggested that the 'passionate' and 'erotic' love evident in the West is replaced by a more pragmatic concern in Chinese societies, where love and intimacy are overall less significant (e.g. K.K. Dion and K.L. Dion, 1993; K.L. Dion and K.K. Dion, 1993; Hsu, 1981; J. Hsu, 1985). Shaver *et al.* (1992) compared students in North America and Beijing. Clustering emotional terms, Shaver *et al.* (1992) reported that love is seen as primarily positive in the US, whereas many aspects of love are more negative in China. This is reinforced by ethnographic investigations in mainland China. Ruan and Matsumura (1991) talk of the 'misery' of close relationships in Chinese societies, where even the holding of hands in public can be scorned by others, and where the very opportunities for romantic liaisons (such as those provided by dance halls) have been controlled by the Communist leadership.

Nevertheless, it is important not to overstate the apparent 'misery' of love in Chinese societies. In a later set of three studies, Wu and Shaver (1993) asked Chinese students to list features of love freely, and to rate how central each feature was to the concept of love. They were also instructed to list the positive and negative aspects of love separately. Although the Chinese were more willing to list negative features of love, and to rate these as more central to the concept of love, there were also many similarities between conceptions of love in the US and China. Thus, positive features were more readily listed and seen as more central to the concept of love, and a factor analysis suggested that beliefs could be broken down into similar factors of intimacy, passion and negativity in both cultures.

Within societies there are undoubtedly significant variations in beliefs about love, although these have rarely been explored in a cross-cultural context. Goode (1959) hypothesised that the maintenance of strong kin lines are greater in the upper classes, as there is 'more to lose' here. Other research has examined sex differences in romanticism within different cultures. A number of Western studies have suggested that men are more romantic than women (e.g. Knox and Sporakowski, 1968), possibly because they can 'afford' to be less pragmatic (Brown, 1994). This result was confirmed by Brown (1994) among Korean students using the Knox–Sporakowski scale (1968), reflecting the limited opportunities for Korean women to support themselves economically.

Love styles across cultures

Much recent work in the love literature has focused on the notion of *love styles*. Lee (1973) identified six love styles: 'eros' (romantic and passionate love, heavily influenced by physical attraction), 'ludus' (game-playing, non-committal love), 'storge' (companionship or friendship love), 'mania' (obsessive, dependent love), 'pragma' (logical, practical, 'shopping-list' love) and 'agape' (altruistic and selfless love). Most of the research on cultural variation in love styles has taken place with ethnic groups within North America. Hendrick and Hendrick (1986) administered their love-style questionnaire to more than 800 students at the University of Miami, and found Asian (Oriental) students to be more storgic and pragmatic, and less erotic, than Black or White US students. In a replication study, K.L. Dion and K.K. Dion (1993) studied an ethnically heterogeneous Canadian sample at the University of Toronto. The Dions similarly found that Chinese and other Asian respondents scored higher on storge than their Anglo-Celtic or European peers. They also found a greater role differentiation among their Asian respondents, with women from Asian backgrounds less likely to be ludic and more agapic in their love styles. Rechtien and Fiedler (1988) found Hispanic men and women more likely to endorse highly emotional concepts of love than their Caucasian counterparts. Goodwin and Findlay (1997) examined cultural variations in love styles among British and Hong Kong Chinese student respondents. They found Chinese respondents to be more pragmatic and agapic and less erotic than British respondents. Finally, in Sprecher *et al.*'s (1994) comparison of North American, Japanese and Russian students, Americans were also higher scorers on the erotic (passionate) love scale compared to the other two samples, as well as endorsing storgic (friendship) love more strongly. Interestingly, the 'traditional' findings in the literature that men are more ludic in love than women and that women are more 'manic' (e.g. Hendrick and Hendrick, 1986) were replicated in the US sample, but not in the Russian and Japanese findings. This leads Sprecher and her colleagues to suggest that gender differences in love styles may not be as universal as previously acclaimed.

An analysis of the literature of a culture can also help us to identify different aspects of love within a society. For example, Gupta (1976) claims that infatuation and romantic love are well reported in Indian society, in secular literature as well as in sacred books and scriptures. However, they are not necessarily seen as relevant to the marital relationship, and to talk about such romantic experiences in everyday life is not common, once again reflecting the dissociation between ideals of love and actual daily interactions and practices. In Urdu literature, the 'highest' form of love is similar to a caring, agapic love, with humans striving towards the love of God through their human relationships (Gupta, 1976).

One recent body of work (Hatfield and Rapson, 1996) has examined the influence of attachment styles (or 'love schemas') as determinants of passionate and companionate love. Several researchers have argued that these early infant attachment styles can be seen reflected in adult love attachments (e.g. Simpson, 1990). In Sprecher *et al.*'s (1994) study of students in North America, Russia and Japan described on p. 64, the US sample contained the greatest proportion of respondents with a 'secure' attachment type (exhibiting security and comfort in their relationships: 49 per cent showed this pattern compared to only 37 per cent of the Japanese and 35 per cent of the Russians). In contrast, a greater proportion of the Japanese and Russian respondents were 'avoidants' (demonstrating a fear of closeness: 46 per cent of the Japanese and 47 per cent of the Russians, compared to 37 per cent of the Americans).

Doherty *et al.* (1994) have argued that attachment styles may actually be more significant than cultural variations in forming attitudes to love. In their study, they interviewed 124 male and 184 female students in Hawaii from four ethnic groups: European-Americans, Japanese-Americans, Pacific Islanders and Chinese-Americans. As may have been predicted, they found significant differences on individualism–collectivism scales, with the European-Americans the most individualist, followed by the Japanese-Americans, Pacific Islanders and Chinese-Americans. They found only weak evidence of a relationship between individualism–collectivism and love styles, but a stronger relationship between attachment styles and passionate and companionate love scores. Thus, those who scored highest on the anxiety–ambivalence attachment style (where individuals report a love life full of emotional extremes) also scored highest on passionate love, while those with a 'secure' attachment style were more temperate in their passion. Those with an 'avoidant' attachment style were least likely to have experienced passionate feelings. Companionate love was highest amongst those who were most secure, with the avoidant being the least companionate lovers. Although the respondents were all students studying within the US, this mixing of the personality and cultural levels of analysis offers a promising direction for further research. Future workers must, however, try to 'unpack' the manner in which culture may contribute to personality values and attachment styles which may then lead to the adoption of particular love styles or behaviours (after Singelis and Brown, 1995).

Love and fatalism: the concept of yuan

Many important 'culture-bound' or 'emic' concepts in the study of relationships may be more universal than is often assumed. According to a traditional Chinese saying,

> If you have *yuan* for each other, though you are thousands of miles apart, you will still meet. If you don't have *yuan*, even if you are face to face, you will never know each other.

The concept of *yuan* is complex and multi-faceted, but primarily refers to the notion of 'relational fatalism' – the belief that personal relationships are predestined to success or failure, and that the interactants themselves have only limited control over this (Lee, 1985; Yang and Ho, 1988). This idea comes from traditional Buddhist beliefs in Karma, and from Tian-Tian Zhi-Yi's doctrine of the 'ten suchnesses', which view relationship partners as passive recipients of a relationship rather than active creators (Yang, 1995). Such a concept challenges simple communication models of relationship formation, causing us to focus on numerous other factors that might influence relationship development (Chang and Holt, 1991). Of course, this concept may have a complex relationship with actual practices. While there is evidence to suggest that this notion is still recognised and valued, even amongst 'modern' university students (Yang and Ho, 1988), the belief in *yuan* may be more like a ritualistic tradition used, *post-hoc*, to explain relationship success or failure (Lee, 1985). Furthermore, to 'follow *yuan*' does not necessarily mean one must reject the role of the participants in the relationship's success: there is still much that can be done within the constraints of these situational forces. Lee (1985) notes how one can accumulate *yuan fen* through one's behaviour throughout life, and, as it is important to know one's *yuan* with a person early in an interaction, it is important to engage in relationships and search out a suitable partner.

Yuan is normally seen as a unique Chinese response to personal relationships, originating from the unique religious and philosophical history of Chinese culture. Yet in some ways it might be argued that this belief in a 'mysterious', 'predestined' love is equally strong in Western conceptions of romantic love (Keller, 1992). For example, the Dions describe romantic love as 'an external force that is allegedly intense, mysterious and volatile' (Dion and Dion, 1988: 267), and romantic attitudes scales devised in the US frequently include items that test belief in a mysterious 'one and only', or 'falling in love at first sight' (both assessed in the Knox and Sporakowski (1968) and Sprecher and Metts (1989) romantic attitudes scales). From a psychoanalytic perspective, Winarick (1985: 380) summarises the feelings of many in Western societies when he writes: 'It is as if the whole process of choosing a love involves bumping into the right person and accidentally discovering the right chemistry.'

To assess the extent to which the concept of *yuan* may be shared by students in a Chinese society and in the UK, Goodwin and Findlay (1997) questioned 200 undergraduates in England and Hong Kong using a specifically designed *yuan* scale. As might have been anticipated, Chinese students were significantly more likely to endorse the concept of *yuan* than were the British respondents. However, British scores on the items were still surprisingly high: British respondents scored on scale mid-points for items such as 'A relationship is something that develops outside human control'. That this was found among a group of middle-class and relatively successful respondents may reflect a broader relationship fatalism in the UK, at odds with the broader values of self-mastery that normally characterise such individualistic nations (Smith *et al.*, 1995). The full implications of this fatalism for the development of relationship behaviours has yet to be explored, however.

Love and relationship quality

One enduring debate has been the extent to which free-choice matches are happier than arranged marriages. This is a difficult issue to assess. Expectations for marriage differ, and in those traditional societies where arranged marriages hold sway, divorce or even separation are often difficult or impossible (Hatfield and Rapson, 1996). From one perspective (cited in Xiaohe and Whyte, 1990), 'love matches start out hot and grow cold, while arranged marriages start out cold and grow hot'. From this perspective, parents are seen as being in a stronger position to judge the long-term happiness of their offspring, the latter seen as being too young and immature to make a sensible decision (Xiaohe and Whyte, 1990). Some evidence seems to support this view: in India, for example, Gupta and Singh (1982) found that, although newlyweds who freely chose their partners reported more intense love than those in arranged marriages, the opposite was the case for couples who had been together for more than ten years. In their study of Hindu Gujarati couples, Goodwin, Adatia *et al.* (1997) also found that older respondents reported the highest levels of marital satisfaction in their arranged marriages.

Blood (1967) examined the importance of partner choice on marital satisfaction in a survey in Tokyo, comparing the free-choice matches and arranged marriages of 444 married couples. Contrary to expectation, Blood failed to find arranged marriages 'starting cold and becoming hot', but instead found that both arranged and love-matches showed a steady decline in satisfaction over the years. Blood's data showed that, where there were advantages to the arranged marriages, these were for husbands, with women from arranged matches reporting less satisfaction than those from free-choice partnerships. This is consistent with other data examining unmarried women in Korea (Hong, 1986). Here, length of love relationship was negatively related to degree of romantic idealism.

Xiaohe and Whyte (1990) conducted a partial replication of Blood's study in Chengdu, the capital of the Sichuan Province of mainland China. They tested a representative probability sample of 586 ever-married women aged between twenty-two and seventy. Their data indicated that women in arranged marriages are consistently less satisfied than those who had chosen their own partners. In an analysis which also included more than fifty other measures (including family income, age at first marriage and year of marriage), freedom of mate choice proved to be the strongest predictor of marital quality.

The changing nature of partner selection

The role of love in marriage has fluctuated since antiquity (Goode, 1959). An increasing degree of freedom in partner choice is evident in many countries throughout the world (Rosenblatt and Anderson, 1981), with Hatfield and Rapson (1996) viewing this as one of the major social movements of our time. Nevertheless, as Hatfield and Rapson acknowledge, this process of change is a complex one, often leading to conflicts between individuals and generations.

Simpson *et al.* (1986), in the US, replicated Kephart's (1967) question about the significance of romantic love as a prerequisite for establishing a marital relationship. They found that, while less than a quarter of women saw love as such a prerequisite in 1967, this had increased to 80 per cent in 1976. The degree to which men endorsed this statement had also increased significantly, with 86 per cent of males now supporting the sentiment. Simpson *et al.* interpret this change as a move away from 'pragmatic' partner preferences to a desire for the more 'intrinsic' satisfactions in a relationship.

Several factors have conspired to emphasise the greater role of partner choice and love in marriage. Greater education and wage labour have led to increased independence (e.g. Strange, 1976, in Malaysia), with high status and geographical mobility associated with the desire for 'free choice' in partner selection (Rosenblatt and Anderson, 1981). Governmental proclamations can also help emphasise free choice (e.g. Xiaohe and Whyte, 1990, in China). In Bengal, India, increased mobility through new forms of employment, and the residential dispersal of the family, have contributed to the breaching of traditional caste endogamy (Corwin, 1977).

The movement towards 'free' partner selection has, however, developed at different speeds throughout the world. Korean data collected in 1965 found that 20 per cent of those surveyed agreed that individuals should be forced to marry whoever their parents selected, and an additional 60 per cent believed parents should have equal say in the matter. Data collected some twenty-eight years later from Korean students indicated only a small change in this pattern, and in 1989 almost 40 per cent of all Korean marriages were arranged (Brown, 1994). In an oft-cited sentiment, Brown (p. 188) concludes that 'in the Korean view, marriage is too important to be left to the principals themselves'.

Resistance to the growth of 'free choice' in partner selection was also evident in a representative sample of married women questioned in Turkey by Fox (1975). Based on the work of Goode and Parsons (discussed in Chapter 2) Fox reasoned, that as countries become more modernised, familial control over the offspring declines with a consequent increase in free-choice matches. As hypothesised, Fox found that free-choice matches were more frequent among women of city rather than village origins, as well as among those with exposure to urban areas in childhood. Those who had been educated beyond the age of fifteen were also almost three times more likely to have chosen their own partner (60 per cent of the more educated had chosen their partner compared to 23 per cent of the less educated). However, the importance of Islam acted as an important counterbalance, with the arranged marriage represented by the religious as an important way to preserve family honour. Thus, the vast majority of respondents had undergone an arranged marriage (72 per cent), and there were only slight differences in the number of free-choice partnerships between those under forty-five and older respondents. Similarly in Kuwait, the level of interaction between the sexes prior to marriage is still heavily circumscribed by Islamic teachings, which continue to limit freedom of courtship and pre-marital intimacy between the sexes (Al-Thakeb, 1985). Religion has also been a factor in changing marital practices among the Bajju of southern Nigeria. McKinney (1992) documents how, prior to the 1930s, the typical practice was polygyny. During the 1930s, however, the establishment of Christianity meant a disapproval of multiple marriage partners. While wives were relieved that their husbands were no longer taking second wives, the wives' sexual freedom to move from one household to another was also lost, which reduced the husbands' incentives to keep their partners happy.

Several major political trends have greatly influenced mate selection. Arranged marriages were the dominant trend in China for all classes for many centuries, and were only seriously questioned at the beginning of this century (Xiaohe and Whyte, 1990). The growing Western influence on China's educational and cultural system led to an increase in the role of young people in mate selection in the years preceding the Chinese Communist takeover in 1949. The Marriage Law of the People's Republic of China (1950) denounced the 'arbitrary and compulsory feudal marriage system ... which ignores the children's interests' (cited in Xiaohe and Whyte, 1990: 714), and led to an acceleration from arranged to free-choice marriages (Whyte and Parish, 1984). Parental dominance in marriage choice declined from between 60 per cent and 70 per cent pre-1949 to under 10 per cent at the time of Xiaohe and Whyte's study. However, as we discussed earlier in this chapter, the economic impact of de-collectivisation has encouraged a return to early marriages, with partner choice heavily influenced by parents and the extended family (Honig and Hershatter, 1988).

A further example of the complexity of the changing pattern of partner choice, and the significance of religion and state practices as significant mediating variables, comes in the important work of Tashakkori and Thompson (1988, 1991) in Iran. Tashakkori and Thompson examined the impact of the Islamic revolution of 1979 on personal relationships. Using large, cross-sectional samples, their first study (1988) showed how a post-revolutionary sample, collected in 1982, was more traditional than a pre-revolutionary sample collected in 1974. This traditionalism was demonstrated through a new desire for earlier marriages, an increase in willingness to allow parents to select the marital partner, and a desire for larger families. These 'new' traditional tendencies were especially marked among those from lower educational backgrounds. However, such views were *not* as strong as the authors had expected (given the political proclamations of post-revolutionary Iran) and were not consistent across all segments of the population, with women in particular desiring more egalitarianism. In particular, there was evidence of some 'modernisation' among the educated young, who also desired more egalitarian family relationships

In their second study (1991), Tashakkori and Thompson compared intended age of marriage and fertility and role/career intentions and aspirations, using data collected from high-school children in 1982, 1984 and 1986. This provided further evidence that the attempts to 're-traditionalise' values were not completely effective. There were none of the predicted changes in the intended age of marriage, intended family size or preferences for male offspring, and there was an increasing tendency for women to seek labour-market participation and further education. Tashakkori and Thompson concluded that, despite the 'revolutionary education' provided by the regime, the very experience of education itself was helping drive students towards more 'modern' relationship intentions.

In some instances, 'Westernisation/modernisation' has led to decreases in partner choice and the 'love' (free-choice) marriage. Oppong (1980) argues that, in her Ghanaian sample, there is evidence of a *decrease* in the influence of love and free choice on marriage. Traditionally, the route for marriage was through the initiative of the young loving couple, with marriage a bond of friendship or affection. Divorce, too, was easily obtainable by the refunding of drinks payment through guardians or lineage heads, with a simple declaration of the 'absence of love' being sufficient ground for divorce. The move towards a cash-crop economy among the Akan has been associated with greater migration and social mobility and larger gaps in income and lifestyles. Younger people, particularly mobile young men from lower socio-economic groups, have been reluctant to take on marital contracts, while elite marriages have demonstrated how women are increasingly dependent on their men for social status and wealth. As a result, marriage has become an increasingly stressful institution based on instrumental gain.

Finally, increasing free choice in marriage partners does not necessarily mean the widespread establishment of 'dating cultures'. While individuals in many parts of the world may now have a far greater role in choosing their partners, the Western model, in which boy meets girl at a party or other social group setting, is still relatively rare. In some cases, this may be because the young people themselves feel awkward when with the opposite sex, despite the overwhelming number of love-matches (e.g. Honig and Hershatter (1988) and Xiaohe and Whyte, 1990, in China). In Japan, there is a clear and growing preference for free partner choice, alongside idealised notions of love, companionship and mutuality similar to those held in the West (Reischauer, 1988; Salamon, 1977). However, widespread shyness and the tendency to socialise in groups means that there is less early pairing of couples than in the West (Reischauer, 1988). Thus it would be wrong to predict an inevitable movement towards the Western style of highly individualistic dating patterns in societies where free-choice marriage is on the increase. While dating agencies, singles clubs and the like are now appearing in a wide range of societies, social activity is still likely to be circumscribed by the existing cultural norms for social interaction.

Summary

The ways in which romantic partners are chosen varies significantly across cultures, with a large proportion of the world's marriages arranged by family members. These choices are usually determined by the 'value' of the partner to the family (and sometimes to the wider community), and payments are often offered to reflect this value. In most societies, however, there is evidence of some 'compromise' in marital arrangements, with the individuals concerned given some opportunities to suggest a possible mate or to veto a chosen partner. *Love* is a widely valued emotion across cultures, although the presence of love does not necessarily lead to marriage in all societies. Partner selection is changing across the world, with more marriages being through the 'free choice' of the individuals concerned. However, a number of economic, political and religious factors serve to influence this process, and these often have complex, and unpredicted, effects on marital choice.

4 The developing relationship

Introduction

In Chapter 3, I reviewed work on cross-cultural variations in relationship formation, preferences for a partner and love, and I pointed to some of the ways in which the partner selection process may be changing. In this chapter, I first consider types of marriage and the rules and norms that underlie marital relationships in different societies. I also consider issues of relationship satisfaction and commitment, and the extent to which relationship alternatives may be a significant factor in relationship dissolution across cultures. This then leads me to consider what happens when things go wrong in an established relationship, and in the last section of the chapter I examine the prevalence of divorce in different societies and of violence across cultures.

As is the case throughout this book, the research I cite reflects the differing concerns of different social scientists in these areas. Social psychologists have been particularly concerned with variations in the rules of equity and exchange, whereas anthropologists have been more occupied with problems of violence in different societies. As a consequence of the varied methods employed by these different disciplines, work on exchange rules has focused on brief interactions among students in the laboratory. Cultural variation has been largely interpreted in terms of cultural values such as individualism–collectivism, viewed primarily as personality variables attained during the socialisation process. In contrast, work on violence within societies has been drawn mainly from ethnographic data which relates violence to broader structural and historical variables in a society. The differing philosophies and methodologies that have informed this research have inevitably helped shape the nature of the findings which I will discuss.

Marriage and partnership forms

Marriage, in some form, is now widely recognised as almost universal (Betzig, 1989). Cross-culturally, the main purpose of marriage is to establish a family, produce children, and further the family's economic and social position (Gupta, 1976). In many societies, marriage has also been seen to have social functions, such as enhancing prestige and status.

There are four types of marriage structure (Ingoldsby, 1995b): *monogamy* (prevalent in modern Western societies) plus three plural types of marriage – *polygyny*, *polyandry* and *cenogamy*. Each can be linked to the economic structure of the society and the various demands that the environment poses, as well as established traditions and religious views. Thus, while monogamy may suit a consumer-based society such as that found in the West, parental authority and economic security can be better supported in the multiple marriage types of other cultures.

Polygyny – which means 'many females' – is probably the most preferred marital structure in the world when numbers of societies (rather than individual marriages) are counted (Murdock, 1967). In Murdock's (1967) analysis of more than a thousand cultures, monogamy was preferred in only 15 per cent of cultures, while polygyny was practised in more than 80 per cent of the cultures under scrutiny, although in half of these it was only practised occasionally. The most powerful explanation for polygyny links the presence of polygynous behaviour to the woman's role in the production of wealth, and, in areas where polygyny is most prevalent, light agriculture is the dominant mode of work (Ingoldsby, 1995b; Lee, 1982). This interpretation is supported by several cross-cultural studies showing a significant correlation between women's contribution to subsistence and the proportion of men married polygynously (Betzig, 1989). Polygynous societies often involve women marrying shortly after puberty, and this early age of marriage means that more women are available (Ingoldsby, 1995b). Different interpretations can be provided for women's position in polygynous societies. For example, in rural Turkish society, the first wife is essential to help with agricultural work, while the function of a second wife is to help with domestic work. This functionalist perspective can, however, be criticised as simply rationalising a situation which is only 'functional' for powerful men in this society (Vergin, 1985).

Polyandry refers to multiple husbands for one wife. The Ethnographic Atlas, with data on 863 societies, suggests that polyandry is very rare, occurring in only four societies (Eriksen, 1995). Three features seem to characterise polyandrous societies: a marginal economy, sexual freedom, and female infanticide. In most cases additional wives are also permitted, leading to group marriage (cenogamy). When a Toda woman marries a man, she is also married to his brothers – even those who are as yet unborn (Ingoldsby, 1995b). Female infanticide among the Toda means that men greatly outnumber women, but polyandry provides a wife for brothers who would otherwise remain without a partner (Cassidy and Lee, 1989). Polyandry in this society tends to be a response to poverty and reflects the demand for low birth-rate (Cassidy and Lee, 1989). In other cases, such as the Abisi in Nigeria, a woman will be married to three men on the same day, two being a formalised arranged marriage by the parents and a third being a 'love marriage'. Women may move back and forward among these husbands as they choose. In this latter case, poverty is not the issue, and this marriage form offers other advantages, such as the extension of affinial ties (Ingoldsby, 1995b).

Finally, *cenogamy*, or group marriage, is where husbands and wives share the same spouses. This is not a preferred structure in any society, but operates more as an 'additional extra' in polyandrous societies (Ingoldsby, 1995b).

One form of partnership that has been greatly discussed in recent years is that of cohabitation. In the United States there was a marked increase in rates of cohabitation during the 1970s and 1980s (Brehm, 1992). In many cases cohabitation was used as a 'trial marriage' by the participants, to assess their compatibility prior to marriage, although there is no evidence to suggest that premarital cohabitation has a positive association with later marital satisfaction or stability (Brehm, 1992). Millar and Warman (1996) compared official governmental policies towards cohabitation across sixteen member states of the European Union. They found three main ways in which cohabitation was treated in civil law. In most societies, there was simply 'no recognition' – no formal governmental regulations concerning the settlement of disputes over property and the like. A second model, of 'partial recognition', gave cohabiting couples the rights of married couples if they had made a suitable contract. This was available as an option in Germany, Denmark, Norway, the Netherlands and Sweden, although in practice relatively few couples took this option. Finally, 'official recognition through registration' was available in Norway and Denmark. Registration was also available for homosexual couples in Norway, Denmark and Sweden, giving homosexual couples similar rights to those of married couples. Across these European countries there seemed to be little evidence to suggest that cohabitation is treated similarly to marriage, with most arrangements for settling disputes not enshrined in legal regulations.

In Sweden, there is a high rate of cohabitation and a declining marriage rate. Although cohabitation is generally seen as part of the pre-marriage courtship, half of all children are born to cohabiting unions, and Swedes cohabit for a long time prior to marriage by European standards (McKenry and Price, 1995). Cohabiting couples have a higher rate of dissolution than married couples, which can be attributed to their age (cohabiting couples are younger) as well as their smaller number of children and lower socio-economic status (Hoem and Hoem, 1988). Cohabitors may also be *different* to those who do not cohabit along other personality dimensions and values (Newcomb, 1987): work among older cohabitors in Holland, for example, has found that cohabitors are likely to be lower in religious commitment (De Jong Gierveld, 1992).

Relationship norms and rules

In Chapter 3, I suggested that mate selection rules about inclusion and exclusion exist in all societies. Relationship norms and rules also help shape established relationships across cultures. Such rules may be both explicit (in the form of legal restrictions) or implicit, with the most explicit rules for relationships and conduct evident in societies where relationship formation is involuntary and prescribed (Moghaddam *et al.*, 1993).

Michael Argyle and his colleagues (e.g. Argyle and Henderson, 1984; Argyle *et al.*, 1986) have suggested that rules are developed to allow the attainment of relationship or situational goals. Rules can offer rewards by aiding relationship maintenance, and can be used to minimise conflicts (as in the rule that we should not be jealous of another's relationship). Argyle *et al.* (1986) asked respondents in England, Italy, Japan and Hong Kong to assess the salience of thirty-three rules across twenty-two different relationships. They found both similarities and differences in rules across cultures. Rules existed for every relationship in all four cultures, with four rules (respect the other's privacy, look the other in the eye during conversation, do not discuss confidences with another, and do not criticise the other person publicly) rated as important in all of the twenty-two relationships across the four cultures. Privacy was the most important rule across relationships and cultures. The public criticism rule was more strongly endorsed in Japan and Hong Kong than in Italy and Great Britain, reflecting a collectivist desire to avoid loss of face and to maintain group harmony. In Britain, Hong Kong and Italy, respondents endorsed more rules for *intimate* relationships than non-intimate relationships, and had more rules about the expression of emotions, opinions and affection. In Japan there were more rules for *non-intimate* relationships (those with work superiors, subordinates, doctors and teachers).

Exchange rules in established relationships

The last two decades have seen a growing body of research on rules for exchange in relationships. There are now numerous exchange theories examining exchanges within established relationships, although all share the assumption that social behaviour is determined by rewards and costs or the expectation of such rewards and costs (Hinde, 1997). For example, Homans' (1961) law of distributive justice examines the relationship between profit and investment in an interaction. Thibaut and Kelley (1959) investigate social interdependence, comparing existing relationships with other possible and real relationships. Equity theory (Walster and Walster, 1978) views individuals as trying to maximise their outcomes while recognising that the equitable proportioning of rewards and costs in a society will be best achieved by treating others equitably. Those in inequitable relationships (which can include ones in which they over-benefit) will attempt to restore equity by leaving the relationship, or by manipulating the actual or perceived rewards and costs to themselves or their partner. These theories, while undoubtedly offering an important understanding into some (primarily short-term) relationships, do however suffer from a number of problems. For example, measuring what someone feels about relationship outcomes is highly complex, and it is often difficult empirically to separate predictor variables from the outcome variables being assessed (Hinde, 1997).

Rodman (1972) examines the role of exchange theories in a cross-cultural analysis of power in marital interactions. This analysis compares the resources provided by each of the spouses in a relationship and relates this to their relationship power, with the spouse who contributes the most seen as having the greater power. Rodman discusses four cultural systems – *patriarchy, equalitarianism, modified patriarchy* and *modified equalitarianism.* Modified patriarchy occurs in nations in the process of moving away from traditional patriarchal relationships. Such nations include the Southern European countries of Greece and Turkey. Transitional equalitarianism states are those where norms are becoming more equalitarian but where full equalitarianism has yet to be attained. The US is seen as such a country. Rodman claims that it is in these more transitional societies (in a state of modified patriarchy or transitional equalitarianism) that norms concerning power structures within the marriage are weaker, and that resource accounts of power relations are more appropriate. Thus, in the modified patriarchal society, the adoption of modern egalitarian norms means that the husband's power decreases as the wife's increases. In contrast, in traditional patriarchal societies and egalitarian societies, gender roles are 'more set'. This contextualisation of exchange theory is important in allowing for the analysis of differences in aspirations and values across various segments of a society. As each group is differentially exposed to ideas which challenge their existing views, new forms of power relationship might be anticipated. Rodman's analysis also suggests some of the complexities of social change within a society. As Lee (1987) notes, modernisation may lead to greater sexual equality for women. However, it may also cause a weakening in women's power, as women become less central to the economic process.

Other cross-cultural work using exchange theories has examined the distribution of rewards among friends and work colleagues. This work has divided the allocation of rewards into three categories of distributive justice: equity (each is rewarded according to his or her contribution); equality (rewards are distributed to each equally) or need (each is rewarded according to his or her need) (Erez, 1994). According to Sinha and Verma (1987: 124), individualist cultures

> … foster contractual relationships which are based on the principles of exchange. People calculate profit and loss before engaging in a behavior. Affect is missing in such relationships.

Individualists thus prefer to use principles of equity, with each getting 'what they deserve'. In contrast, the more relational (collectivist) self tends to stress equality rather than equity orientations in distributive justice (Kashima *et al.*, 1988; Triandis *et al.*, 1985). Collectivists are more likely to consider the implications of their actions and share material (and non-material) resources (Hui and Triandis, 1986). For example, in two studies examining the distribution of justice among Indians and North Americans (Berman *et al.*, 1985; Murphy-Berman *et al.*, 1984), Indian subjects were more likely to allocate bonuses and recommend pay cuts on the basis of need. Individualists, however, are more universalistic in their social exchanges (i.e. they treat everyone alike), whereas collectivists are highly particularistic – much depends on your relationship with your interactant (Hofstede, 1994b). Members of collectivist cultures are sensitive to social evaluation, trying to maintain a positive evaluation within their group and placing priority on the maintenance of harmony. For out-groups, the rule of equality does not hold in collectivist societies (Erez, 1994; Leung and Bond, 1984). Using a hypothetical rewards allocation scenario, Tower *et al.* (1997) compared Russian (collectivist) and British (more individualist) students. They found that, overall, Russians were influenced by the identity of their co-worker as a friend or stranger in distributing rewards. In contrast, equity was the guiding principle for the British students regardless of the identity of their co-worker.

Rewards may also depend on whether the reward allocation situation is public or private. Leung and Bond (1984) found that both Chinese and American respondents gave more to themselves in a private rather than a public condition. Leung and Park (1986) compared the use of distributive justice rules in work settings and neighbourhoods in the United States and Korea. In both countries, the equity rule was more highly rated in the work setting, but in the neighbourhood setting those allocators using the equality rule were more favourably rated (Erez, 1994).

Fijneman *et al.* (1996) questioned the validity of the individualism–collectivism dichotomy in distributive justice, arguing that emotional closeness is more important than culture. They questioned students in five countries (Hong Kong, Greece, Turkey, the Netherlands and the US). Respondents were asked to indicate 'how emotionally close' they felt to people in ten social categories, their 'input readiness' for such relationships (their willingness to help the other person with caretaking or by providing money) and their output expectations from such relationships (i.e. the degree to which support was expected from these others). Their findings indicated that the ratio between input and output, as well as the patterning of input and output over social categories, was similar across all their samples, with the ratings of emotional closeness accounting for most of the variance between the social categories. Other research reinforces this argument. Li (1996) questioned 324 students in China. He identified four types of helping behaviour which he termed *altruistic intentions, exchange intentions, relation-*

ship intentions and *normative intentions*. Here, the critical factor in judging the intentions of others was the degree of relationship closeness with the donor, with altruistic helping judged as more likely from those who were closer to the receiver.

These findings echo Mills and Clark's (1982) distinction between 'exchange relationships' (strangers, acquaintances, business contacts) and 'communal relationships' (close friends, close family and romantic partners). Even in communal relationships in the individualistic United States, benefits are given on the basis of needs. Communal bonds are more selfless, and receiving a benefit does not create an obligation of direct repayment (Mills and Clark, 1982). Indeed, tit-for-tat exchanges may even be offensive, and promoting an exchange orientation within a close relationship can undermine long-term harmony (Basic Behavioral Science Research for Mental Health, 1996a). In exchange relationships, benefits are given with the expectation of repayment. Here, there is a direct tallying of services or favours provided: people give with the expectation of receiving comparable benefit in return.

Exchange rules may also vary on the cultural dimensions of masculinity–femininity (Hofstede, 1980) and societal fatalism (Douglas, 1982). Organisations within feminine societies reward people on the basis of equality as opposed to equity (Hofstede, 1994b). Thus, equality is more highly rated in Sweden than in the US (Erez, 1994), reflecting the greater levels of femininity in Sweden (Hofstede, 1983) and the greater egalitarianism of the Scandinavian countries (Schwartz, 1994). In fatalistic cultures, receivers may be very cynical about the rewards they receive (Pepitone and Triandis, 1987). However, there is as yet little systematic work on societal fatalism and distributive justice.

Foa and Foa (1974) describe a circumplex model of social exchanges, dividing resources into six categories: love/positive affect; status (a judgement conveying prestige, regard or esteem); information; goods (tangible objects); and money and services (activities carried out on a person's body or belongings). These are arranged along two dimensions.

Particularism refers to 'the extent to which the value of a given resource is influenced by the particular persons involved in exchanging it and by their relationship' (p. 80). Love, for example, is highly particularistic and moderately concrete. *Concreteness* ranges from concrete to symbolic and refers to the form in which this resource is expressed. Services and goods are highly concrete, although services are more particularistic than goods. Although the distinctions between these resources are not absolute, Foa and Foa use these divisions to predict the relative frequencies of resource exchanges, claiming that frequency of exchange follows the proximity of these resources along two-dimensional space (for example, money is more likely to be exchanged for goods than for love). Furthermore, resources that are close together are more likely to occur together and be seen as similar. Foa and Foa discuss interpersonal structures in different societies, claiming that the order of the classes remains invariant. For example, while love and status may be less differentiated in traditional compared to modern societies, love is more similar to status than information in each case. While Foa and Foa do well to point us towards similarities in the ordering of resource categories, there are of course considerable differences in the determinants of relationship formation and satisfaction in different cultures (Hinde, 1997; Pepitone and Triandis, 1987). Furthermore, as we have seen, much resource exchange depends on the type of relationship in which the interaction is taking place and the nature of the task being conducted (Hinde, 1997). This makes the generation of specific hypotheses about resource exchange across cultures very complex.

There can be little doubt that exchanges of resources play an important role in both the instigation and development of close relationships. Yet, as Hinde (1997) notes, using exchange theories drawn from studies of the effects of food on hungry animals to investigate interpersonal relationships is problematic, and vague concepts of rewards, costs and profits can be used to explain almost anything. While exchange theories, modified for cultural context, seem powerful in some settings, a great deal remains unexplained, with the more emotional aspects of close relationships only poorly comprehensible from such a perspective (Safilios-Rothschild, 1976). Furthermore, existing sexual inequalities in most societies mean that unequal exchanges are the norm in marital exchange across societies, making interpersonal 'exchange' considerations largely peripheral (Safilios-Rothschild, 1976). Thus, while exchange theories provide a useful heuristic for future theory generations, such theories must be more firmly located within the socio-cultural conditions in which a couple operates in order to provide useful insights into relationship behaviours.

Relationship commitment and satisfaction

A number of researchers have commented on the ways in which satisfaction and commitment may be differently experienced across cultures, with such variations following the different functions that such relationships may serve. Relationship commitment and investment in Western research are typically viewed in terms of resource/exchange theories. For example, Rusbult (e.g. Rusbult 1983) offers an investment model which distinguishes between *satisfaction level* (love and other positive feelings for a partner) and *commitment level* (psychological attachment and intentions to maintain a relationship). Satisfaction increases when the relationship fulfils important needs, while commitment strengthens when the perceived quality of the alternatives is lower. Individuals also become committed as a consequence of greater investment in the relationship (for example, putting in time and effort to the relationship, or having a child).

Some researchers have argued that the 'individualistic' calculations inherent in investment theories and related concepts are inherently 'Western' concepts, with little relevance for more collectivist cultures (Wallach and Wallach, 1983). According to Johnson (1998), relationship commitment can be seen as comprising three components: personal (the individual's desire to stay in the relationship, reflecting the attractiveness of their partner and their attraction to the relationship); moral (the individual's sense of personal and social obligations) and structural (the pressures to stay together and the social costs of breaking away). This last component, which emphasises the importance of the social structure, has, however, been largely neglected, with very little research conducted across cultures on the structural determinants of relationship commitment.

Lin and Rusbult (1995) examined the applicability of Rusbult's (1983) investment model in Taiwan, questioning American and Taiwanese university students. In general, they found this investment model to apply as well in Taiwan as it did in the US. However, they did find that the Americans were less committed than the Chinese respondents to their partners, supporting Dion and Dion's (1988) assertion that commitment can be challenging in individualist societies because of its inherent threat to autonomy.

Gao (1991) examined the stability of the romantic relationships of Chinese students in China and American students in the US. Four factors appeared to contribute towards relationship stability in both cultures:

1   openness (a willingness to reveal whatever is on each other's minds);
2   involvement (a willingness to invest an extensive amount of time in the relationship);
3   a shared non-verbal understanding; and
4   a shared and positive assessment of the relationship.

Gao's findings suggest that, while cultural differences can be expected during relationship initiation, they are less predictive of relationship stability. However, it should be noted that Gao was using a small sample (nine Chinese dyads, eight North American – all students) and future study needs to extend such research to a larger and more representative sample.

From an exchange theory perspective, relationships are likely to be threatened when an attractive alternative appears (e.g. Levinger, 1979). Udry (1981) identified two major types of alternatives: those concerning the replacement of a partner, and those associated with the economic costs of a new partner, or the psychological and physical costs of remaining alone. In a study conducted in the US, Udry questioned some four hundred couples, asking them whether they could find a better partner and how they would be affected by leaving their present partner. Relationship alternatives were found to be strong predictors of marital disruption in the following year, independent of marital satisfaction. Other North American research has supported these findings. Rusbult *et al.* (1986) found that alternatives were negatively correlated with relationship commitment, while Kelley and

Thibaut (1978) claimed that the strength of alternatives were positively correlated with a partner's bargaining power in their relationship.

However, the opportunity for taking an alternative partner is likely to be severely reduced in a culture where structural factors serve to make relationship dissolution costly (Hatfield and Rapson, 1996; Rosenblatt and Unangst, 1979). Marriage is a 'socially serious' event in China and in Chinese communities throughout the world (Xiantian, 1985). Structural barriers to the break-up of Chinese relationships include rejection by relatives (Xiantian, 1985) as well as significant personal costs (such as the 'loss of face' described by J. Hsu, 1985). Another factor encouraging harmony is the concept of *yuan*, discussed in Chapter 3. From a Western viewpoint, *yuan* can be seen as a form of mediator of alternatives: we cannot easily find *yuan* with another, thus our alternatives are automatically reduced. Couples believe that they are together because of *yuan*, and thus their coupling is inevitable. Relationships must be cherished and tolerated (Chang and Holt, 1991), although this does not mean that the couple should not work at the relationship (Yang, 1995). One final reason to expect harmony within Chinese relationships is the need patterns of the Chinese peoples. Given the high affiliative, nurturant and succorant needs evident among those of a more collectivist orientation, we might anticipate that dyadic needs play a larger part among the Chinese than among their more individualist counterparts, where the individual needs of autonomy are more evident (Hui and Villareal, 1989). This would provide a further interpersonal bonding that would supplement the broader structural forces encouraging relationship commitment. Perhaps unsurprisingly, therefore, divorce rates are low among Chinese couples, even when the couple is living overseas (Schwertfeger, 1982). Intermarriage is still difficult for many in overseas communities, with US–Chinese data showing that it is most likely to occur among those who are the most unconventional and rebellious (Sung, 1990).

Japanese marriages are often characterised as instrumental units for production and reproduction, rather than the affectional units represented in North American literature (Kamo, 1993). The notion of *ie* – a 'multigenerational property-owning corporate group which continues through time' (Long, 1987: 7) is one dominant social representation of the Japanese family (Kamo, 1993). Although mate selection is now mainly an individual (rather than a family) choice, Kamo claims that, even after marriage, there is less emotional involvement between Japanese couples than their American counterparts.

A comparative study by Ting-Toomey (1991) seems to support this proposition. Ting-Toomey reasoned that those in individualist countries would be more likely to expect romantic affairs to fulfil their needs than those in collectivist societies. She questioned 781 men and women from the US (a highly individualistic country), France (moderate on individualism) and Japan (low on individualism), finding US students to be the most committed to romantic partners and Japanese the least. Weaknesses in conjugal relationships in Japan may be replaced instead by stronger inter-generational ties (Lebra, 1984).

Kamo (1993) compared the predictors of marital satisfaction across cultures using data from a large sample of Japanese couples in Japan and data from the American Couples Survey (Blumstein and Schwartz, 1983). In the American sample, a spouse was likely to be satisfied with the marriage if he or she was young, perceived the relationship as beneficial to him/herself, and shared many friends with the spouse. For the Japanese respondents, sharing friends and going out with friends in common were also positively related to marital satisfaction, and perceived benefit from the relationship was positively related to marital satisfaction for the Japanese *wives*. Perceived benefit from the relationship was not positively related to satisfaction for the Japanese *husbands*. Among these Japanese husbands, the more household work they performed, the less satisfied they were with their relationship. This may reflect the great social pressures on the man to be away from his family and to spend time with his workmates after work (Salamon, 1977). Perhaps most significantly, there was also a direct relationship in Japan between the husband's income and both spouses' marital satisfaction, something not found for the American couples. This supports the idea that instrumental aspects of marriage are more important in Japan than the US. Kamo (1993: 565) concludes:

> Earning a large income is one of the critical factors when a marriage-able Japanese woman chooses her future husband. When marriage is 'empty' in terms of emotional needs, Japanese spouses could be satisfied as long as it provides economic security.

Needless to say, other factors may be involved. For example, it might not be income *per se* that is important, so much as the level of optimism/life satisfaction of the husband (which may result from the greater autonomy associated with higher-paid jobs). Furthermore, the lack of association between perceived benefits from the marriage and marital satisfaction for Japanese men (found among the other three groups in this study) is inter-preted as evidence that Japanese husbands see their relationship as a collective entity rather than a process of interpersonal negotiation. However, it is not clear why this emphasis on marriage as a 'collective' enterprise was not found among the Japanese wives.

Several structural variables have been identified as likely to influence marital satisfaction. Recent British research (Ferri and Smith, 1996) has underlined the significance of employment for relationship satisfaction. For families with no earners, the stress of economic disadvantage is predictive of a high degree of marital unhappiness and vulnerability to depression. Work on African-American families (Orbuch and Veroff, 1997) has shown that, even within one country, there may be considerable ethnic variation in the factors which underlie relationship evaluation. Financial security may be more important for how a Black rather than a White husband feels about the marriage, while White husbands may rate sexual fulfilment in marriage as more significant. Honig and Hershatter (1988) in China note how financial constraints, and in particular the large expenses of a traditional family wedding, often weaken the finances of the couple and their wider family for years to come. Honig and Hershatter describe how the sharing of tiny rooms in China, often with other siblings and their families, can severely restrict and put stress on the couple's relationship.

Relationship dissolution and conflict

Divorce

Provisions for divorce exist in almost all societies, and from a historical perspective the relationship breakdown figures currently of so much concern in the US and Western Europe may be comparatively modest (Eriksen, 1995; Lee, 1982; McKenry and Price, 1995). All industrialised nations have undergone recent rises in divorce rates (Goode, 1993), with divorce rates varying greatly even within Europe. For example, in 1991 there was an annual divorce rate of 13.3 per thousand married couples in the UK compared to only 2.3 per thousand in Greece (United Nations, 1995). Greece's low divorce rate is typical of Southern Europe, where legal barriers to divorce are strong (McKenry and Price, 1995).

Certain common grounds for divorce can be found across cultures. These include adultery, sterility, desertion and cruelty (Kephart and Jedlicka, 1988). Betzig (1989) examined reasons for divorce in 160 societies using the Standard Cross-Cultural Sample developed by Murdock and White (1969). She found the prime reason for conjugal dissolution to be infidelity, although it was women's infidelity more than men's which put the marriage at greatest risk. Betzig interprets this from an evolutionary perspective, with women's infidelity being more threatening to the reproductive potential of the married couple. The second most cited reason for divorce was sterility, and the third cruelty or maltreatment. In the vast majority of cases this cruelty involved the husband's maltreatment of his wife. Betzig's analysis focused primarily on pre-industrial societies: extending this to more modern societies, Betzig notes how couples with fewer children are more likely to divorce even when the study was controlled for the length of the marriage. Surprisingly, economic reasons for divorce are rarely mentioned in Betzig's analysis. Others have argued that social and economic developments are major influences on divorce, with changes in the role of women likely to be a major contributor to rising divorce rates across a wide range of cultures (McKenry and Price, 1995).

In addition to these common causes for divorce, important local factors are also important in relationship breakdown. In Japan, the increase in divorce rates over the past thirty years has been partly attributed to the Japanese economy and the corresponding increased employment opportunities for women (which has made independent living more practical). This has combined with more favourable societal attitudes towards divorce and the decreased role of the extended family (McKenry and Price, 1995). It is important to note, however, that divorce still creates scandal in Japan, and break-up may tarnish the reputation of the children of the divorced parents (Hutter, 1988).

In Poland, where divorce figures are very low by European standards, it is women who usually file for divorce (Fuszara, 1997). This often follows psychological or physical abuse associated with the misuse of alcohol by their male partner. Unusually, women in Poland claim they are both emotionally and materially better off following the divorce, with many women in Poland being professionally employed and not dependent on their male partner. Other reasons for divorce in Poland underline the economic realities often important for personal relationships in post-Communist Europe. Couples who had managed to obtain more than one residence may divorce in order to retain scarce living apartments (one of these apartments would otherwise have had to be returned to the co-operative if they had stayed married). In this situation, the couple may still live together and use the second apartment to generate much-needed income.

The high rate of marital dissolution in Russia is also often linked to the husband's alcoholism (Perevedentsev, 1978). However, low remarriage rates are also reported in Russia, with less than half of all divorced individuals remarrying (compared to 80 per cent in the US), leading to a marked loneliness among divorcees (McKenry and Price, 1995). These low remarriage rates are linked to the lack of available housing, as well as the desire of women to retain professional and independent lifestyles (Moskoff, 1983).

Xiaohe and Whyte (1990) report that divorce is still uncommon in China, with less than 4 per cent of their respondents having divorced (compared to more than a quarter of respondents in a similar study in the US conducted by Whyte, 1990). However, there is evidence of a recent increase in divorce rates, with divorce figures doubling following the introduction of the 1980 Marriage Law (which made absence of love a primary criterion for relationship breakdown). A large number of divorce cases resulted from unhappy marriages that were formed in the turmoil of the Cultural Revolution period (Honig and Hershatter, 1988). Urban women 'sent down' to the countryside may have married a Youth League or Party member as a means of securing their survival, and the new social policies of the late 1970s (which allowed educated youths to return to the cities) called into doubt many rural marriages made during the Cultural Revolution period. Sudden changes in status and role, particularly pronounced in the turmoil in the years following the Cultural Revolution, also led to a widening gulf in the social status of the couple, and strained previously egalitarian relationships. And in the materialistic 1980s the failure to deliver promised material goods also led to dissatisfaction (Honig and Hershatter, 1988). In addition, until recently, much interaction between couples was dictated by the state, as state bodies had the power to allocate jobs to couples many hundreds of miles apart (Ruan and Matsumura, 1991). This separation of couples led to significant dissatisfaction in many Chinese marital relationships. Nevertheless, divorce is still a difficult option, having the potential to cause considerable shame for both the individual and the family. Housing for divorcees is particularly difficult, especially in urban areas where accommodation is scarce (Honig and Hershatter, 1988).

Intriguingly, given the social constraints and taboo against divorce normally associated with traditional arranged marriages, freedom of partner choice in China has a small but significantly positive correlation with marital stability, with love matches being more stable than arranged marriages (Whyte, 1990). Although reasons for divorce vary between rural and urban areas (Naltao, 1987), as is the case in many countries, those who marry young are more likely to become divorced (McKenry and Price, 1995).

A period of political unrest has also been blamed for the rising divorce rate in Iran. McKenry and Price (1995) claim that a large number of people rushed into marriage during the Islamic revolution, and family instability was exacerbated by the uncertainties of the Iraqi war and the difficulties faced by the middle classes in adapting to the strict Islamic value system (McKenry and Price, 1995). As in other countries, divorce is more common where women marry younger and work after their marriage (McKenry and Price, 1995; Nassehi-Behman, 1985). Family disintegration in rural areas may be largely due to the migration of men to the urban centres in their search for work. However, Nassehi-Behman (1985) also notes that divorced women are liable to become targets of sexual harassment and abuse, and that, in spite of family support, such women often experience marked loneliness.

Economic modernisation and the greater education and work opportunities for younger women are seen as major factors in divorce in African societies. In Ghana, those who have lived in urban regions, influenced by modernisation, have higher divorce rates, and again divorce is higher among couples who marry young and those where the women work (Amoateng and Heaton, 1989). If the man becomes an economic liability by being unable to work, divorce is also more likely (McKenry and Price, 1995). In Nigeria, divorce rates are also expected to rise as urbanisation increases. Divorce is also anticipated to increase in rural areas, where it is now less essential for women to work (McKenry and Price, 1995).

Some cross-cultural work has been conducted on premarital relationship dissolution, although this work rarely employs samples representative of the countries studied. Hortascu and Karanci (1987) asked Turkish students about the causes of recent relationship breakdowns. Their results showed that these Turkish couples gave similar reasons for their break-up to those reported in the Western literature (e.g. Hill *et al.*, 1976, in the US), citing personality incompatibility and living too far apart as the main reason for their separation. However, as the authors note, this study was conducted with one of the most modern groups in Turkey (students studying near the capital) and, given the influence of family and economic forces on less 'modernised populations', one might anticipate different results in more rural areas and amongst more diverse populations.

While divorce may be seen as a much-needed escape from the tensions of marriage, few societies place a positive value on divorce (McKenry and Price, 1995). However, the mechanisms that allow an individual to divorce differ greatly across cultures, and in many cultures one of the partners (usually the man) has greater rights to obtain a divorce than the other (Hatfield and Rapson, 1996). Furthermore, in most cultures, demographic factors interrelate with men's preferences for a younger partner to make it harder for a woman to remarry than a man (Goode, 1993). In Saudi Arabia, a man does not have to give formal reasons for his divorce, while a woman cannot divorce unless this is specifically stated in her marriage contract. Custody of the children goes to the father and the man remains in the family home with the children, while the woman must return to her parents' home (Minai, 1981). In Egypt, women find it much more difficult to initiate divorce than men: while the Muslim man can simply repudiate his wife three times *(talaq)*, the woman must go to court and petition for her divorce and divorce is only permitted on certain grounds – that her husband has refused to support her, he has a serious defect, has a bad moral or social effect on her, has been absent for long periods, or is imprisoned (Rugh, 1984). Sow (1985) argues that divorce restrictions in Islamic society often run contrary to traditional arrangements which existed in the pre-Islamic era. In the traditional family, the woman could take refuge in the home of her uncle or brother, and her parents could pronounce the divorce. Under Islamic rules, divorce remains the man's prerogative.

The direct relationship of cultural values to relationship breakdown has rarely been assessed. In a historical analysis, Simmel (1971) suggests that individuation in a society can make the achievement of satisfaction more difficult, as the individual constantly searches for a 'unique partner'. Fine (1994) related cultural values to divorce laws. In an analysis of the divorce laws of five Western cultures (US, England, Wales, France and Sweden) he noted that most countries have moved away from traditional fault grounds for divorce to grounds designed to allow for divorce with lesser acrimony (as, for instance, in the new Family Law Act of 1996, which comes into effect in England and Wales in 1999). At the same time, there has been increasing legislation to improve the situation of children following divorce. The highly individualistic US has emphasised the notion of individual rights in its divorce laws, whereas Sweden, while also valuing individual rights highly, has reflected this society's more egalitarian orientation by placing a high value on public support networks. At the same time, across the cultures the 'liberal' divorce laws of the 1970s and 1980s have been increasingly chal- lenged in more recent years. Fine (1994) argues that these changes in divorce and marriage legislation have been bi-directional in influence: while they have followed existing cultural values, they have at the same time been important in helping to change societal perspectives on marriage and divorce.

Brodbar-Nemzer (1986) examined the relationship between active group commitment and divorce, interpreting group commitment as an index of social integration and collectivist orientation. Arguing that divorce can be seen as a strong reflection of a group's attitudes towards marriage, Brodbar-Nemzer (1986) studied more than 4,000 Jewish households in New York, asking them about their Jewish denomination (orthodox or liberal) and behaviour (e.g. attending synagogue, visiting Israel, belonging to Jewish organisations), and their friendship networks (the proportion of closest friends that were Jews). He found a direct relationship between Jewish commitment and disinclination towards divorce, attributing this relationship to a stronger sense of social integration, and more positive attitudes towards the family, among the more 'committed' Jewish community.

Relationship violence

Humans act aggressively and violently to different degrees, in different ways, and for different reasons, across cultures. Different cultural attitudes and rules influence how societies both define and assess sexual and non-sexual abuse (Levinson, 1989; White and Sorensen, 1992). Writers from a feminist perspective have stressed the way in which learned gender-role socialisation and coercive cognitive schema combine to perpetuate sexual aggression (e.g. Buckhart and Fromuth, 1991). In a minority of societies, violence is practically unknown. Levinson (1989), using Human Relations Area Files data from 330 societies, estimates that in about 16 per cent of societies marital violence is unknown or very rare, with non-violent societies characterised by a cooperative and egalitarian family life.

The study of relationship violence is a politically highly-charged area. Thus, although researchers in the US have created headlines by finding that Black and Hispanic couples are more likely to use violence on one another, these ethnic differences disappear once researchers allow for economic circumstances (Hatfield and Rapson, 1996). Lockhart (1987) examined the effects of race and social class in a study of African-American and White couples. There were similar rates of domestic violence among poor African-American and poor White couples. Among the middle-class couples, domestic violence rates were higher for the African-American than the White couples, while upper-class African-Americans had a lower rate of violence than upper-class Whites. This was interpreted as reflecting the insecurity and stress that many African-Americans feel when they attain a relatively unfamiliar middle-class status.

In a study of 115 Korean heterosexual males in a large Korean city, Ridley *et al.* (1996) found that a number of relationship beliefs distinguished abusive from non-abusive men. Non-abusive men were relationally closer, had fewer dysfunctional love beliefs (reflecting over-dependency or posses- siveness), believed that power and force tactics were inappropriate, had a more positive self-perception, took greater responsibility in dealing with problems, promoted greater equality in relational power, and were more satisfied with their relationships. Hardin *et al.* (1996) argue that an extreme 'working model' of love can lead to unrealistic expectations and responses in a relationship. This can lead to anger and frustration when these expecta- tions are not met, leading, in some cases, to abusive behaviour.

Differences in the cross-cultural perceptions of wife-beating make rela- tionship interventions across cultures problematic. Levinson (1989) cites the case of Christian missionaries in Brazil who, by discouraging divorce, kept together people who were clearly unsuited. This seems to have contributed, inadvertently, towards a marked increase in wife-beating among the mission- aries' new converts.

Sexual aggression and rape

Sanday (1981) distinguished between 'rape-prone' societies, where sexual assaults by men or women are either permitted or ignored (18 per cent of the societies she studied) and 'rape-free' societies, where rape is practically unknown (47 per cent of the societies she studied). Using ethnographic accounts from 156 largely pre-industrial societies, she found rape-prone soci- eties to be violent societies where both inter- and intra-group violence was common. Such societies also tended to view women as 'property'. Rape-free societies were distinguished by a belief in male and female complementarity. She argued that

> ... rape in tribal societies is part of a cultural configuration that includes interpersonal violence, male dominance and sexual exploitation ... rape is not an integral part of male nature but a means by which men programmed for violence express their sexual selves.
>
> (Sanday, 1992: 25ff)

Box (1983) claims that British society prepares the man for his role as 'potential rapist', and provides a whole 'cultural library of excuses' for his actions. At the same time, however, male rapists are viewed by the popula- tion at large as extreme psychopaths, freaks who are somehow 'outside' of society, while the woman is often implicitly (if not explicitly) blamed for an attack (White and Sorensen, 1992). Haebich (1997) also argued that accep- tance of violence and rape myths are culturally determined. She examined male sexual aggression among students in Finland and the US. Sexual aggression was defined in this study as 'any sexual behaviour ... that is achieved by coercing a female partner through various tactics including verbal threats, physical force or weapons'. In her study she found that, while many of the personality factors predicting sexual aggression were similar in the US and Finland, imagined sexual aggression only predicted actual aggression in the US. This suggests that social restraints intervene more directly in Finland to influence the expression of sexual frustrations.

Tang So-Kum *et al.* (1993) examined non-offender male students in Hong Kong, suggesting that motivations for sexual aggression may depend on cultural levels of aggressiveness, sex guilt and aggression desirability. Their study indicates that, in a society with low sex guilt and high aggressive drives, such as the US, variations in sex guilt predict sexual aggression. In a society with low aggressive drive and high sex guilt (Hong Kong), variations in aggressive drive predict sexual aggression. This suggests that both sexual and aggressive motivations may be important, depending on the prevailing cultural levels of aggression or sexual inhibition. Such work is important in helping contextualise sexual aggression within the wider social norms of a society.

One intriguing psycho-dynamic hypothesis suggested by Segall (1988) links the rape of women to child-rearing practices. In cultures where child-rearing is assigned to female adults, early childhood gives the male little opportunity to learn male roles. To assist him in learning such roles, some societies will provide severe male initiation ceremonies which involve extreme displays of aggression. In such examples of 'compensatory machoism', men are encouraged to escape their 'womanliness' in an atmosphere where female rape is acceptable. A similar notion is suggested by Broude (1983). Using coded data from more than two hundred societies in the Standard Cross-Cultural Sample, she suggested that male boasting, sexual hostility and infidelity may be seen as attempts by men to compensate for insecurities about their masculinity.

Cultural differences in individualism and collectivism can be used to explain some of the international variations in relationship aggression and rape. Gordon and Donat (1992) argue that the strong ethos of social exchange in the individualist US (discussed on p. 78) may lead certain men to feel that once they have kept 'their side of the bargain' (having paid for a meal, taken the woman out in their car, etc.) then their partner should also keep hers (i.e. engage in sexual intercourse). Failure to do so may lead to the man feeling 'justified' in sexually assaulting the woman. In more collectivist societies, however, direct social exchange is less evident, with interaction governed by broader values reflecting collective goals. In these societies, therefore, expectations of reciprocal exchange are less common.

A second, related example refers to the way in which women in individualist societies are frequently caught in a 'double-bind' situation, being both attracted to their partner but having to deal with the possibility of unwanted advances (Burgoyne and Spitzberg, 1992). This situation often leads to equivocation, misunderstanding and potential aggression. Such problems may be less likely to occur where there is strong regulation of pre-marital interaction by other parties (for example, in Iran: Hanassab and Tidwell,

1989). This may explain why rape is reported less among Hispanic women in North America, who usually originate from the collectivist societies of South America (Sorensen and Siegel, 1992). At the same time, of course, aggression against out-group members (including those from the dominant culture) may be less restrained.

Within the US, different reports of sexual assault may mirror the varying histories of different ethnic groups. During the times of slavery in colonial America, it was deemed 'impossible' to rape Black women because of their 'inherent sexual nature', and there were no penalties for the abuse of Black women by White men (Wyatt, 1993). Seen in this context, it is perhaps unsurprising that African-American women even nowadays are less likely than White Americans to report sexual assault to the authorities, antici- pating a lack of support from the community and wider society if they do so. Such pessimism is supported by evidence from police and courtroom procedures (Borque, 1989). African-American women are also more likely than their White counterparts to see sexual assault as an inevitable part of their lives, thus encouraging them to make less effort to guard against its occurrence and perpetuating the risk of attack. Culture here acts as a form of 'collective memory', making significant historical events major predictors of relationship practices and beliefs for many successive generations.

Summary

Marriage takes a number of forms across cultures, ranging from monogamy to cenogamy, and each of these different forms can be related to different ecological demands as well as to enduring political and religious beliefs. Certain relationship rules (such as respecting privacy) have been found in a diversity of cultures, although rules for exchange and distributing justice are likely to be moderated by both cultural values and the relationship with the interactant. In some societies, such as Japan, satisfaction within a marriage may be tied more strongly to inter-generational relationships, whereas Western models of relationship commitment, with their emphasis on rela- tionship alternatives, frequently ignore the important structural variables central to relationship maintenance in many cultures. Although certain factors, such as infidelity, are strong cross-cultural predictors of relationship breakdown, the opportunity for obtaining a divorce favours men in many societies. Relationship violence is likely to be partly predictable from the general levels of aggressiveness within a culture, as well as the degree of egalitarianism and the social expectations for sexual exchange persisting within that society.

5   Sexual attitudes and behaviour

Introduction

The study of sexual behaviour is a controversial one in most societies. In Britain, for example, funding for the largest-ever survey of British sexual behaviour was blocked by the British Cabinet, and was only eventually completed due to the intervention of an independent charitable foundation (Wellings *et al.*, 1994). Jahoda (1990: 16) notes how the cross-cultural analysis of sexual practices can both create and sustain prejudices. He recalls the writings of François Peron (1775–1810) who, during one of his voyages, encountered a group of natives keen to see whether a sailor was white 'all over'. The sailor's erection was greeted by the natives with surprise and delight. Peron concluded that the natives' response demonstrated that they were sexually inadequate. Interestingly, this notion of the 'savage' as 'sexually inadequate' is at odds with a more prevalent prejudice, that such 'primitive people' were retarded in their mental development by their excessive preoccupation with sex (Jahoda, 1990).

Prejudices are also sustained by research which appears to glory in the 'bizarre' or abnormal practices of others. Ritualistic practices, such as penile blood letting rites in Ilahita, are described in dramatic terms, although their fuller cultural significance (which largely concerns the assertion of masculine power) are rarely discussed (Tuzin, 1995). Taken out of context, such reports can only add to a continuing discourse of discrimination, which sees 'other cultures' as perverse and immoral. As I will argue in this chapter, such perceptions may be of particular significance where there is widespread concern about the transmission of sexual disease. In this chapter, I continue my discussion about cultural norms and relationships by considering relationship rules concerning incest, extra-marital relationships and pre-marital sex. I also consider how sexual attitudes have changed over time, and the relationship between sex and love and jealousy and envy. I then move on to consider some of the issues surrounding sexual orientation. In the latter half of the chapter, I discuss some of the more negative aspects of sexual behaviour, including sexually transmitted diseases and sexual exploitation. I end by warning of some of the problems we face when attempt to assess sexual practices and mores across cultures.

Social norms and sexual behaviours

Rules of behaviour: incest and extra-marital relationships

As I discussed in Chapters 3 and 4, cultural rules play an important role in determining the 'appropriateness' of a relationship partner. Nearly all known human societies prohibit sexual relations between those seen as blood kin (Eriksen, 1995; Schlegel, 1995), although there are some variations about how such blood kin are defined and how incest is sanctioned (Davenport, 1987). A large number of explanations have been given for this taboo, with some stressing the value of forging new alliances, while others have argued that those who have grown up together are unlikely to feel attracted to one another (Eriksen, 1995).

Evolutionary theorists (e.g. Thornhill and Thornhill, 1987) have argued that individuals will not typically engage in behaviour contrary to their reproductive interests. Such behaviour may well be the case in incestuous liaisons. These theorists distinguish between three types of incest: mating between very close individuals (such as parents and offspring and siblings); inbreeding between close relatives, and breeding between those who are related by affinity rather than genetics. Incest rules against mating are rarely focused on close kin, who, evolutionists argue, are unlikely to mate, but concentrate on relations between more distant kin who, if they mate, threaten the reproductive interests of the rule-making men. Incest rules can also function to ensure that females are kept as sexually isolated as possible from men, preventing sexual interactions within lineage and restricting relatives from concentrating their wealth or power. The one exception to this rule seems to be the marriage of siblings by royal or tribal chiefs. Here, dynastic or political interests may override the incest taboo (Schlegel, 1995).

In Chapter 4 I identified extra-marital liaisons as a major contributor to relationship dissolution across the world, and there are norms governing non-marital sex in most of the world's cultures (Frayser, 1985; Rosenblatt and Anderson, 1981). Even the suspicion of having extra-marital sexual relations can have severe consequences in some cultures (Hatfield and Rapson, 1996): in Egypt, a Kenuzi husband can kill his wife even if he merely suspects her of infidelity (McCammon *et al.*, 1993). In Morocco, the law excuses a man who kills his wife caught in the act of adultery, although a woman is not equally excused (Davis and Smith, 1991). On the Chinese mainland, extra-marital relations have become one of the major reasons for divorce (Honig and Hershatter, 1988), with some 80 per cent of divorce cases in the Canton region mentioning extra-marital affairs in their proceedings, and some 10 per cent of couples reporting having had extra-marital relationships (Ruan and Matsumura, 1991). In response, some Chinese cities, worried about the apparent explosion in the numbers of such affairs, have made adultery a crime.

In Britain, the largest-ever survey of sexual activity, which questioned a random sample of 19,000 respondents, found that fewer than 5 per cent of married men and 2 per cent of married women reported having more than one partner during the past year, and less than 1 per cent of married men and 0.2 per cent of married women more than two partners over this time period (Wellings *et al.*, 1994). Those who were cohabiting behaved more like single people, with more than one in seven cohabiting men and one in twelve cohabiting women having more than one partner over the previous year. Multiple partnership was greatest not among the single but among the separated, divorced and widowed, regardless of age or sex. These results are comparable with North American data. In a US survey of more than 600 spouses, 96 per cent claimed they had been monogamous in the previous year (Greeley *et al.*, 1990).

Double standards, which allow men but not women to have affairs, seem to be prevalent in many societies (Frayser, 1985). Frayser found that no society gave women the option of having affairs while at the same time denying this right to men. For example, although the Japanese do not seem to share Western puritanical views about the sinfulness of sex, far greater licence is given in sexual activity for men than women (Reischauer, 1988). There is also evidence of a 'double standard' after marriage in many Chinese societies. In a study conducted by Kok in Singapore (1989), both young men and young women were found to be relatively conservative in their initial sexual experiences, but after marriage, more than 15 per cent of men were involved in casual sex, usually with commercial sex partners. In the US, men have extra-marital sex earlier in marriage than women, and have more extra-marital sexual partners (Glass and Wright, 1992).

A number of studies have examined attitudes towards extra-marital relationships. In most societies there is relatively little tolerance of such affairs (McCammon *et al.*, 1993), although Scandinavian countries and the Netherlands seem more tolerant than most. Buunk (1980) found Dutch couples to be more positive towards extra-marital sex than those in the US. Christensen (1973) asked students in nine cultures whether sexual infidelity was always wrong. This research found college students in Denmark and Sweden relatively tolerant (only 7 per cent of Danes and 31 per cent of Swedes thought such affairs were always wrong, compared to 71 per cent of their Taiwanese respondents). It should be noted, however, that this latter research was conducted in the early 1970s, well before the current concerns about HIV/AIDS and other sexually transmitted diseases. More recent work has shown attitudes towards extra-marital sex to be strongly negative in Britain. Only 2 per cent of respondents in Wellings *et al.*'s (1994) survey claimed extra-marital sex was not at all wrong, and three-quarters of respondents believed it was 'always' or 'mostly wrong'. Furthermore, two-thirds of the men surveyed, and three-quarters of the women, believed that cohabiting partners should be sexually exclusive, with young people supporting monogamy as strongly as elder respondents. These results are comparable to those found in the US, where 88 per cent of people thought extra-marital sex always or almost always wrong, and only 3 per cent thought it was not wrong at all (Davis and Smith, 1991). Of course, as we saw in Chapter 3, in many societies a number of partners may be permitted (mainly pre-industrial or Islamic cultures), with some of these partners having a primary sexual purpose. While the deprivation of marital sex seems to contribute to non-marital sexuality in some cultures, this is not evident in others (Rosenblatt and Anderson, 1981). Indeed, in some cases, extra-marital affairs may even strengthen the marriage by providing an extra source of income, or by providing a child for an otherwise infertile couple (Rosenblatt and Anderson, 1981).

Pre-marital sex

There is considerable variation across cultures in the extent to which pre-marital sexual relations are permitted (Ingoldbsy, 1995b; McCammon *et al.*, 1993). A number of factors are likely to be significant in determining attitudes towards pre-marital sexual relationships. One reason for rejecting pre-marital sexual relationships is the fear that such relationships may complicate planned relationships, and in many cultures where marriage is arranged, contact between young people of the opposite sex may be severely restricted (Rosenblatt and Anderson, 1981). As I argued in Chapter 3, this is most likely to occur in collectivist cultures, and indeed young people in the primarily collectivist countries of Asia, the Middle East and South America generally strongly disapprove of pre-marital sex, whereas young adults in the more individualist UK, Belgium, France and Scandinavia accept relatively permissive sexual standards (Hatfield and Rapson, 1996: 126). Thus Sprecher and Hatfield (1996) found young Americans more tolerant of pre-marital sex than the more collectivist Russian or Japanese students, although in all three countries these students disapproved of casual sex. Rates of pre-marital sex in Singapore are low, with representative studies of women finding that very few engaged in casual sexual intercourse, and that nearly all acts of pre-marital intercourse were with a person who later became the regular sexual partner or husband (Kok, 1990). Wellings and her colleagues in Britain (Wellings *et al.*, 1994) explored attitudes towards pre-marital sex. Only 8.2 per cent of men and 10.8 per cent of women in her sample believed it to be always or mostly wrong, showing far more permissiveness than comparable American data. This acceptance was greatest among the young, but even for the oldest cohort in the sample (aged 45–59) only one in seven men and one in five women disapproved of pre-marital sex.

Sub-cultural ethnic differences are also likely to be important in sexual behaviour. In their study of sexual behaviour in Britain, Wellings *et al.* (1994) found that those from an Asian background (who might be assumed to be from a more collectivist sub-culture) were less likely to have reported sexual intercourse before the age of 16 (less than 1 per cent of Asian women reported losing their virginity before the age of 16). Black men were likely to have reported earlier sexual intercourse. Roman Catholic men were more likely to report sex before 16 than those of any other religious affiliation. Within the US, there are large ethnic differences in the percentage of births to unmarried mothers. Births to unmarried mothers make up 21.8 per cent of White births but 67.9 per cent of African-American births (Wolf, 1996). In general, African-Americans were found to have a less puritanical attitude towards sex than White Americans (Staples, 1982) and begin sex at an earlier age (Banks and Wilson, 1989).

Although collectivist societies are generally hostile towards pre-marital sex, non-industrialised societies may be far more tolerant. Frayser (1985) gathered data from sixty-two hunting, foraging and agricultural societies from the *Standard Cross-Cultural Sample* and found that two-thirds of these non-industrial societies permitted men and/or women to have pre-marital sex. In an analysis of more than 800 societies in Murdock's Ethnographic Atlas, two-thirds of societies were found to impose little restriction on pre-marital sex, with the most permissive societies being in the Pacific regions (Wen-Shing and Jing, 1991). For example, the Marquesans on Nuku Hiva Island (Eastern Polynesia) encourage pre-marital sexual explorations by both boys and girls as young as 10 years of age (McCammon *et al.*, 1993). In Africa, penetrative sex may also begin at a relatively young age: in a 1984 survey, nearly a third of Zimbabwean women aged 15 to 19 had had at least one pregnancy (Wilson and Marindo, 1989). Demographic and educational factors may have a significant effect on the sexual attitudes and behaviours of teenagers. In a study of more than 500 unmarried Zambian women, ranging in age from 13 to 21, Pillai and Roy (1996) found that high academic self-esteem and high social class were correlated with liberal attitudes towards sex. Finally, the physical conditions of child-rearing may also be particularly significant. Among the much-studied !Kung there is a relaxed attitude towards sex, with parents sleeping with their children in the same beds and having sexual relations while the child lays next to them. Sex play is seen as a natural part of childhood, and older children can lose their virginity without this being condemned (Wolf, 1996).

Despite fears of 'waking the sleeping child' (Sengoku, 1990), Japanese schools are required to incorporate sexual education classes in their curricula (Tanomura, 1990). Hatano (1991) argues that the great pressure on young Japanese taking university entrance examinations can be seen as a major factor in reducing heterosexual behaviour, with much of the young persons' energies focused on preparatory study. The Japanese Association for Sex Education administered nationwide surveys in Japan on sexual development, sexual consciousness and sexual behaviour among Japanese youth during the 1970s and 1980s. A comparison of the results between 1981 and 1988 indicated an increase in intercourse rate among university students during this period (Hatano, 1990), indicating a greater acceptance of pre-marital sexual activity.

In rapidly changing societies, there may be marked differences between ideology and practice in sexual relationships. For example, although there is evidence that many young women in Asia no longer see pre-marital chastity as a major goal, they *perceive* their activities as being far more restrained than their Western 'liberal' counterparts (e.g. Kok, 1990, in Singapore; Shieh, 1990, in Taiwan; Zhou, 1990, in China). Notably, however, in a large study of Taiwanese residents (*China Times Weekly*, 29 October 1993) nearly half the survey's respondents had had their first encounter before marriage. In Hong Kong, a Family Planning Association survey (1987) revealed that 38 per cent of men and 24 per cent of women in their mid-20s had had pre-marital sex. Eight-six per cent of respondents in a large Shanghai study approved of pre-marital sex (Burton, 1990), a finding that may be reflected in the recent large rise in abortions among young women (Ruan and Matsumura, 1991; Tsui, 1989). In mainland China, questions of physical intimacy between unmarried urbanites were widely discussed in the mid-1980s (Honig and Hershatter, 1988; Zhou, 1990), although the advice given to the young depended very much on the generation of the advisor and the sex of the young person involved. Elders were far more in favour of pre-marital abstinence, stressing the risks for women in particular. At the same time, while the press emphasised some aspects of the dangers of pre-marital sex, there was also a greater stress on practical advice on how to deal with problem situations, and the potentially negative impact of sexual activity. This can be seen as indicating a significant movement away from both traditional and socialist moralities, which were largely puritanical in their attitudes towards sexual activity (Tsui, 1989).

In Eastern Europe, Hillhouse (1993) argues that urbanisation and migration (traditionally associated with the individualisation of a culture) reduced traditional social controls and allowed pre-marital sexual behaviour to be more openly acknowledged. Changing attitudes towards sexual activity are well documented by Wellings and her colleagues in their study of sexual activity in Britain (Wellings *et al.*, 1994). For those women born between 1931 and 1935, the median age for first sexual activity was 21. This had dropped to 17 for those born between 1966 and 1975 (aged between 16 and 24 at the time of interview). Similar trends were also evident for men. Nineteen per cent of women born in the early 1970s had lost their virginity before the age of 16, compared to less than 1 per cent born in the early 1930s. Men and women in the upper social classes (social class one of five) were two to three years older than those from the lowest (unskilled) class at the time of first sexual intercourse, and those with higher education were also more likely to have had experienced first sexual intercourse at a later age.

Wellings *et al.* (1994) also found that first sexual experience in marriage is now almost unknown in Britain. This has changed dramatically in the last half-century: for those women born in the 1930s and 1940s more than 38 per cent remained virgins until they were married, compared to less than 1 per cent born in the late 1960s and early 1970s, and similar changes were reported for men. Older members of the sample (aged between 45 and 59), and women in particular, were likely to attribute their first sexual intercourse to resulting from 'being in love': curiosity was a stronger reason for first sexual intercourse among the younger members of the sample.

Of course, in many societies the issue of when individuals (usually women) decide to have intercourse is of less relevance. Wyatt (1993) notes how, in many parts of the world, children are sold into prostitution or married very young against their choosing. In these cases, issues of power and exploitation once again come to the fore.

Sexual attitudes and behaviour

Sexual encounters have very different meanings and consequences in different cultures (McCammon *et al.*, 1993). Even experiences which are generally seen as physiological in origin may be culturally influenced. For example, Abramson and Pinkerton (1995) note how a greater proportion of women are orgasmic in 'sex-positive' cultures (where oral sex, greater fore-play and female pleasure are encouraged) than in sexually inhibited cultures. In some societies, such as the Mangaians of the Polynesian Islands, sexuality is expressed in a very open way, with adults copulating in the same room as their kin (Marshall, 1971). The woman was expected to be sexually active from childhood, and to be an active participant in sexual activity. In contrast, in a small Irish agrarian community, women were found to be sexually passive and sexual activity was highly private (Davenport, 1977).

In China, medical texts on sexuality date back further than 100 BC, and in Ancient China courtly love and sex (including homosexual sex) was consid-ered virtuous among both rulers and subjects (Hatfield and Rapson, 1996). However, although we have relatively little information about the sexual behaviour of the Chinese, there is clearly a great deal of misunderstanding about sexual matters in some Chinese cultures. In the words of Wen (1995), 'It is clear that many Chinese people still hold the folk view that sexual desire and activity needs to be carefully regulated, otherwise it would be harmful to your health.'

Within marriage, many Chinese women know little about sex, with some couples reporting that they were still unsure whether or not they had had intercourse after several years of marriage! Recognising this ignorance, the official mainland Chinese press began to publish sex manuals for the newly married in the early 1980s, although not without a touch of propaganda about the role of sex in 'socialist reconstruction' (Honig and Hershatter, 1988). A great deal of anxiety arose concerning masturbation, particularly among young males (Honig and Hershatter, 1988). Even during the 1980s, young people were warned in sexual education lessons to wash their faces in cold water if they became sexually aroused (Honig and Hershatter, 1988).

A continuing debate in China concerns the sexual morality of unmarried women (Honig and Hershatter, 1988). Much of this is rooted in the political tides that first swept through this country in the early days after the revolution of 1949, followed by the Cultural Revolution and the reaction to this in the 1980s. One marked area of change has been in the public attitude towards female adornment. Such adornment was rejected during the austerity of the Cultural Revolution, during which plain dress was required so as to show identification with the masses. However, the assertion of individual identity through beauty was embraced in the years of reactance following the death of Mao. Nevertheless, despite the assertion of individuality, women are still viewed as being at risk from predatory males, and virginity squandered while young could lead to social rejection. Thus, women were given the double message that, while they should make themselves sexually attractive, they should at the same time keep clear of sexual activity until safely married.

In a detailed review of the cross-cultural evidence, Hatfield and Rapson (1996) argue that throughout the world there is a tendency for people to engage in more sexual activity and experimentation. They point to the 1986–7 demonstrations by university students in China, in which posters advocated greater sexual freedoms. At the same time, in the US the 'sexual revolution' which helped herald an increase in early and greater sexual activity may since have been reversed, with the fear of AIDS accompanied by the rise of the New Christian Right (Wolf, 1996). Sexual attitudes should therefore be seen as part of a continuing political and social debate concerning the 'correct' balance between the individual expression of needs/desires and the restrictions placed by wider social obligations.

Sex and love

According to Hatfield and Rapson (1996), passionate love and sexual desire are closely related – they are, in Hatfield and Rapson's terms, 'kissing cousins' (p. 90). However, a number of studies have indicated sex differences in women's desire for love in a partner, suggesting that women are more likely to see love and sex as more closely related than men (Foa *et al.*, 1987; Wellings *et al.*, 1994; Wyatt, 1993). Women in the US are more likely to have a greater emotional involvement with their extra-marital sexual partners, often claiming to feel that falling in love justifies their affair (Glass and Wright, 1992). Women are also more likely to report that they like their lovers better than their husbands, whereas the opposite pattern is evident for men with their female lovers (Patterson and Kim, 1991).

Foa *et al.* (1987) conducted three studies to examine sex differences in love and sex among heterosexual and homosexual respondents. Two of these studies were conducted in the US, and one in Sweden. Respondents sorted statements referring to sex (for example, having sexual intercourse, showering with someone), love (sharing feelings, caring about someone) and a third 'service behaviour' category (such as making lunch for someone or ironing their shirt). Women (and particularly single homosexual women) were more likely to group love and sex together. A comparison of the Swedish and the US scores showed that Swedish scores were more in the 'feminine' direction in their categorisations, with sex and love more closely grouped together. Using Hofstede's (1980) data, Foa *et al.* (1987) relate this to the greater femininity of Swedish culture.

Sexual jealousy and envy

Jealousy and envy are important subjects for study across cultures, not only because of their obvious implications for behaviour but because they may provide important insights into the continuing controversy between socio-biological accounts of relationships (which stress the genetic determination of jealousy responses) and socio-cultural accounts (which emphasise cultural variety in jealousy and envy) (Hupka *et al.*, 1985). Hupka *et al.* defined jealousy as 'the emotions, cognitions, and behavior associated with the appraisal of threat ... arising from the potential, actual, or imagined involvement of one's loved one or mate in a relationship with an interloper', and envy as 'the invidious comparison of one's qualities and achievements with another's' (p. 425).

Hupka et al. (1985) compared romantic jealousy and envy among students in Hungary, Ireland, Mexico, the US, the Soviet Union, Yugoslavia and the Netherlands. While a factor analysis of this data suggested that there were some core factors indicative of jealousy and envy across cultures, there were also significant cultural differences in the exhibition of jealous and envious behaviours. Individuals in all seven cultures were keen to project an image of themselves as people capable of establishing and maintaining close relationships, rather than as envious individuals who resented the relationships of others. However, triggers for jealousy responses differed across cultures. For example, Hungarians were significantly more likely to become upset than Dutch respondents if they saw their lover kissing someone else.

In a second analysis, using data from the same countries, Buunk and Hupka (1987) reported that in nearly all these nations, kissing, flirting and sexual involvement with another evoked jealousy, while hugging and the sexual fantasies of their partner produced a more neutral reaction. Respondents from the former Soviet Union were the most negative about the majority of these behaviours, while in other nations (such as the former Yugoslavia) there was a mixture of responses (a very negative reaction to flirting but the least negative reaction to kissing and sexual fantasies). There were also notable sex differences which held across all seven nations, with women more upset when their partners kissed someone else, and men reacting more negatively to their partner's sexual fantasies of another. Buunk and Hupka (1987) see this mixture of universality and cultural variation as offering partial support for both socio-biological and socio-cultural accounts of jealousy.

Sexual orientation

Sexual orientation is rarely an uncontroversial topic, with homosexuality in many cultures a politically charged topic (Peplau, 1998). Until 1967, male homosexuality was a criminal offence in Britain, and it was only removed from the list of psychiatric disorders by the American Psychiatric Association in 1974. Abramson and Pinkerton (1995) point out that there are a variety of economic and political reasons why homosexuality might be pathologised. One reason may be that, by influencing non-reproductive sexuality, homosexuality reduces the potential number of workers in a society.

Most non-industrialised societies permit homosexuality (McCammon *et al.*, 1993), although much may depend on the life stage of the individuals concerned. In Melanesian societies, sexual contacts between males may occur as part of male initiation. Although forced upon the boys at first, homosexuality may be enjoyed more by participants when older (Greenberg, 1995). Schlegel and Barry (1991) examined attitudes towards homosexual activity among adolescents in more than fifty mainly pre-industrial societies. In general, adolescent homosexual behaviour was widely regarded as a childish substitute for prohibited heterosexual activity. They found little relationship between attitudes towards adolescent homosexual and heterosexual activity, although there was a correlation between attitudes towards adolescent and adult male homosexual behaviour. Despite relative tolerance towards homosexuality in youth in many societies, same-sex families are rarely socially acknowledged or given the legal status or legitimacy of other family forms (Stanton, 1995).

Deciding what percentage of the population is heterosexual, gay or bisexual is notoriously difficult. It is often unclear whether we should focus on self-definitions, sexual desires or actual behaviour. Unfortunately, different definitions have been used in different countries, making cross-cultural comparison difficult (Hatfield and Rapson, 1996). Furthermore, different methods for collecting data have led to different responses. For example, in Britain, Wellings *et al.* (1994) surveyed nearly 19,000 people aged 15 to 59 during 1990 and 1991 (Wellings *et al.*, 1994). Here, the researchers asked about sexual orientation in two ways. First, they asked their subjects about sexual attraction – who they were attracted to. Second, they asked about sexual experiences. This included 'any kind of contact with another person that you felt was sexual', and ranged from kissing or touching to intercourse. In *face to face interviews* these researchers found that 90 per cent of men and 92 per cent of women were exclusively heterosexual in both their experiences and attraction. Only 1 per cent of men had had sexual experiences exclusively or mostly with other men, and fewer than 0.3 per cent of women had been exclusively or mostly lesbian. When given the opportunity to respond to *booklets in sealed envelopes*, respondents admitted to more *actual* homosexual activity than in the interviews. Here,

6.1 per cent of men and 3.4 per cent of women reported actual homosexual contact, and approximately half of this activity involved genital contact. Homosexuality was more likely to be reported by those in the two upper social classes, with almost 10 per cent of men from the professional and managerial classes reporting homosexual experiences, compared to only 3.2 per cent of skilled manual workers. Having attended private (boarding) schools was probably a major factor in this social class variation, with those attending such schools reporting greater homosexual activity at some stage in their lives, although this was only likely to have been short-lived. Men were more likely to have had their first homosexual experience in their teens, while women were equally likely to have their first lesbian experience at any time until their fifties. The greatest proportion of men reporting homosexual experience were aged between 35 and 44, with the lesser activity reported by the younger age groups, suggesting that concerns about HIV/AIDS played a role in their behaviour. Most homosexual activity was not exclusive – more than 90 per cent of respondents who had had a same-sex partner during their lives had also had a partner of the opposite sex. In terms of number of partners, the great majority of homosexual men did not report a great number of partners, contrary to public perception. However, a small proportion were highly sexually active, with highly sexually active men and women significantly more likely to have had a homosexual partner at some stage.

Lauman *et al.* (1994) interviewed more than 3,000 men and women between the ages of 18 and 59 across the US. They found that, although only 2.8 per cent of men and 1.4 per cent of women classified themselves as homosexual or bisexual, 10.1 per cent of men and 8.6 per cent of women said they had some same-sex desires or experiences. In the Netherlands, 12 per cent of men and 4 per cent of women reporting having had homosexual sex (Zessen and Sandfort, 1991) while in Finland 4 per cent of men and 3.8 per cent of women reported having had some homosexual experiences (Kontula, 1993).

While there is some evidence of a slowly growing tolerance to homosexuality in China (Liu *et al.*, 1992), few Chinese admit to being homosexual. Until very recently, homosexuals in mainland China were actively persecuted, and often charged with 'hooliganism' (Ruan and Matsumura, 1991). This led to not only a fear of penal servitude, but a feeling of emotional isolation too. Contact between gay men was closeted, with meetings occurring in only a few limited places, and contact between lesbians was even further restricted. This was reinforced by a strong, publicly-held prejudice against lesbians as 'immoral' people (Ruan and Matsumura, 1991). In a recent survey (*China Times Weekly*, 29 October 1993) most Taiwanese and mainland Chinese had heard of others' homosexual experiences but only 0.3 per cent of Taiwanese and 0.1 per cent of mainland Chinese admitted to personal homosexual experiences. However, there may be large differences between different sub-groups of this population. Of college men, 7.6 per cent reported having been attracted to another man, but only 2.3 per cent of peasants and 0.5 per cent of city dwellers reported such experiences (Liu *et al.*, 1992).

When analysing attitudes to homosexuality (rather than actual or reported behaviours) Minturn *et al.* (1969) found homosexuality to be condemned or ridiculed in nearly half (48 per cent) of the fifty-two non-industrial societies they analysed. A National Opinion Research Centre survey (Davis and Smith, 1991) found 75 per cent of Americans thinking homosexual relations always or almost always wrong. In Britain, Wellings *et al.* (1994) found that 70 per cent of men and 58 per cent of women believed sex between two men is always or mostly wrong, with similar percentages reporting condemnation of sex between two women. Only 20 per cent believed homosexuality not to be wrong at all. Younger people were not significantly more tolerant than older people

In Eastern Europe, homosexuality has often been repressed. In the former German Democratic Republic, the gay movements of the late 1960s reached East Germany through personal contacts and the media (Hillhouse, 1993). Ironically, however, given their general hostility to homosexuality, it was in the church that East German homosexuals received the most protection, with the church protecting gays and lesbians as part of a continuing rivalry with the state. In direct response, the Socialist Unity Party became more tolerant in its own attitudes and sought to spread a gay and lesbian identity in East German society and even to fund gay and lesbian clubs. Ironically, an attempt to give homosexuals the same civic rights as all other citizens was one of the last acts of the old GDR parliament. German unification led to the revoking of these liberal proposals (Hillhouse, 1993).

Sexually transmitted diseases

The spectre of HIV/AIDS presents a great challenge to a large percentage of the world's population, and has become a central topic for relationships analysis. In Africa and Asia (the areas of greatest infection), HIV is primarily a heterosexually transmitted disease (WHO, 1995) and in the US, women represent the fastest-growing segment of the HIV-infected population (Cooper, 1992). HIV has led to some rapid changes in governmental legislation. In Thailand, for example, a 'condom-only' law for commercial sex establishments was introduced in 1991, and non-governmental organisations have sprung up rapidly to provide health education (Manderson, 1995). Nevertheless, sex is still marketed as an important opportunity to earn much-needed tourist dollars in a number of poorer countries (Manderson, 1995).

Attitudes to AIDS vary extensively across cultures (Beardsley and Pederson, 1997). Attempts to stem the rapid growth of HIV infection in Africa have met with only limited success, with AIDS knowledge being limited in most poorly-developed countries (Ndeki *et al.*, 1994). Ocholla-Ayayo (1997) tried to explain the widespread nature of AIDS in East Africa.

A number of factors were cited as possible contributors, including the relatively wide variety of marriage forms (including polygamy), greater sexual freedom, and an increase in casual prostitution resulting from economic instability. An awareness of AIDS does not seem to have significantly changed behaviour, with high rates of sexual activity with casual partners reported by a range of occupational groups.

Cameron (1996) examined the individual and relational barriers that influence an individual's use of condoms among college students in the US and Kenya. Individual barriers reflect individual beliefs, attitudes and self-perceptions, while relational barriers incorporate the individual's perceptions of the relationship, and include perspective-taking and relationship trust. Cameron found greater individual and relational barriers to condom use in Kenya than in the US. Wilson *et al.* (1991), undertaking research in Zimbabwe, stress the considerable interpersonal skills needed to practise abstinence or condom use without causing tension within an interpersonal relationship. They argue that the social/interpersonal dimensions of the disease may be more significant than 'core disease dimensions' (assessments of susceptibility to the disease or ratings of its severity). These social factors, they argue, might be particularly significant in African societies, which stress adherence to cultural and community values. Once again they report relatively little evidence of a change in behaviour.

It is, of course, important to remember that AIDS in many countries poses no more of a threat than malaria, typhoid, or any one of the other fatal diseases which are so much part of everyday life in parts of Africa. For example, life expectancy is only 54 in Kenya, with 47 per cent of deaths being due to infectious or parasitic diseases (WHO, 1997). Bailey and Aunger (1995) argue that natural selection has left us with a strong desire for sex, and that psychological mechanisms overriding this may be overcome only in extreme conditions. Given the relatively long dormancy period of the HIV virus and the prevalence of other life-threatening diseases, it may be difficult to persuade those at risk to forfeit normal sexual practices because of the risk of such a 'long-term' disease.

The structure of the local environment may be an important determinant of contraceptive behaviour. Entwisle *et al.* (1989) examined the effects of village, household and individual characteristics on contraceptive use, questioning a large sample in rural Egypt. They argued that a range of community factors influence contraceptive behaviour by altering the value of children to parents and households, affecting the costs of child-bearing and influencing barriers to the use of contraception. They found that contraceptive behaviour varies with the village setting, with greater contraceptive use when agriculture was more commercialised, when the population was more educated, and when more family planning workers were employed.

HIV is a rising concern in Chinese nations. Liu (1992) estimates that approximately 5,000 people in Hong Kong are now infected with the HIV virus, but that this number is rising rapidly. Particular factors affect the propensity to engage in sex, including educational level (sexual activity does not usually begin until studying has finished) and occupation, with small-business people those most likely to visit prostitutes. Udomaratn (1990) reported that, of the Thai students he questioned, 41 per cent had had sexual experiences, mainly with prostitutes, and that one in five failed to use protection. In mainland China, officials have claimed an extremely low rate of HIV infection (*People's Daily*, 6 August 1989), although, given the ideological fallout associated with this disease, figures are hard to obtain. What is clear is that information is still only very limited, and practically nothing is known about the sexual activities of some social groups, such as divorced women.

Little research has been conducted into sexual health and the wider sociopolitical factors associated with it in Eastern Europe (Visser and Ketting, 1994). Where investigations have been conducted, they have demonstrated a great deal of misinformation about sexual matters, and about AIDS prevention in particular (Visser and Ketting, 1994). Thus, for example, Lunin *et al.* (1995) found that only 29 per cent of Russian 16-year-olds thought condoms should only be used once. This is perhaps unsurprising given that the frank discussion of sexual matters was strongly taboo in Communist Eastern and Central European countries (Goodwin, 1995). In much of the former Soviet Union, HIV/AIDS has remained a highly political subject. In Georgia, for example, an article in *Akhali Taoba* (3 December 1996) reporting official numbers of AIDS cases was contradicted a week later by the Department of Social and Economical Information, which in turn reported that there were no AIDS cases in Georgia (*Kavkasioni*, 11 December 1996). In Russia, a widespread belief that HIV is an 'outsiders" problem associated with 'the decadent West and Africa' contributed to a controversial AIDS law requiring the compulsory testing of foreigners. In Poland, infection has become easier due to the high rates of mobility, while a strongly influential Catholic Church has blocked a number of attempts to encourage discussion about sexuality (Danziger, 1996).

Most of the existing research on sexually transmitted diseases (the majority of which concerns HIV/AIDS) uses survey instruments which attempt to link individual knowledge, attitudes and beliefs to sexual practices (Moore *et al.*, 1996). However, there are both theoretical and empirical problems with the link between AIDS-related knowledge, attitudes and practices (see Joffe, 1996; Joffe, in press, for an overview). One particular problem with this approach is the assumption that individuals make considered, rational health choices. It fails to capture the tacit cultural and emotional dynamics that influence their beliefs and practices (Joffe, 1996). There is mounting evidence that sexual decisions are based upon a number of factors including the degree of commitment to the relationship: a heuristic exists whereby sex is viewed as inherently 'safe' once the relationship is a more committed one (Flowers *et al.,* 1996). Thus actual individual desires may be underpinned by non-conscious factors (Joffe, 1996).

Joffe (1996) argues that we need to employ a social representations approach to understanding HIV (Moscovici, 1984). This approach is explicitly concerned with examining cultural assumptions underlying sexual practices, and combines an interest in both individual thinking and wider societal representations (as expressed, for example, in the mass media). Social representations of HIV operate on a number of conceptual levels, helping protect culture and sub-group identities as well as serving the individual in affirming his/her actions and beliefs and justifying individual experiences (Stephenson *et al.*, 1993). Research informed by this approach is particularly concerned with the way in which different groups protect their identities by way of group-specific representations, both minimising their own perceptions of risk and allowing them to perpetuate existing prejudices against others. Recent studies of HIV using this perspective have begun to tap into the way in which people 'make sense' of an otherwise abstract scientific concept, anchoring it within existing models of disease and out-group discrimination (Joffe, 1996).

Joffe (1996) provides semi-structured interview data from a study of lay representations of sixty Britons and South Africans, a third of whom were gay men. Questions focused on where HIV originated, how it spread, which groups may be worst affected and the respondent's own sense of personal risk in relation to the syndrome. Joffe also investigated national, government-sponsored HIV/AIDS prevention campaigns in the two countries. She suggests that the early medical information transmitted on HIV focused overwhelming on 'out-groups', with the disease originally reported in 1981 as 'Gay Related Immune Deficiency' because early symptom-holders were all gay. According to the British press, it was gay people's promiscuous behaviour that was at the root of the risk, with their 'perverse' or deviant practices combining to produce a deadly 'sin cocktail'. This was coupled with a Western fascination with the syndrome's 'African aetiology', and a continuing debate about the extent to which the African model of sexual relationships was particularly conducive to the spread of HIV (Ocholla-Ayayo, 1997). Joffe found that over three-quarters of her White respondents in both Britain and South Africa saw AIDS as originating in Africa, while an even greater proportion of Black respondents in both samples saw the syndrome as originating in the West. This placement of responsibility for the threat 'out there' – evident in both cultures – helps maintain social order and existing dominant representations (Joffe, 1996) so that HIV/AIDS becomes, in the words of McAllister (1992: 196), 'the most explicitly politicised of medical conditions'. Joffe concludes that any attempt to understand AIDS-related thoughts and actions must account for the identity-protective role that such representations enjoy.

There are significant sub-group variations in safer sex practices in most countries. For example, affluent men in many cultures are more likely to use prostitutes, a group with a relatively high incidence of HIV infection (Towianska *et al.*, 1992). In Britain, Wellings *et al.* (1994) reported that men were more likely than women to have had 'unsafe' sex, defined here as having had two or more heterosexual partners in the past year but not using a condom during that time. The largest proportion of these were aged between 16 and 24, although the divorced/separated/widowed were five times more likely to engage in 'unsafe' sex than married people. 'Risk takers' (such as those who drink and smoke) also partake in riskier sexual behaviour, enjoying a greater number of sexual partners.

Prostitution and sexual exploitation

Prostitution in mainland China was established as early as the seventh century BC, and was prevalent throughout the country until the clampdown under Communism in the 1950s (Ruan and Matsumura, 1991). In the mid-1980s, however, there was a strong revival of the practice, with some commentators claiming that it was then more prevalent than in the years prior to Communism (Ruan and Matsumura, 1991). However, a growing fear of sexually transmitted disease, coupled with strong ideological opposition to the practice, led to a second and harsher wave of suppression in the late 1980s, although the long-term effectiveness of this later clampdown has yet to be assessed.

In Britain, almost 7 per cent of men reported that they had paid for sex at some time during their lives, with nearly 2 per cent claiming they had visited prostitutes within the last five years (Wellings *et al.*, 1994). This was most likely among older men: while 3.4 per cent of men aged 45–59 had their first sexual experience with a prostitute, none of those aged 16–24 reported this. Separated, divorced and widowed men were the most likely to have paid for sex during the previous five years, and those men in the upper social classes (classes one and two of five) were the most likely to have paid for sex at some time.

Phizacklea (1997) points to the close links between the sex and tourist industries, with sexual pleasure considered to be part of the 'package deal' for visitors to some Southeast Asian countries. Migration for women in many societies has only been possible in a limited number of professions, one of which is that of the sex worker. In some cases this migration involves the elaborate deception of the migrant, with this deception sometimes perpetrated by members of the woman's own community. Thus, a woman may be invited to work in an apparently 'respectable' job abroad, with her flight paid by a community member back home. On arrival she realises that she is trapped, working in the sex industry with no legal migrant status and little money to repay her flight costs. At the same time, of course, her participation in the sex industry helps reinforce negative stereotypes about Southeast Asian women as being subservient and highly sexed.

Assessing sexual practices and mores: a cautionary note

It need hardly be said that what people report in relationship surveys is unlikely to be a direct account of actual behaviour (McCammon *et al.*, 1993). This may be particularly true with research into sexual practices, yet researchers are rarely critical of the responses they receive in their work in this area (Berk *et al.*, 1995). Berk and colleagues (1995) found that their subjects could not reproduce in questionnaires sexual activities they had reported in diaries shortly beforehand, with subjects reporting more sexual activities in their questionnaires than in their diaries. There were also gender differences in reporting sexual behaviours, with women more likely to over-report oral sex than men in their diaries. Wilson *et al.* (1989) reported that African women were less open than men in answering questions about sexual behaviour. Hart and Poole (1995) argued that respondents to health surveys in collectivist societies are particularly likely to be non-compliant due to the out-group status of the interviewer. Western-funded prevention programmes (such as those in the area of HIV/AIDS) may be most likely to be treated with the greatest suspicion, and will rarely lead to substantial behavioural change (Maclachlan, 1993). This does not mean that all findings should be totally discounted. It does, however, mean that researchers should be particularly sensitive to the political and social contexts in which the data is collected, and should, where possible, aim to derive data from a number of complementary sources.

Summary

Rules prohibiting incest exist in all societies, while rules about pre-marital and extra-marital sex are far more culturally variable, although there is some evidence of a greater liberalism in sexual attitudes in many cultures. Both gender differences and cultural differences are evident in the relationship between sex and love and in attitudes towards jealousy and envy. Homosexuality forms part of a politically-charged debate in many societies, although there are signs of a greater tolerance in attitudes in some previously hostile cultures. Sexually transmitted diseases such as HIV are also heavily framed within existing political rhetoric, with many nations still denying the evidence of widespread sexual disease in their society. Finally, prostitution can be seen as part of a broader set of social problems that beset some of the world's poorer economies. Tackling the exploitation associated with this profession necessitates an examination of the large-scale problems of entrapment and immigration rights, as well as addressing the cultural stereotypes associated with 'sex tourism' in many societies.

6   Family relations across cultures

> Families shape the quality of our lives. Emotional and economic links
> among family members stretch across households and decades, influencing
> our outlooks on life, motivations, strategies for achievement, and styles for
> coping with adversity. Family relations are the earliest and most enduring
> social relationships. As a result, family life experiences deeply affect the
> competence, resilience, and well-being of each of us.
>
> (Basic Behavioral Science Research for Mental Health, 1996a: 622)

Introduction

The family forms a vital link between society, family and the individual
(Cowan *et al.*, 1993). It also constitutes a major topic for debate in many
societies, a political 'hot potato' discussed, often in vague and contradictory
terms, by politicians and the media alike. In this chapter, I begin by
discussing different family structures and values, with a particular emphasis
on how these values may be challenged or reaffirmed in changing societies. I
then consider the related issues of child-rearing and children's rights and
gender roles in the home, with a particular emphasis on how practices may
vary between sub-groups within cultures as well as between nations.

Kinship and family structure

A considerable amount of anthropological literature discusses kinship
arrangements (Georgas *et al.*, 1997). In many societies kinship is the single
most important cultural institution, organising careers, marriages and
personal identities. Even in the most 'modern' of societies, in which the
nuclear family may predominate, families are often financially important to
their members, and can help dictate political allegiances and career and life
opportunities (Eriksen, 1995). Indeed, Eriksen (1995: 109) argues that
nationalism in modern societies represents a 'metaphoric kin group'.

In most of Europe and North America, kin from both sides of the family
are of similar importance to family members, although a slight bias towards
the father's side is evident in the adoption of the father's surname. In

patrilineal (largely non-Western) societies, only men and their children are members of the lineage, with inheritance rights following the men. Women in such societies are in a weak position, and are often viewed as 'outsiders'. In the rarer cases of matrilineal kinship, political power still usually remains with the men, even where descent is traced through the women (Eriksen, 1995).

In most societies, the husband has close associations with his close male relatives, and lives in close proximity. This is known as *patrilocality*. In *matrilocal* societies, the wife resides with her husband and children near to her female relatives, although she may move closer to the husband's family later in the marriage. In *bilocal* arrangements, the family may choose which relatives to live close to. Such patterns of residence are likely to be dependent on economic factors. In hunting societies, hunting is a male preserve, and it is important that men stay in the same familiar area. Agricultural societies are more likely to be matrilocal, while in industrialised families it is less in the interests of the individuals to cooperate with larger kinship groups, and residence patterns may be more diverse (Stanton, 1995).

In the West, the concept of kinship is based on biological relationships. In Africa, the concept is broader, with kinship incorporating a wider religious and social community (Sow, 1985). This broader conception of the family can lead to misunderstandings. Stanton (1995) recites the case of a business owner who had a Native American Indian (Iroquois) employee. The businessman was frustrated by this employee who frequently asked permission to attend the funeral of his 'mother', 'father' or 'brothers'. The business owner suspected that the worker was using this simply as an excuse to miss work, and did not believe that the employee could have so many 'mothers' or 'fathers'. In doing this he was failing to comprehend that the Iroquois may refer to some twenty people as 'mother' and consider one hundred people brothers or sisters.

Nuclear and extended families

Two main types of family form are identified in the literature: the elementary, or nuclear, family, and the joint, or extended, family. The *nuclear* family consists of three social positions: husband/father; wife/mother and children (Lee, 1987). It is the presence of these positions (and not the size of the family) that makes the family nuclear (a family that includes a husband, two wives and eleven children is still nuclear but polygynous). The joint/extended family usually consists of three or more generations under one roof, although in the 'non-residential extended family' family members may live in adjacent homes but share meals and communal life (Stanton, 1995; Stopes-Roe and Cochrane, 1989). The presence of an extended family within one household may have both positive and negative implications for its members. While extended family members can provide important support, they can be interfering and restrict the autonomy of resident individuals and couples (Goodwin, Adatia *et al.*, 1997; Sillars, 1995).

The form of family structure adopted is likely to be dependent on both enduring cultural values and social and economic circumstances. The joint family is likely to be an important source of secure labour and inheritance, as well as welfare aid and support. This may be particularly important when wage labour is not the principal economic form (Suda, 1978). Joint families often evolve a hierarchical and authoritarian structure in order to operate in a smooth manner, and are likely to stress obedience and respect for authority and family reputation (Stopes-Roe and Cochrane, 1989).

The historical persistence of extended family households has often been exaggerated, a point recognised some time ago by Goode (1963) in his international analysis of family systems (see also Al-Thakeb, 1985; Tsui, 1989; Vergin, 1985). In China, for example, the extended family was under attack at least as early as the 1940s by the modern educated classes, who saw it as a restriction on the development of personality. In the words of Levy (1949: 302), in Hong Kong 'the traditional family is being wiped out without being replaced'. In particular, the large extended family in rural China is more of a myth than a reality, with census evidence showing the nuclear family to be the dominant form (Anderson, 1992; Chu, 1985; C.F. Yang, 1988). The reasons for this may be economic. High mortality rates among the poor in China have made it difficult for them to afford an extended household (Tsui, 1989). One increasingly common form of living in China is the 'stem' family, which consists of parents, their unmarried children, and one married child with a spouse and children. Children live with their parents simply because of a lack of housing, an arrangement adopted with some reluctance on both sides (C.F. Yang, 1988). This format is frequently maintained for the first few years of the young couple's marriage and allows the married children free accommodation and baby-sitting while the young mother is out at work (Tsui, 1989). Rather than contributing more to their elders than they receive in return, the traditional extended family pattern is reversed, with the young now taking more from their parents than they give (Tsui, 1989). Thus the Chinese family shows a strong adaptive ability to suit its environment and socio-political conditions, with the modern family in a continuous state of flux, ranging from the traditional conjugal format to the relatively isolated nuclear structure (Lau, 1981; Tseng and Wu, 1985). This underlines the functional value of the family, which serves to provide solidarity and very material support in an often difficult world (C.F. Yang, 1988).

In Turkey, as in China, the extended family is rare and is the dominant form mainly among large landowners, the only people with enough land to support such a family (Vergin, 1985). Al-Thakeb (1985), reviewing evidence from nine Arab countries, concluded that the Arab family is large but nuclear in structure. Indeed, Al-Thakeb argued that the extended family has *never* been the predominant family form in Arab cultures. As we will see, however, the presence of an independent conjugal family does not mean that family-kin relations are weak: on the contrary, there are strong levels of interaction between family members in Arab cultures. By living in close proximity to siblings, the advantages of the nuclear and extended family are combined, providing valuable opportunities for economic cooperation and emotional support (Al-Thakeb, 1985).

In Iran, housing problems in large cities have reduced the potential for the extended family, while intensive migration among the rural population has led to the weakening of larger kinship groups (Nassehi-Behman, 1985). This has contributed to the separation of extended families, with new couples leaving parents and creating their own nuclear units. At the same time, although old kinship networks have weakened, new ones have been built around careers.

In Japan, the modern Japanese family structure is similar to that of the American nuclear family, or perhaps the American family of sixty years ago (Reischauer, 1988). Once again, adapting to economic realities, retired parents are likely to live with their children out of economic necessity, although they may have their own separate wing of the house (Reischauer, 1988).

Personal relationships within Britain's ethnic minorities are likely to be influenced by three types of factors: the 'traditional' relationships they have brought with them from their country of origin, their adaptation to their changed environment (including the social support structures available to family members), and relationship patterns within the dominant White community (Modood *et al.*, 1994). Britain's ethnic minority groups exhibit very different patterns of family structure. While those of Caribbean origin are more likely to cohabit and have a number of dependent children, South Asians are more likely to be married (Ballard and Kalra, 1994) and may live in 'semi-extended' arrangement, with separate nuclear households existing in close proximity (Goodwin, Adatia *et al.*, 1997; Sillars, 1995). South Asians are also more likely to have created their own former kin network in Britain, with family members brought in from overseas. As we shall see, these ethnic differences in networks are reflected in the different family values held by Britain's ethnic minorities.

Family policies and values

Family values in Chinese societies

In Chinese societies, 'the family is still the basic unit of society' (Xiantian, 1985: 86) and is central to self-identity (J. Hsu, 1985). The Chinese family is often seen as the 'prototypical' collectivist family (Liebkind, 1996). Basic beliefs underlying the Chinese family can be traced back to the teaching of Confucius in the fifth century BCE (Meredith and Abbott, 1995). Such Confucian ethics teach individuals to value the collective welfare of the family more than individual welfare, and to take responsibility in community affairs (Schneider *et al.*, 1997). Three of the five major relationships in Confucianism are those involving family members: these are, in order of importance, those of father/son, older/younger brothers and husband/wife (K.S. Yang, 1988, 1995). Other characteristics of this family are hierarchical power with submission to parental authority, the mutual dependency of parents and children across generations, and the dominance of social interactions with family members over other activities (K.S. Yang, 1988: 98). The traditional extended family provided not only material security, but also psychological security in terms of ancestral lineage (Chu, 1985). When a Chinese family migrates overseas, responsibility towards the family, the interdependence of family members and respect for parents are still important principles, with many households remaining multigenerational abroad (Feldman and Rosenthal, 1990, 1991). The family may even provide a model for other, non-family organisations, with structural patterns, ethics, role relations and attitudes learned from family life seeping through into non-familial structures (K.S. Yang, 1995).

Although the tradition of Confucianism is well established in Chinese societies (J. Hsu, 1985), Tsui (1989) argues that there has been an increasing development of individualistic attitudes among the young in China, and a growing interest in material comfort and small, conjugal families (see also Anderson, 1992; Chu, 1985). The reasons behind this change are complex, but a number of macro-structural factors have probably been significant. One factor is obviously the greater exposure to alternative, Western models of the family. Certainly the young are keen to spend their earnings on themselves and their conjugal family. A second factor is directly related to the politics of mainland China, where the extended family as an economic unit was challenged by the land reforms of the Communist state (Chu, 1985). The confusion and turmoil of the Cultural Revolution, and its cry for a challenging of traditional authority structures, meant that traditional patterns of social relations based on respect for elders no longer held sway, and this led to a pragmatism and rejection of conservatism and authoritarian styles of upbringing (Lau *et al.*, 1990).

A third force undermining the traditional Chinese family is the increase in market orientation (Pollay *et al.*, 1990). The severity of the market, and the lack of formal support for those who have failed, has led to the forming of 'utilitarianistic familism', where traditional extended family ties are replaced by new ties of economic convenience (Lau, 1981). In some situations, these new formations have superseded family loyalties. Relations are now being built with a wider group of individuals who serve the interests of the family group (King and Bond, 1985). There is increasing use of nonkinship, 'pseudokin' networks to aid in achieving particular – usually materialistic – goals (Lau, 1981; Lee, 1985). New members are 'inducted' into the family group by core (usually 'blood-related') members (Blau *et al.*, 1991). Ironically, this has contributed to a 'new kind of familism', not alien to the Confucian philosophy, with new, close, non-kinship networks replacing many former family functions (King and Bond, 1985: 41). The utility of instrumental networks has tended to be ignored by researchers concerned primarily with the importance of kinship networks in Chinese societies. Yet we might hypothesise that such networks are likely to increase in prominence with the projected decrease in family size on the Chinese mainland.

Indeed, governmental restrictions on family size provide a further factor contributing to changes in Chinese family values (Tsoi, 1985). This restriction has been reinforced by the increasing availability of contraception to Chinese couples (*South China Morning Post*, 5 November 1993: 11), with only 10 per cent of mainland Chinese now using no method of birth control (*China Times Weekly*, 29 October 1993). This restriction on family size is leading to increasingly small family units which can no longer offer the resources of the extended kin network. The consequences of this promise to be profound. China's rural elderly in particular are closely bound to their families, and many couples are worried that their children will be unable to support them in retirement (Meredith and Abbott, 1995). Governmental restrictions on family size have thus indirectly produced an economic problem which threatens to absorb large amounts of government funds (Meredith and Abbott, 1995).

For all this, it is too early to declare the 'death of the family' in Chinese communities (J. Hsu, 1985). There is still a persisting loyalty and sense of commitment that goes beyond most Western family obligations. There is also evidence of a rejection of simple self-interest and a continuing belief in family cooperation (Ho and Chiu, 1994). Given the continuing political uncertainties of life in many Chinese societies, it seems unlikely that the need for psychological and material support from the family will decline.

Family values in European families

Georgas *et al.* (1997) studied the relationship between family structures and family bonds across five Western European cultures – Greece and Cyprus (chosen to represent collectivist cultures), and the Netherlands, Britain and Germany (representatives of individualist cultures). They argued that a combination of emotional closeness, interactional and functional interdependency and persisting normative obligations and roles bind individuals to their families. In their study of university students in these five countries, respondents were presented with an emotional distance scale, an indicator of their geographical proximity to relatives and a frequency rating of meetings and contact by phone with these relatives. Their results indicated systematic differences in family structure and function between the North Western (individualistic) societies of Britain, Germany and the Netherlands and the Mediterranean societies of Cyprus and Greece, with those in collectivist societies enjoying greater intimacy and more contact with family members. Notably, however, these cultural differences were only evident for relations with the extended (and not the nuclear) family. Their findings suggest that, while the extended family may be more functional for family members in southern Mediterranean cultures, there was little evidence of a simple 'de-personalisation' in the nuclear family in any of these European cultures. Instead, the nuclear family remains a strong and supportive feature of everyday life across Europe (Christakopoulou, 1995).

A recent British study of family attitudes also demonstrated the persisting importance of the family (McGlone *et al.*, 1998). In a large and representative survey, respondents overwhelmingly rated the family as more important than their friends, and preferred spending time with family members. Families were seen as having a strong supportive role in helping meet material and emotional needs. Family contact was seen as particularly important by those with dependent children, with manual workers having the greatest level of contact with relatives. However, a comparison of data collected in 1986 and 1995 suggested some fall in the level of contact with relatives over the last decade, with non-manual workers in particular decreasing their level of interaction with family members. There also appears to be some decrease in 'family centredness' in the younger generation, suggesting attitudes towards the family may be becoming less positive over time.

Diversity among ethnic minority groups

Family orientation and collectivism are closely related (Sillars, 1995; Triandis *et al.*, 1986). Among North America's more collectivist ethnic minority groups, the family plays a central role (Sillars, 1995; Triandis *et al.*, 1984). Wilkinson (1987: 204), in a detailed analysis of five ethnic minorities in America (American Indians, African-Americans, Mexican-Americans, Asian-Americans and Puerto Ricans), observed that, despite the differences between these communities, 'families remain the primary types of social arrangements'. Each group, she notes, has experienced social discrimination and exclusion, with families affected by the group's experiences of, and responses to, being a minority in America. The African family was radically altered by slavery, with the husband's position greatly undermined through the removal of his traditional role as family protector. The conquest and subsequent dislocation and cultural disintegration of American Indian life can be related to some of the family problems now evident on the reservations. For Puerto Ricans, residence in large cities has also created its own problems, with high rates of unemployment and a physically dangerous environment threatening family stability. While all of these families have changed and adapted to meet their new environments (often by extending kinship arrangements, or by maintaining closeness and mutual aid with family members), certain community-wide problems have proven difficult to overcome. Wilkinson cites the growing economic insecurity of African-

American husbands as contributing to the rising divorce rate among this community.

Freeberg and Stein (1996) examined the concept of 'familism' among Mexican-American and Anglo-American families, defining familism as 'the set of attitudes which reflect the relative importance given to family membership in terms of support, sacrifice and involvement' (p. 458). They found Mexican-American young adults reported higher levels of familism than Anglo-Americans from similar economic backgrounds. This is consistent with other studies showing Hispanic-Americans to have strong feelings of attachment and loyalty with family members, exhibiting the strong bonds which extend beyond the nuclear family in Latin cultures (Dunkel-Schetter *et al.*, 1996; Marin and Triandis, 1985). African-American communities also value the family and children highly. For these communities, the extended family is of particular importance, with extended kin particularly valuable for providing housing in difficult economic circumstances (Wolf, 1996). However, the presence of high interdependence between family members does not mean that autonomy is not valued in this community, with many African-American families promoting both individual autonomy and strong cooperation within the family (Sillars, 1995).

Kelly (1996) asked European-American and African-American students to provide metaphors as to the nature of their family (for example, 'my family is like a team'; 'my family is like a military confinement'). While many of the themes suggested extended family characteristics among both ethnic groups (indicating that the traditional White nuclear family may be becoming extended through divorce), Kelly did find that supportive metaphors were more characteristic of the African-American families, while 'isolation' metaphors were more characteristic of the European-American families.

In Britain, Asian families differ in the extent to which they seek to pass on family values to their offspring, although this desire for cultural propagation may vary according to events both in Britain and abroad (for example, during the Gulf War, hostile media coverage of Muslims in Britain led to a great sense of support and solidarity across Muslim communities (Singh Ghuman, 1994)). The degree to which families change as a result of migration is often hard to predict. Stopes-Roe and Cochrane (1989) note that long-established Sikh families might be expected to have experienced considerable changes in their customary attitudes and practices as a result of their time in Britain. At the same time, however, living in an extensive and well-established Sikh community in Britain may encourage the rearing of children along traditional lines, and the greater economic security of the well-established migrant may encourage wives to return to traditional household duties. Differences in the experiences of different South Asian groups in Britain are reflected in Stopes-Roe and Cochrane's (1980) findings that family support in their Indian sample was more strongly correlated with mental health than was the case for Pakistani or Irish immigrant populations. Poor mental health in the Pakistani community may result more from the downward social mobility experienced by many Pakistanis when coming to Britain, as compared to the economic success found by many Indian migrants.

Religion and the family

The Muslim world is composed of a number of different areas, including the Arab countries, Turkey, Iran, Malaysia and a number of African nations (Behman, 1985). The principal characteristics of the Muslim family are endogamy (with preferred marriage between paternal cousins), early marriage and high fertility, and the residence of married sons with their parents. The family system is largely patrilineal and male-dominated (Behman, 1985).

The impact of Islam does, however, vary across societies. In many African societies, Islam is compatible with a pre-modern, hierarchical and traditional society but is inconsistent with established patterns of lineal dualism and female decision making (Sow, 1985). Despite the presence of strong Western influences in Kuwait, Islamic teachings still have a powerful influence on families. This is particularly evident in the persistence of strong kinship kin ties and obligations, and the maintenance of the husband's authority over wives and children (Al-Thakeb, 1985). In Iran, the patrilineal and patriarchal traditions of the family have been challenged by new cultural models which challenge traditional hierarchies (Nassehi-Behman, 1985). In Turkey, secularisation has led to a questioning of the status of the husband as the head of the family (Vergin, 1985).

According to Hindu scriptural texts, a person should go through *grah-stashrama*, a stage of life which includes the procreation of children (Gupta, 1976). High prestige is given to parents of large families, and particular emphasis is placed on a male heir. In India, large families provide security for the old and ill as well as the unemployed, in a country where such assurances can rarely be obtained from the state. When a family has many children, early marriage becomes an economic necessity. Early marriage also restricts the opportunity to 'transgress' across kin or caste group (Gupta, 1976).

Modernisation and family change

The family is not a static institution, but one which evolves through time (Sow, 1985). By influencing the living conditions under which individuals operate, Kagitcibasi (1996) argues, economic and social change is now having major but complex impacts on the family, leading to modifications in both family structures and value systems.

Changes in the family can be brought about by broad, universal developments (such as Westernisation and modernisation), by specific economic developments in a region or culture (such as industrialisation or urbanisation), and by unique socio-political environments created by deliberate government interventions (Sow, 1985; K.S. Yang, 1988). Economic developments in a society can lead to a number of possible outcomes which influence everyday family interactions. Economic changes can lead to smaller family living spaces, changes in work locations, and new work opportunities for both sexes. According to some, this has led not only to the decline of the extended family, but has also challenged the protective and emotional functions of the nuclear family (Sillars, 1995). In their classic sociological accounts of industrialisation, Durkheim (1933) and Tonnies (1957) described the impact of industrialisation on social bonds. According to these theorists, the mutual obligations between group members in pre-industrial societies created strong bonds and encouraged cohesive relationships. In industrialised societies, a lack of such interdependency between individuals encourages more fragmented relationships. According to these accounts, the 'independent' family of modern industrial societies is independent of its kin, contented to 'go it alone' as a separate unit, with role positions becoming increasingly unclear (Kagitcibasi, 1996). For example, Katakis (1978) studied two groups of 12-year-old children in Greece, one group on the island of Patmos and the other in an Athens suburb. Her results show that previously unifying family values and roles now led to tension and insecurity, with young people unsure about their role as family members and as citizens of a wider society.

India has seen massive social transitions over the last two decades. In Sinha's model of social changes, rapid socio-economic changes in a country induce adaptive changes in the family that in turn lead to changes in socialisation and child-rearing practices. These in themselves have led to psychological and behavioural consequences for the individual. Writing in 1988, Sinha claims:

> A rapid rise in education, and legislation covering economic, social, and political spheres pertaining to land, property rights, inheritance, the rights of women, marriage and divorce, and minimum wages, have radically altered the land ownership pattern, power, and relational norms in villages, family interactions, and in the politicization of the castes. Conferring rights on women and making divorce laws easier have dealt a fatal blow to the traditional pattern of joint family ...
>
> (Sinha 1988: 49)

Sinha lists a number of major changes that have occurred in the family in India since independence. 'Nucleation' represents the movement away from the extended family towards the nuclear family form. 'New' child-rearing values which stress greater psychological separation between children and their families have led to inconsistencies in child-rearing behaviours, and the disappearance of clear-cut role models for the child. Changes in the status and role of women introduced by the Hindu Code Bill have allowed women greater egalitarianism and allowed them to make a larger contribution towards the family income.

Structural social changes can lead to a complex variety of outcomes. For example, just before the Second World War the Indian government introduced a large irrigation programme. In Wangala (near Bangalore) the government introduced *per capita* quotas encouraging peasants to share their land with their heirs. The loss of traditional parental control over land reduced the influence of fathers and allowed greater psychological autonomy for their sons. At the same time, women became more important for the organisation of surplus income, and now adopted a larger role in the running of the household. In another nearby village (Dalena), young people also gained greater autonomy resulting here from an increase in schooling provision. However, because agriculture in this village was located in drier lands than in Wangala, women were required to be become more closely tied to the land, and did not develop the greater family authority found nearby (Epstein, 1962).

Changing family forms can have pronounced effects on the most dependent members of the family. Goldstein *et al.* (1983) questioned the position of the elderly in Nepal, challenging the assumption that the persistence of the extended family meant that their position is secure. They interviewed forty-six high-status elderly adults (aged over 60) in Kathmandu. Traditionally, all members of these Hindu households worked the family land, and sons brought their wives into the extended family until the death of the father. Parents expected to be served and respected by their sons and daughters-in-law. The centre of the father's authority was his ownership of the land which provided the family with their main source for economic survival. Goldstein *et al.*'s (1983) findings suggest that, contrary to the religious and traditional ideal of this community, a large number of sons did not support their elderly parents. The demise of the importance of farmland meant that sons would often work in salaried employment, reducing the fathers' monopoly over economic resources. In a situation of growing poverty, this means that there were hard decisions to make about the distribution of this valuable income, and for people with children the shame of not being able to care for an elderly parent was less than that of not being able to support their own young children. The father's authority was further undermined by increased education among the young, which led to the questioning of parental control. Elderly parents therefore no longer received the love, attention and respect they took for granted, as they literally had 'nothing to offer' their offspring. Instead, the elderly became pressurised to earn their own income, something they found humiliating in itself. This should not be seen as the simple 'march of modernisation'. Instead, these changes in family status should be seen against the complex backdrop of increasing poverty in the country. Furthermore, inter-generational problems now openly being discussed are not necessarily new ones created by

'Westernisation', but may be older problems brought to the fore by shifts in economic circumstances.

In Chapter 2, I discussed the 'modernisation' hypothesis and the impact of purported modernisation on the development of personal relationships. Kagitcibasi (1988) challenges the assumption that the Western family has moved from communality to individualism as a result of industrialisation. Instead, she argues that family independence and interdependence go hand in hand in many cultures. She presents three patterns of the family in context (Kagitcibasi, 1994, 1996). First, the *interdependent* family is the traditional 'functionally extended family', characteristic of 'collectivist' societies. Here there is both material and emotional dependency on the family. When young, the child is dependent on the parent, but later the young adults provide security for their elders. There is a preference for sons (who are better at providing assets in these societies) and for high fertility (to ensure survival of enough children).

In contrast, the *independent* family (characteristic of individualist societies) has little overlap with the interdependent model. Independent families stress their separateness from other families, with members also being keen to distinguish individual family members. In these families autonomy is stressed, and as the costs of children are high there is low fertility. There is also little material or emotional dependency on family members. Finally, the third pattern of family relations is one of *emotional dependency*. Here we have social structural and economic change alongside cultural continuity, with the resulting synthesis forming a new adjustment to environmental demands. Although material dependencies may decrease with socio-economic development, Kagitcibasi argues that emotional dependencies do not necessarily decrease, and may even increase, with a greater stress on the 'companionship' value of children. Socialisation values continue to stress family and group loyalties but individual loyalties emerge too, with the child's autonomy no longer perceived as a threat to the family.

A number of examples serve to illustrate this 'third model' of emotional dependency. Bradley and Weisner (1997) discuss whether or not the Kenyan family is in decline. They claim that, although institutional family structures are becoming more diverse, many family functions (such as supporting and caring for children and the elderly) are as strong as ever. 'Old', 'traditional' values are made to fit in with 'new' valued aspirations and achievements. Elders, although highly respected, face new challenges: increasingly dependent on their children's earnings, they are also faced with performing hard physical tasks, undertaking child-caring and farming roles previously left to children (who are now at school). Bradley and Weisner view the process of adaptation as a continuous struggle to provide for basic needs, to teach community morals, and to maintain a coherent existence in spite of changing external circumstances. Thus, relatives are given shelter, the successful older man pays for his younger sibling's schooling, families strengthen their ties with their villages and attend community festivals together, and elders adopt new roles in the household.

Vergin (1985), in Turkey, claims that it is the very social changes that have characterised recent Turkish society that have led to emotional withdrawal into the family circle. Here the impact of 'Westernisation' may be greatest among the rural immigrants and shanty-town dwellers, where sons now often earn more than their fathers. This has contributed to a new egalitarianism in urban life. Finally, Cha (1994) provides a historical interpretation for changes in family alliances in Korea, demonstrating how collectivist traditions can be transferred from the family to other social institutions. In the 1950s, after the Korean war, materialistic values such as money, power and status emerged as a result of economic hardships. The industrialisation of the 1960s also promoted self-reliance and diligence, with these values actively propagated by the military government. In the 1970s the value of individual rights and traditional values of loyalty and filial piety declined. Instead, as the extended family and clan receded in significance, they were replaced by the school as a focus for collectivism. Nevertheless, Cha claims that modernity is *positively* related to family orientation, with the nuclear family model highly valued and superseding more traditional allegiances to country and clan (Cha, 1994).

Family policy across cultures

The impact of governmental policies on family relations is often neglected by personal relationships researchers, yet in many countries the provision of day care for children, community care for the elderly, and financial support for the young and those with children play a vital role in everyday lives. Millar and Warman (1996) examined family obligations, as defined in law and social policy, across sixteen European countries. They found that family obligations in these countries could be divided into three broad categories.

In Denmark, Finland, Norway and Sweden, emphasis was on individual entitlements. Consistent with these countries' high scores on individualism, femininity and egalitarianism (Hofstede, 1983; Schwartz, 1994), autonomy was seen as an important driving principle, and there were high levels of gender equality. Those in need both expected and received state, rather than family, support. Care of the elderly was not seen as a family obligation but a broader social commitment, with cash benefits targeted at the individual rather than the family. Where family support was expected, this was largely seen as the responsibility of parents to children, rather than vice versa.

Eight, mainly Northern European, countries (Austria, Belgium, France, Germany, Ireland, Luxembourg, the Netherlands and the UK) defined family obligations primarily in terms of the nuclear family. Benefits and taxes recognised these family relationships and services were intended to support family care. While equality between men and women was formally present, this was undermined by what Millar and Warman (1996) term a 'gender fault line', with gender role assumptions most prevalent in Austria, Germany and Ireland, but less evident in France (as indeed Hofstede (1983) would predict on the basis of these countries' masculinity scores). In some countries (Austria, Germany, the Netherlands, Ireland, Luxembourg and the UK), there is an assumption that the mother cares for the children, and school hours and a lack of child care provision reflect this. In Belgium and France, child care is seen as a responsibility of the state and not just the family.

Finally, in Southern Europe (Greece, Italy, Portugal and Spain) the extended family is more important, and involves obligations towards a wider family network which includes grandparents, siblings, uncles and aunts. A strong sense of family privacy means the (extended) family is seen as best 'left alone' without state intervention. Marriage is most likely to be a long-standing relationship, with relatively few people living outside families based on marriage. Services that exist are mainly for those without families. State provision of child care for children is relatively poor and is more likely to be social or educational in nature (rather than providing direct financial support for working parents). Furthermore, older children, often in their thirties, are seen as dependants on their parents, with young single people living with their parents for a relatively long period (in Spain, for example, 70 per cent of single people aged between 18 and 29 lived with their parents). Care of the elderly is mainly seen as a family function, although women perform most of the unpaid care work, whether this is for the children or the elderly.

Across these sixteen European countries, Millar and Warman (1996) found certain themes to be common. Marriage remains important in most countries and enjoys special status and protection in law and policy. However, it is parenthood rather than marriage that is increasingly being seen as the major life-long obligation. Cash benefits and payments to support carers exist in all these countries, although such payments include a range of types and are given to meet a variety objectives. In Northern Europe in particular there are considerable governmental pressures to 'reinvent' the family as a means of support. This not only satisfies a yearning for the 'good old days' but, through the means-testing of social assistance, has the potential to save these countries considerable money.

Across Europe, family policies have been influenced by economics, political ideologies and religion (Kurczewski and Maclean, 1997). In Italy, family policy changes are rarely openly debated for fear of awakening memories of Fascist propaganda campaigns (Millar and Warman, 1996). In the former Communist societies of Central and Eastern Europe, state-sponsored social security for families has been greatly undermined by the economic crises that have followed the fall of Communism (Laciak, 1997). This has left many people shocked by the new responsibilities they now face, both for themselves and their dependants (Kurczewski and Maclean, 1997). At the same time the family has taken on new life as a source of refuge from a harsh external world (Goodwin and Emelyanova, 1995b), as well as a 'social glue' for societies in which there are few larger social binds (Kurczewski and Maclean, 1997). In Poland, the central role of the Catholic Church has meant that the very discussion of family planning and sex education has been severely curtailed (Danziger, 1996). In Bulgaria, family issues have been intertwined with debates about growing multiculturalism in this society (Kurczewski and Maclean, 1997). These examples emphasise the strong ideological roots that underlie discussions about family, and the considerable political impact of family policies.

Child-rearing

There are a large number of similarities in the ways in which parents socialise their children across cultures and in the effects of this socialisation on child development (Heath, 1995). Concerns about the nature of 'youth' and their (negative) attitude towards parental authority have also been long discussed across a number of cultures. Hofstede (1994b) gives examples of 'the modern disrespectful young' reported on Egyptian scrolls dating back some 4000 years!

Steinberg *et al.* (1989) describe parenting styles along three dimensions:

1   psychological autonomy (the degree to which parents encourage children to be autonomous/independent);
2   parental involvement (the degree to which parents are actively involved in their children's lives); and
3   behavioural control (the degree to which parents try to control their children's behaviour/activities).

Collectivist societies encourage obedience to authority and interdependence with others (Ellis and Petersen, 1992). In collectivist societies, family obligations are highly ritualised, whereas in individualist societies children are encouraged to develop their own opinions (Hofstede, 1994b). Lanaro *et al.* (1997), in Canada, gave school students from a range of ethnic groups an individualism–collectivism inventory and a parental monitoring scale. Collectivist children perceived their parents as more controlling and less involved with them than individualist children. In a nine-culture study into the value of children, Kagitcibasi (1982) reports that Turkish parents most desired their children to 'obey their parents', and only 18 per cent of parents stressed independence and self-reliance in child-rearing. Similar findings were evident in collectivist Thailand, while in Korea and Singapore (fast industrialising countries) the promotion of independence and self-reliance was even more important than in the US. Phalet and Claeys (1993) reported that Turkish youth desired both loyalty to the family and individual self-realisation. This was in contrast to a similar group of Belgian respondents who sought only self-realisation.

The Confucian tradition has a strong influence on child socialisation (Ho, 1987). Children in Western societies are taught to value independence and individualism, while in Chinese cultures a broader social responsibility is emphasised (King and Bond, 1985). In Chinese cultures, children are traditionally taught inhibition of expression and respect for significant elders (King and Bond, 1985). In traditional Chinese societies, a son's respect for his father (filial piety, or *hsaio*) may involve a continual display of obedience throughout his life (Hsu, 1983; Meredith and Abbott, 1995). He may also be obliged to make a financial contribution to his parents even after he has left home (Argyle, 1982). Traditional Vietnamese culture also emphasises filial piety, with the child expected to respect and obey its parents (Wolf, 1996)

In China, there is continuing evidence for strong parental nurturance and support even when the child has grown up (C.F. Yang, 1988), although the Chinese parenting style is largely authoritarian and involves high levels of regulation from parents in order to ensure 'proper' behaviour. This does not mean that children fail to develop autonomy, but may mean that they do so at a later age than children in the more individualist West (Schneider *et al.*, 1997).

As has been suggested throughout this book, political events and decisions in the People's Republic of China have had complex but profound effects on family life. Whyte (1992) examines the contrasting forces at work in China following the de-collectivisation of rural China in the early 1980s. One force, which Whyte terms 'tradition-restoration', sees the re-emergence of the Chinese extended peasant family as a production unit after almost thirty years of collectivised agriculture. Strong parental control over the family farm might be expected to lead to a greater proportion of young people's time being directed by their parents. At the same time, a second force, that of modernisation, has been accompanied by greater migration within the country, leading to the formation of new alliances which weaken patrilineal solidarities, and providing new opportunities for autonomy among the young. The result is a mixture which does not readily comply with simple 'Westernisation' hypotheses. Thus, young women may work in towns and express their autonomy by choosing their own partners. They may, however, also send some of their earnings home to their family, and might expect a large dowry from this family at marriage.

Hofstede (1994b) also relates child-rearing practices to cultural variations in power distance and masculinity–femininity. In large power-distance societies, such as Latin American cultures, children are expected to obey their parents. Where there is low power distance and high femininity, mothers and fathers tend not to dominate and there is a greater emphasis on the feelings of the child and greater gender role equality in the family. One interesting comparison has been made between the child-rearing practices of Israel and Japan, both moderately collectivist societies but scoring differently on the dimensions of power distance (Japan is higher on power distance (Hofstede,

1983)). In Japan, children are strongly bonded to their families (Lebra, 1992), with the Japanese mother keen to harmonise her needs with those of her child (Kornadt *et al.*, 1998). Japanese children are constantly in contact with their mothers, and are rarely left alone (Tobin, 1992). Young Japanese are often carried around on their mothers' backs, and there is constant non-verbal interaction between parent and child (Reischauer, 1988). Doi (1962) describes the term *amae* (meaning 'to look to others for affection'), which refers to a deep sense of interdependency originating in the child–mother relationship. The child also develops an acceptance of authority from the mother, which expands into a greater desire for approval and acquiescence with the group in later life and the development of particularistic (as opposed to universalistic) relationships (Reischauer, 1988). In contrast, Israeli parents promote a greater sense of early independence and self-sufficiency in their children (Heath, 1995). As a result, the Israeli mother may encourage the child's ability to be alone as an example of his/her emotional independence, while the Japanese mother may value the child's development of social relationships. Interestingly, the same behaviours by the child may be differently interpreted in the different cultures (Orlick *et al.*, 1990). The child who dresses himself/herself is seen by the Israeli mother as demonstrating instrumental independence, and by the Japanese mother as demonstrating the child's obedience (Heath, 1995). In North America and Germany, parental control may also be associated with perceived parental hostility and rejection, while in Japan and Korea it is associated with warmth and acceptance (Kagitcibasi, 1996). High levels of parental control are seen as 'normal' in Japan and Korea, and might therefore be perceived by the child in a positive manner (De Vos, 1960).

Lee (1987) has examined the impact of political structure on the values taught to children. In autocratic cultures, self-reliance is more dangerous and less promoted. Societies where there is close supervision of performance emphasise conformity, in contrast to societies where there is greater autonomy. Where social change leads to a lessening of autocracy in the political sphere, we can expect socialisation patterns which encourage greater self-direction in the young. However, the impact of these changes differs across different social systems, with different political, family and religious factors influencing socialisation. Thus, work on the Mizos of India, a male-dominated patrilineal culture, has shown that greater parent–child interaction has only a limited effect on girls' achievement because of wider societal values which restrict their access to formal education (Sudhir and Sailo, 1989).

In Britain, different ethnic groups have different attitudes towards the socialisation of their children. Asian, and in particular Muslim, parents are highly protective of their daughters, fearing British society's drugs problems and its undue emphasis on sex (Singh Ghuman, 1994). Stopes-Roe and Cochrane (1990a) gave their Asian-British respondents Kohn's thirteen child-rearing values, and asked them to identify the three most desirable of these (see Table 6.1).

As can be seen from this table, honesty was the most frequently selected quality by all respondents. Obedience and being good at school were more stressed as desirable child-rearing values by Asian respondents, particularly Asian parents. Asian respondents stressed self-direction values less than the Whites, with the effect again more marked for parents than children. These findings were independent of the Asian parents' sense of British identity or contact with British people or customs, although for younger Asian respondents there was a significant (negative) relationship between observance of customs and emphasis on self-direction. Many of the younger people questioned in Stopes-Roe and Cochrane's (1990a) study appreciated the strengths and supporting nature of their families, but also valued personal independence and individual decision making. As is the case with families in many other cultures, the greater education of children led to some questioning of hierarchical relationships. Schools were seen as reducing parental responsibilities, while children enhanced their status by learning skills important for the whole family (Nassehi-Behman, 1985, in Iran; Sow, 1985, in Africa).

Table 6.1   Rank orders of respondents by generation and ethnic groups on Kohn's scale of thirteen child-rearing qualities

	Parents		Young people	
	Asian	British	Asian	British
Qualities				
Conformist				
Honest	2	1	1	1
Obedient	1	6	2	4
Good at school	5	12	9	11=
Good manner	9	7	3	7=
Sex-appropriate	10=	11	13	11=
Neat and clean	10=	13	12	13
Self-directing				
Considerate	4	2	6	3
Good sense	6	3	5	5=
Responsible	7	5	7=	7=
Interested	13	8	7=	9=
Self-control	12	9=	11	9=
Both				
Successful	3	4	4	2
Friendly	8	9=	10	5=

Source: Adapted from Stopes-Roe and Cochrane (1990).

Employment and family relations

The employment activities of different groups are critical for providing the resources for successful family living and for offering the opportunities for interaction with family members (Kohn, 1989). Social class and occupational differences may be central to our understanding of the socialisation process, with different social and occupational groups holding different values about how to raise their children (Kagitcibasi, 1996). Parental background and social class are regularly associated with academic success across cultures (Heath, 1995), with the active investment of parental time in children more common among those from higher social classes. This investment has a positive impact on academic achievement, and contributes to enhanced life satisfaction and well-being (Man, 1991).

Goodwin and Emelyanova (1995a) asked 600 Russian students, entrepreneurs and manual workers about how a good father or mother should act towards his or her child, how children should treat their parents, and the qualities they would wish to develop in a child. Respondents were asked to answer these questions 'in their own words', with response content analysed to extract key themes. Overall, most respondents saw the main duties of both parents to be kind and attentive to their children. However, there were significant occupational group differences in some of the other responses provided by the respondents. Significantly more students and entrepreneurs than manual workers stressed the importance of the parents' tutorial role in raising their children. There were also marked differences in the values that the respondents wished to develop in their child. Thus, while 'humanity and the collective good' was given prime place by 70 per cent of the manual workers, only 40 per cent of the students and 27 per cent of the entrepreneurs cited this as the most important value to be developed. Instead, students and entrepreneurs were keener to develop individuality and intellect in their offspring.

One way of interpreting these findings is through the important work of the sociologist Mel Kohn. Kohn (1987; Kohn *et al.*, 1990) has argued that the degree of control people have over their work influences their values, and these values are then passed on to their children. Class position greatly affects the opportunities for occupational self-direction and control (Kohn *et al.*, 1990: 1006). Blue-collar workers are occupied in more repetitive tasks where conforming to authority is vital, while creativity and self-direction are more valued in white-collar occupations. As these criteria for success differ at work, so do the values conveyed by the adults to their children.

Working from this perspective, Tudge and his colleagues (Tudge *et al.*, 1997) examined parents' values and beliefs in cities in four cultures: Russia, Estonia, South Korea and the US. They examined the extent to which social class distinguishes parental values and beliefs, and the way in which children's actual behaviour reflected their parents' values and beliefs. They found that, across the countries studied, middle-class parents were more likely than their working-class peers to value self-direction in their children and to espouse beliefs about child-rearing consonant with these values. Furthermore, the children's own behaviours were largely in accordance with these values, with middle-class children more likely to engage in behaviours that would help them become self-reliant once they entered school (being involved in academic lessons, learning skills, playing with academic objects and conversing with adults).

The degree to which children themselves are expected to do manual work varies significantly across cultures. In Whiting and Whiting's (1975) classic study, children in agrarian culture were expected to work from an early age, performing both household jobs and outside labour. In the nine-country 'value of children' study (Kagitcibasi, 1982), children's material help was considered particularly important by parents in less-developed countries and by rural respondents. As Kagitcibasi (1996) notes, where children carry heavy responsibilities, childhood as a *distinct entity* is less evident. This may be changing, however, with increased urbanisation and parental education lowering the importance of child work.

Children's rights

What are the basic rights of child? The UN Convention of the Rights of the Child (UN General Assembly, 1989) sought to codify children's protection needs and rights. Yet there are clear cultural differences in interpreting how these needs should be applied (Murphy-Berman *et al.*, 1996). These cultural variations in children's rights emphasise important differences in the ways in which children are raised across cultures.

First, consider the idea that children are individuals with their own rights. As Murphy-Berman *et al.* (1996) observe, while some countries (such as Canada) strongly emphasise the child's right to freedom of choice of religion, Islamic states may oppose the right of children to choose their own religion. As we have seen throughout this chapter, individualistic cultures are more likely to stress an independent orientation in a child, in contrast to the strong group loyalty emphasised in collectivist cultures. The granting of freedom of expression may be more problematic in highly collectivist and hierarchical societies, where individual rights may conflict with the interests of the family group or the wider nation.

Responsibility for a child may also differ cross-culturally along the dimension of 'egalitarian commitment' (Schwartz, 1994), which stresses loyalty beyond one's own narrow group interest. The egalitarian emphasis of the Convention of the Rights of the Child may fit less well in a society where commitment to the child only extends as far as the family (Murphy-Berman *et al.*, 1996). Even terms such as 'family' and 'best interests' are likely to be open to considerable variation in definition (Saks, 1996). Saks gave eleven delegates from different countries attending the Convention a list of ten different practices and asked them whether or not the Convention permitted these practices. These included the use of corporal punishment and the right of the parents to insist that a fourteen year-old follows their religious beliefs. On all but one of these ten there was disagreement about whether or not the Convention permitted these practices.

Decision making and gender roles

Across the world, males tend to be more self-assertive, achieving and dominant, while women are more socially responsive, passive and submissive (Segall *et al.*, 1990; Williams and Best, 1982). From an evolutionary perspective (e.g. Archer, 1996; Kenrick *et al.*, 1990), male dominance and female nurturance have their roots in natural selection, where there are selection advantages for individuals who exhibit such behaviour. However, as Segall *et al.* (1990) note, there are wide variations in the magnitude of these sex differences and these variations follow the ecological demands of the environment. Sex differences in socialisation are greater in societies where strength is significant (Barry *et al.*, 1959). In high food-accumulating societies, females are trained to be more compliant and nurturant, whereas in hunting or gathering societies there is little need for either of the sexes to be compliant (Segall *et al.*, 1990). Sex role division of labour may also be less functional in highly industrialised nations (Schlegel and Barry, 1986).

Williams and Best (1990) examined the gender roles of student men and women in fourteen diverse countries (five from Asia, five from Europe, two from North America and one each from Africa and South America). Traditional ideology was represented by items such as 'the first duty of a woman with young children is to her home and family', while 'egalitarian' ideologies were tested by statements such as 'a woman should have exactly the same freedom of action as a man'. The four countries with the most egalitarian sex role ideology scores were the Netherlands, Germany, Finland and England, all high on Schwartz's (1994) egalitarianism dimension. Higher egalitarianism was evident in countries high on Hofstede's (1980) individualism dimension and those with higher socio-economic development, a lower proportion of Muslims, and more Protestant Christians.

Munroe and Munroe (1997) claim that sex differentiation is perhaps strongest in Africa. Power in African society is complexly held, however. At the top of the hierarchy are oldest brothers and household heads. The wives of family heads in a polygamous system are ranked by age and order, and both they and their children may partake in certain decision-making processes (Sow, 1985). At the same time, the post-colonial period in many African countries, along with industrialisation, the growth in schooling for children and the re-organisation of agriculture, have led to profound changes in the traditional duties performed by men and women in many societies. Thus, for example, Babukusu women in Kenya find themselves doing extra tasks which would normally have been done by men (now seeking work in the towns) or children (who are now in school) (Wandibba, 1997).

In Japan, the most 'masculine' culture in Hofstede's (1980) data set, women often appear meek and long-suffering. Certainly a combination of Confucian philosophy and a long feudal tradition restricted women's role in society, with the wife's duties consisting of bearing children, serving her husband and attending to family needs (Ingersoll-Dayton *et al.*, 1996). Even now, few women are in career-track positions, and these tend to be women who are not married (Wolf, 1996). Japanese women are usually treated as temporary workers, and are likely to be excluded from the life-long employment and seniority system enjoyed by men (Reischauer, 1988).

However, there are some signs of change in the modern Japanese family. Women are now demonstrating increasing signs of disenchantment with marriage and motherhood (Brinton *et al.*, 1991). The dramatic fall in fertility rates among Japanese women over the last fifty years (Kumagai, 1984) has led to more women working outside the home, and is seen by Kumagai (1984) as an important step towards greater autonomy for Japanese women. Furthermore, the mechanisation of housework has now given women at home far more free time and increased their opportunities to lead fuller lives outside the home (Reischauer, 1988). However, although young Japanese college women may desire equality with men, they are less likely to plan their careers than their American counterparts, with fewer expecting to pursue graduate degrees and more expecting to stop working when they marry (Hill and Hicks, 1998).

Ingersoll-Dayton examined patterns of independence among elderly Japanese and US couples by asking respondents to tell the story of their relationship, to reflect on their lives together, and to discuss the turning points in their marriage (Ingersoll-Dayton *et al.*, 1996). All of the Americans in the sample had freely chosen their spouses, whereas most of the Japanese had their marriages arranged by a matchmaker.

Three major themes emerged from this analysis. First was the theme of marriage as separateness and togetherness. Roles were clearly separable in the Japanese marriage, particularly in the early days of marriage, when husbands worked in the workplace and wives looked after the family and household. These findings are similar to those reported by Salamon (1977) in her study of younger middle-class women in Japan. Here, husbands were drawn away from their families and spent little time with their wives. In contrast, the American couples often referred to themselves as 'we', seeing themselves far more as a partnership (Ingersoll-Dayton *et al.*, 1996).

Second, Ingersoll-Dayton *et al.* (1996) found that roles were negotiated using quite different rules. American couples were more likely to refer to notions of equity, whereas Japanese respondents focused on their dependency on one another. Thus, if a Japanese wife was now elderly and frail, the husband might study cooking and take the role of household cook. Finally, while ignorance about their partner meant a limited opportunity for emotional closeness early on in the Japanese relationship, there was evidence of an increased emotional closeness in later life among these Japanese respondents. This was in contrast to increased separateness and distance among the American couples. This detailed research suggests that apparently simple cross-cultural differences need to be completed by a lifespan perspective in the analysis of marriage roles across cultures.

Mexico is also a highly 'masculine' culture, ranked sixth in Hofstede's (1980) index of masculinity. Diaz-Guerrero (1991) examined the effects of time and habitat on what he terms 'historic-sociocultural premises' (HSCPs), ethnographically-derived beliefs that are widely held within a particular society. In a questionnaire given to single-sex and mixed-sex schools in Mexico City in 1959, children were asked to rate 123 HSCPs. In a repeat study some eleven years later, respondents were more likely to reject such HSCPs as 'the place for women is in the home'. Respondents were also increasingly likely to question the superiority of males and the need to be obedient to parents. However, other, more recent Mexican data (Rodriguez, 1990) demonstrated less evidence of attitudinal change. In her study of Nahuatl Indians over ten years (1978–88), Rodriguez found little change in agreement with notions such as 'men should wear the pants in the family'.

The role of women in Hindu society is complex. While in Hindu theology female goddesses possess considerable power, they are also the consorts to more powerful male gods (Singh Ghuman, 1994). In marriage, segregated gender roles mean that the woman's central role in Hindu societies is that of homemaker (Mishra 1994). In India, despite a rising women's movement, women's roles are strongly determined by region, tradition, educational level and land rights, with women in Southern India attaining greater status in the family (Dyson and Moore, 1983).

In a study of seventy Hindu Gujarati couples in Britain (Goodwin, Adatia *et al.*, 1997), marital roles were found to be partly dependent on the position of the couple in the family, with the eldest couple being responsible for the parents and in-laws while younger couples enjoyed greater role flexibility. In general, little evidence was found of serious role-conflict among members of this community, with family friction mainly restricted to disagreements about conflicting social arrangements (for example, when family weddings on both sides of the family were held on the same day). Where paid work was performed by both members of the couple, this also failed to lead to the family conflict often reported in the European and North American literature (e.g. Ferri and Smith, 1996; Whyte, 1990). Instead, couples where both partners worked adopted more egalitarian marital roles.

In Britain, the relationship between gender roles and employment was investigated using data from the National Child Development Study, a longitudinal birth cohort study which has traced the lives of all those born in Britain in one week in 1958. In a study of 6,000 fathers and mothers, Ferri and Smith (1996) found that the more mothers were involved in work outside the home, the more fathers shared equally in child care and

housework. Fathers' hours of employment also affected their own contribution to child care – those that worked long hours did less at home, regardless
of their wife's employment situation. However, considerable gender segrega-
tion in roles remained, and even in families where both parents worked
full-time, mothers took the main responsibility for domestic life.

In the US there are ethnic differences in the effects of household participation on marital quality. African-American marriages tend to be more
egalitarian than White marriages, and although African-American women
are mainly responsible for household work, there is a greater sharing of
housework and child care (Sillars, 1995). This may result from the considerable amount of work undertaken by African-American wives outside the
home (Orbuch and Veroff, 1997). Orbuch and Eyster (forthcoming) found
that the husband's participation in household jobs and child care was a
predictor of marital well-being for Black but not White wives. Within the
Hispanic-American family, the cultural ideal of femininity is central, with
women more likely to be housewives than in comparable African-American
or non-Hispanic White communities (Wolf, 1996). However, in the Mexican-
American family, traditional sex roles are becoming less rigid, with evidence
of increasing egalitarianism and joint decision making in these families
(Dunkel-Schetter *et al.*, 1996). In Vietnam, a woman has traditionally been
under the authority of her father. When married she was then expected to
submit to her husband and, if she became a widow, to her eldest son.
However, the woman did have power to manage the family budget, and
family decision making was a joint process (Rutledge, 1992). Studies of
Vietnamese-American households have found that, once in the US,
Vietnamese immigrants reconstruct extended families that have previously
been weakened through immigration. Distant relatives and friends are added
together as 'fictive' kin to establish large, complex households (Kibria,
1990). This extended family plays a valuable role in helping to adjust to the
new culture, with wives playing an important role in deciding who is to be
part of this extended family.

Cultural ideologies concerning family power do not always transfer into
action. Female submissiveness is more likely to occur in the public rather
than private sphere, and may only be evident in the presence of particular
others (Sillars, 1995). Whiting (1973) notes how Kenyan career women may
be independent outside the home but highly submissive in their relationships
with their husbands. In the study of Hindu Gujaratis in Britain (Goodwin,
Adatia *et al.*, 1997), women were found performing certain 'traditional' roles
when the mother-in-law was nearby, but sharing roles with their partner
when she was absent. One wife in her twenties remarked: 'I would like my
husband to help more around the house but, when the mother-in-law is
around, I find it difficult to ask for help'.

A limited amount of work has examined marital roles in situations of
war. Bar-Yosef and Padan-Eisenstark (1977) argue that, during the Yom
Kippur war, the man's role in the fighting led to the re-emergence and legit-

imisation of traditional sex roles in Israel. The active participation of women outside the family was reduced, and the well-being of the male became the society's central interest, with women expected to focus on providing much-needed emotional support for their partners. However, as the war progressed, the women's discontent with these traditional gender roles re-emerged. This discontent then helped strengthen future egalitarian demands in Israeli society.

Sex roles in Communist societies

China scores high on mastery and low on harmony on Schwartz's (1994) cultural dimensions, indicating a highly masculine culture (Smith and Bond, 1998). In traditional Chinese communities, husbands wielded considerable power, with older sons inheriting power on the death of the husband. In such societies, 'males were expected to behave as males, and females as females' (Ho, 1989: 154), with sex-role differentiation both unambiguous and backed by strong social sanctions. This differentiation began in early childhood and continued into adulthood, and was most marked in the lower classes (Ho, 1989). The father's unquestioned right to be head of the family meant economic autocracy (all the family's material resources were under his name), 'thought autocracy' (all the family had to accept his standards); strict family rules and the hierarchical ordering of family members (K.S. Yang, 1995).

Honig and Hershatter (1988) describe the changing gender roles that have followed the major political transformations of the last fifty years. The Chinese Revolution of 1949 aimed to build gender equality, and openly avowed the liberation of women. Chinese publications discussed the competing claims upon women of outside work and household duties. The Cultural Revolution banned gender as a distinct social category. However, although women took on non-traditional roles at work, they were also exhorted to take on housework burdens at home to further the economic advance of socialism.

One major factor in relations between the sexes in mainland China has been the one-child policy, begun in the late 1970s. Under this policy each new family has been limited to one child (Honig and Hershatter, 1988; Meredith and Abbott, 1995). The Chinese government has introduced a complex system of rewards and punishments to try to maintain this policy. Couples who pledge to have only one child are given preferential jobs, housing, medical services and maternity provisions, but if they violate the policy they face stiff fines and risk being penalised at work (Li, 1995). However, both rural and urban citizens show a preference for sons which dates back to pre-Liberation China, and which reflects a continuing tradition whereby only sons could carry through the family name (Li, 1995). Under the new responsibility system in agriculture, introduced in the 1980s, sons have become even more important in the countryside (Honig and

Hershatter, 1988). In China in 1992, 118.5 boys were reported born for every 100 girls, and an estimated 1.7 million Chinese girls were either aborted or killed (Hatfield and Rapson, 1996). Given China's relatively high infant mortality rate (44 per 1,000 births: *Encyclopaedia Britannica*, 1993), and the fact that a majority of the population still practise labour-intensive agriculture, particular resistance against the one-child policy has come from Chinese farmers (Banister, 1987). This has led to a movement by local officials to allow Chinese peasants a second child when the first was a girl (Greenhalgh and Li, 1995).

In contemporary China, gender is now a subject of considerable controversy. There is some evidence of a growing egalitarianism in family affairs, with both parents now playing a more equal role in a number of key areas of family life. A recent *China Weekly Times* poll revealed that almost 50 per cent of mainland Chinese and 38 per cent in non-Communist Taiwan now share the housework (cited in Goodwin and Tang, 1996). There is also some evidence of changing power relations in the workplace, with Taiwanese women leading the way in demanding a more egalitarian role in society (Chia *et al.*, 1986). Women's aspirations have been raised by contact with Western products. In terms of socialisation, it is now both parents who make important family decisions (Goodwin and Tang, 1996). However, the traditional view of women being secondary to their husbands remains (K. S. Yang 1988, 1995). At home, as in the West, men still gain the most from their marital relationship (Ying, 1991). Furthermore, the role of women in the People's Republic of China as emotional managers is still stressed in magazines, with advice books, press stories and indeed 'scientific' texts underlining the belief that, as a result of immutable biological differences, girls are inferior to boys in intellect, physical abilities and emotional stability (Honig and Hershatter, 1988). In rural areas, parents may still take their daughters out of school to help out on farming tasks, as they believe there is little point in educating them. In urban areas, parents might give their daughters additional household tasks so that they can leave their sons free to study (Honig and Hershatter, 1988).

Totalitarian regimes often place conflicting expectations upon children, with parental attitudes and behaviours contradicting the propaganda taught in state bodies such as schools (Alechina *et al.*, 1997). Sex role development was particularly confusing in the former Communist societies of Eastern Europe, where agency was a dangerous characteristic to develop. In Communist Eastern Europe, discussions of gender roles were rare, with women given little opportunity to challenge prevailing inequalities in society (Kerig *et al.*, 1993).

In Russia, the years of *perestroika* led to a greater discussion of gender and gender roles. Debates about women's roles became caught between a widening feminist discourse and the efforts of the Russian government to encourage 'traditional' sex roles and a return to the 'womanly mission' of family responsibility, a propagation which reflected both traditional gender stereotypes and growing fears of male unemployment (Kerig *et al.*, 1993; Vannoy, 1998). The result was conflicting norms, reflecting both the 'traditional' double standard (which underlines sex differences and gives preferences to men) and the legacy of socialist notions of equality. Thus, a man may have been taught in school about gender equality, but his army experience was one that promoted 'manly' aggressive behaviour (Kerig *et al.*, 1993). For the young girl or woman, existing social practices underlined the advantages of being male, and any adoption of more assertive, 'male' behaviour was liable to be criticised as 'unwomanly'. In a large sample of women in Moscow and two rural areas, Vannoy (1998) found that role conflict often spilled through into marital violence, with one in four Moscovite wives reporting physical abuse in their marriages, with even higher rates of abuse in rural locations. Yet despite the hardships they endured in family life, women remained very positive about the family as an institution, with the family seen as offering a valuable retreat from the hardships of modern Russian life (Goodwin and Emelyanova, 1995b).

In former East Germany, every woman had the right to one day off per month for household responsibilities, and could claim paid maternity leave for the first year after the birth of a child. Extended maternity leave and retirement benefits were available for parents with two or more children. Under the Communist system, women's economic dependence on the male breadwinner was formally abolished, with more women working in East Germany than in West Germany. At the same time, East German employees gave high emotional priority to their families as an escape from boring, but guaranteed, employment (Ostner, 1996).

Changes in the political system following German unification led to changing patterns in work, marriage and the family (Ostner, 1996). Spouses and their children now have to rely on each other in new ways in a system where there are few care facilities for young children. This has led to a great deal of confusion about the woman's 'place' in marriage and considerable emotional and financial difficulties for families from former East Germany.

Summary

In this chapter I have reviewed the changing nature of the family across a range of cultures, attempting to describe how complex factors such as social class, religion, modernisation and migration may have helped shape the current state of the world's families. Kinship arrangements and family forms largely reflect ecological demands, although historical assumptions about the functions and longevity of the extended family in many cultures have been shown to be erroneous. Family values are increasingly stressing the need for individual autonomy in most cultures, although there is evidence of a 'middle way' which blends material autonomy with emotional support, combining many of the best aspects of family life in the modern world. As educational opportunities increase for most children across the world, so they are beginning to challenge old orthodoxies and behavioural restrictions, and this often leads to unpredictable consequences for the whole family. Gender inequalities are still evident in most cultures however, with women carrying the 'double burden' of work and family responsibilities. For all these changes, however, the family, in whatever form, is still a vital refuge from the outside world, and an important shaper of behaviour and identity. As such, it seems likely to persist, despite, and maybe sometimes because of, the challenges posed by societal transitions.

7   Relationships at work

Introduction

In the previous chapter, I briefly described some research relating parental occupation to the development of values in children. But work and family life complement one other in more than just child-rearing. The family can allow an individual to 'escape' from a difficult work environment, providing a welcome refuge from a hostile outside world. Work outside the home can provide a welcome relief from the boredom and routine of domestic life, providing a sense of 'self-actualisation' (Maslow, 1954) and allowing for the attainment of greater self-respect (Kanungo and Misra, 1988). At the same time, however, holding both domestic and work duties can be a strain, allowing little time for other social activities or relaxation (Ruble *et al.*, 1988). Furthermore, difficulties in one sphere of home or work are likely to have a bad effect on the other – for example, when the trials of a workplace are carried home to the family, or when domestic break-ups contribute to absenteeism at work (Scott and Taylor, 1985).

I begin this chapter by describing the link between the psychological needs fulfilled by work and those fulfilled by the family. I also consider some of the ways in which companies in Japan and Korea have tried to structure themselves as 'families'. I then turn again to the work of Hofstede (1980, 1994b) and Trompenaars (1993), which is particularly concerned with cultural variations in values and relationships at work. I briefly consider cultural differences in four 'mainstay' areas of organisational psychology: leadership, decision making, workplace conflict and 'social loafing'. In the final section of this chapter I discuss 'informal' economies, an important area of economic activity rarely discussed in the occupational psychology texts.

Work and the family

Kanungo and Misra (1988) examined the needs fulfilled by involvement in work and family life in Canada (an individualist nation) and India (a collectivist nation). They questioned mid- to senior-level executives from public and private sector organisations in India, and mid-level management personnel from Montreal. In general, they found their respondents rated achievement, autonomy and the opportunity for personal growth as important aspects of the work environment. The fulfilment of more affiliative needs (love, having good interpersonal relationships, etc.) was more important in the family context. Indian respondents rated involvement in family life as more important than work involvement. In the Canadian sample, as work involvement increased, respondents sought less satisfaction from their families, suggesting a compensatory mechanism between the two life spheres of work and home. Canadian respondents with children reported greater involvement in both their family and work, whereas there was no relationship between having children and work involvement in the Indian sample.

Moen and Forest (1990) sought to examine the conditions under which employment affects psychological well-being in Sweden, using longitudinal data collected in three large cohorts between 1968 and 1981. They found that, while employed mothers of young children reported less psychological well-being than employed fathers at all three time points, fewer employed mothers reported psychological strains and daily fatigue in 1981 than in 1968. They interpreted this as resulting from changes in social roles, as well as new workplace options (such as leave of absence and reduced working hours) introduced during the period of this study. Their data also underlined the importance of social class and the work performed for psychological well-being. Professional-level mothers were least likely to feel physically exhausted after their work. Fathers in professional occupations were more likely to feel mentally exhausted, while working-class fathers felt physically exhausted.

In some cultures the workplace can be seen as an extension of the family, with the work manager adopting a similar paternalistic role to that of the father in the 'traditional' family. Kim notes how seniority and gender are important in the Korean business corporation, just as they are in the Korean family (U. Kim, 1994). Kim conducted a survey of the managers of almost a thousand companies in Korea, asking about the provision of social welfare and benefits for the workforce. Workers in Korea preferred the company manager to be a guiding 'father figure'. A large majority of workers also believed that the company should be responsible for the well-being of both employees and their families.

The Japanese workplace has also been seen as analogous to the family environment (Reischauer, 1988). Japanese workers feel a strong desire to maintain harmony in their work relationships, and enjoy the feeling that they all belong to 'the same club' (Maher and Wong, 1994). This identification may be promoted by the singing of company songs and the wearing of company pins (Reischauer, 1988). This sense of warmth may also spread beyond the company to groups of companies who work together, and personal ties are seen as playing a major part in business relations. Government and business leaders often come from the same (high-status) universities, furthering a sense of cooperation between business and the state (Reischauer, 1988).

The employee's lengthy association with a particular company has also served to reinforce the image of the workplace as an extension of the family. Japanese companies have traditionally been famous for their 'lifetime employment' policy, although there is much misunderstanding of this by those outside the system (as Beardwell and Holden, 1994, note, such a policy applies only to a minority of workers working for the great conglomerates, and workers typically retire at 55). Workers in Japan are likely to be promoted on the basis of length of service (Beardwell and Holden, 1994), and those that have entered a company in any given year form a 'class' that remains 'in step' in the company hierarchy throughout their company career (Reischauer, 1988).

In recent years, the more negative aspects of the Japanese management system have been acknowledged. The seniority rule, which may appear to minimise internal competition, is set within a hierarchical structure which inevitably leads to the placing of some above others. During mid-career there can be considerable competition between workers to rise up the hierarchy, with a failure to win promotion leading to a serious loss of face in the eyes of family and friends (Lebra, 1992). Japanese management styles are popularly portrayed as major contributors towards the successes of Japanese industry, but a number of recent studies have questioned the extent to which workers are satisfied with their work and committed to their organisation (Smith *et al.*, 1992). In smaller businesses in particular, paternalistic leaders may fail to look after the interests of their workers, and employee loyalty is weaker (Moeran, 1984). Finally, while the strengths of personal ties between company leaders, and in particular the strong links between the business sector and the state, have traditionally been seen as a source of great strength, recent economic events in Japan have questioned their utility. Indeed, the 'cosiness' of the relationship between business leaders, and between business and the state, may encourage corruption. Such corruption is one major contributor to the economic problems of the Japanese economy in the late 1990s.

Cultural values and the workplace

In Chapter 2, I described two major studies of values and culture conducted by Hofstede (1980, 1994b) and Trompenaars (1993). Both studies were concerned with cultural differences in practices in the workplace. I now return to these studies to describe in more detail their findings as related to relationships at work.

Hofstede's study

As we saw in Chapter 2, Hofstede's (1980) study described four dimensions of culture. Hofstede's first dimension, that of *power distance*, was assessed on the basis of three questions, examining the extent to which employees were willing to disagree with their managers, their preferred management style and their perceptions of their managers' actual decision-making style. In low power-distance countries, such as Austria, Israel and Denmark, there is a preference for consultation with subordinates, and subordinates are quite willing to contradict their managers. Organisations in low power-distance countries are relatively decentralised, and younger managers are more valued than older ones. In high power-distance countries, such as Malaysia, Guatemala and Panama, subordinates and managers perceive themselves as unequal, and subordinates depend more on the management and are expected to 'do as they are told'. Interpersonal contact between levels of the hierarchy is initiated by superiors. This can be stressful for the business manager. Peterson *et al.*, (1995) examined role stresses in the workplace among middle managers in twenty-one countries. Managers from high power-distance countries reported greater role overload than managers from low power-distance countries.

The second dimension identified by Hofstede is that of *individualism–collectivism*. Individualism–collectivism was assessed by Hofstede by presenting respondents with a set of 'work goals', asking them to describe their 'ideal job' by rating a list of fourteen characteristics. Individualism was highly related to having a job which allowed personal time outside of work, allowed for an individual's own approach to the work, and gave a personal sense of accomplishment. Collectivism was related to the presence of training opportunities, good physical conditions in the workplace and a requirement for skills that reflected the employee's dependence on the organisation (Hofstede, 1994b). In a collectivist culture, employees are more likely to be hired as members of an in-group, and those of the same ethnic group are likely to work together. Preference is given to relatives of the employer or current employees. As a result, people at work are likely to know each other already from other spheres of life, with personal relationships being at the 'centre' of the workplace. In collectivist Hong Kong, firms are predominately small and are becoming increasingly smaller (Smith and Wang, 1996). Organisations are based upon filial piety and a strong work ethic. As the size of an organisation grows, the centralised control of the owner is threatened, and therefore sons and relatives are likely to leave to set up their own businesses rather than challenge the stability of the existing organisation (Smith and Wang, 1996).

The cultural dimension of *masculinity–femininity* was also derived from the same set of fourteen ideal work goals used to differentiate individualist and collectivist cultures. Highly masculine cultures are Japan, Austria and Venezuela, highly feminine cultures are the Scandinavian nations of Sweden, Norway and Denmark, and the Netherlands. Respondents from masculine cultures attach great importance to having good earning opportunities, getting management recognition for doing the job well, having an opportunity for advancement and having challenging work to do. Feminine cultures stressed the importance of good relations with manager and colleagues, living in a desirable area and having security of employment (Hofstede, 1994b: 82). Negotiations in feminine cultures are more likely to involve compromise, whereas in masculine cultures the good manager is highly assertive and decisive.

Hofstede's (1980) final dimension, *uncertainty avoidance*, assesses the extent to which unknown or uncertain situations are threatening. Uncertainty-avoidance scores were derived on the basis of three questions, which assessed job stress, a belief that 'company rules should not be broken', and the intention to remain with the company for a long period (Hofstede 1994b: 111f). Workplace rules are very important in strong uncertainty-avoidance cultures. Although managers may face high levels of role overload in uncertainty-avoidance cultures, this is compensated for by less role ambiguity in such societies.

All of these value differences at work, Hofstede claims, reflect the 'cultural programming' carried out by the family and schooling. Because of these cultural differences in values, and the relationship implications they imply, Hofstede (1994b) judges 'green-field ventures' (where a foreign subsidiary is established 'from scratch' using appropriate local employees) to be more likely to succeed than a direct foreign takeover.

Trompenaars' study

Trompenaars' (1993) study of culture and business values and behaviours introduces us to new dimensions of culture – and new avenues for possible relationship conflict. In a *universalist* (but not a *particularist*) culture, 'helping your friends' may be seen as being corrupt. Given that much depends on the nature of the business relationship, contracts in particularist cultures may be less 'concrete', although the commitment between employer and employee may be very strong. Shenkar and Ronen (1987) compared Chinese and North American negotiating behaviours. They found that Chinese communications strongly emphasised social obligations, reflecting both traditional Chinese values of harmony and kinship affiliation and the greater particularism of Chinese cultures.

In *affective* cultures, such as that found in Italy, workers are more likely to express their feelings in the workplace. Trompenaars (1993) found that only 29 per cent of Italians would not express their feelings at work. More *neutral* cultures, such as Japan, are less likely to express themselves in the workplace, and over 80 per cent of Japanese replied that they would not express their feelings at work. Those in neutral cultures may feel that the expression of emotion is 'unprofessional' in the workplace, while those in affective cultures may feel that the detached and cool demeanour of a 'neutral' colleague is a sign of dislike or social superiority.

Diffuse cultures (such as Japan and Mexico) differ from *specific* cultures (such as the Netherlands) in the extent to which work relationships overlap with other spheres of life. Workers in specific cultures segregate tasks across domains, and the manager's superiority ends at the factory gate. In diffuse cultures, a manager is a manager in all areas of life. In diffuse cultures, business negotiations may involve considerable background knowledge about your negotiating partner, as the gap between the world of work and the rest of life is narrow. In diffuse cultures, 'task' behaviours have interpersonal ramifications, and spending 'private' time with your superiors is part of the work experience (Smith *et al.*, 1989). In such cultures, 'getting straight to the point' gives you little time to assess the trustworthiness of your partner, and 'mixing business with pleasure' is part of the business deal itself (e.g. Reischauer, 1988, in Japan; Shenkar and Ronen, 1987, in China). This diffusion between work and 'outside' life may often come as a shock to those from more specific cultures. Trompenaars (1993) gives the example of the British manager of a Central African company who sacked an employee for stealing meat from the company canteen in order to feed a large and hungry family. This dismissal led to the manager's poisoning by the employee with the connivance of several of his workmates, who were appalled by the manager's lack of understanding of the employee's domestic circumstances.

A final relationship dimension described by Trompenaars compares *achieved* with *ascribed* status. Achieved status is acquired by what you do for a company or what you have done in the past. In contrast, ascribed status may be ascribed by age, gender or social connections. Trompenaars found a significant correlation between Protestantism and achievement orientation, and Catholicism, Buddhism and Hinduism and ascription orientation. In many Anglo-Saxon cultures (which are heavily oriented towards achieved status), operating a company using ascribed status can be seen as archaic. In contrast, the greater status given to the older company manager in Japan (a more 'ascribed-status' society) can be seen as quite 'natural' in a culture where the manager's experience is likely to be invaluable to this company. A young 'whipper-snapper' transferring from an achievement-oriented culture can soon alienate those in an ascription-based hierarchy.

In considering these various cultural dimensions and their significance for business life, Trompenaars differentiates between four types of corporate cultures, a framework which closely overlaps with the high/low power distance and the individualism–collectivism divides which I discussed in Chapter 2. The *family culture*, typical in Japan, is both very personal (with close, face-to-face relationships) and hierarchical. Personnel selection procedures reflect this, with open recruitment and testing rare (Love *et al.*, 1994). Instead, corporations may ask for a specific number of workers from trade schools or universities and the educational institution may match the characteristics of the student to the demands of the corporation. Younger members of the company are indulged, older members are respected, with the relationship being similar to that between older and younger brothers. Sanctions are usually moral and social rather than financial. Relationships are diffuse, with the elder member being an influential figure across situations. Companies are likely to be interested in the wider family of their employees, and may aid employees in finding family housing and appropriate schools for children. Consequently, workers may be rewarded not only by long-term employment, but by the availability of cheap company housing, the use of a company holiday resort, and other activities designed to encourage company solidarity (Reischauer, 1988).

What is known as the *Eiffel Tower culture* represents a steep, symmetrical organisation, broad at the base but narrow at the top. Typical examples of such cultures can be found in Germany, Denmark and the Netherlands. Although this culture is similar to the family culture in its hierarchical structure, Eiffel Tower companies are more impersonal and rational, with the manager obeyed only because of his/her role position. Strong personal relationships are not encouraged in such cultures, as these may interfere with job performance, and applicants for posts are treated neutrally and equally. Employees are expected to be precise and meticulous in their work and in their relations with others.

Guided missile cultures and *incubator cultures* are both egalitarian, but they differ in degree of formality. Guided missile cultures are highly task oriented and impersonal – workers are there to do a job, and relationships are thus instrumental, and involve little affection or commitment. These cultures tend to thrive in such individualistic cultures as the US, Canada and Britain. The organisation in which we find the incubator culture is often small, and is both highly personal and egalitarian. Such cultures thrive in low power-distance cultures such as Sweden. The incubator culture has little structure, and people are particularly valued as innovators. Relationships between workers are not necessarily strong (these companies are usually short-lived and aimed at developing particular projects), but there is considerable emotional and ideological commitment to the work being done. Typically, incubator cultures are in the forefront of technology.

Inevitably such typologies are simplifications, as Trompenaars himself freely acknowledges. Much depends on the size of the company, with smaller companies more likely to be 'family cultures' or 'incubators', larger ones 'Eiffel Towers' or 'guided missiles'. Yet the distribution of these companies across cultures does not seem to be accidental, and closely reflects well established differences in cultural values. This makes these typologies a useful heuristic for managers keen to obtain an outline of corporate operations in different cultures.

Leadership

Many discussions of group behaviour assume that the group phenomena observed in North America are universal (Bond and Smith, 1996). However, the manner in which leaders are selected and the way in which they function is likely to vary across cultures. While, in individualist societies, a leader may be chosen by others (in Trompenaars' (1993) terms, roles are ascribed), in collectivist and high power-distance societies such as China, group members are more likely to be chosen by others and to have clearly delineated and prescribed roles. In both Sweden and Japan, there is a high value placed on group orientation as a criterion for advancement, a group orientation less evident in the US or in many north-western European countries (Rosenstein, 1985). However, in Sweden there is also greater room for 'industrial democracy', and management prerogatives are taken less seriously in this low power-distance culture (Hofstede, 1994b).

Misumi (1988) has conducted a longitudinal study of leadership over thirty years in Japan. Misumi and Peterson (1985) reported that, regardless of sex, age, education or social class, the Japanese preferred a manager with a 'father-like' character. Such a manager would be demanding at work, but would also be concerned with the workers' personal concerns that existed outside of the workplace. Japanese leaders are expected to be sensitive to the feelings of others, demonstrated by the warmth of their personalities and the confidence they inspire in others (Reischauer, 1988). Subordinates expect to be consulted and can feel free to make their contribution, with the paternalistic concern of the leader allowing for a feeling of warmth and solidarity (Reischauer, 1988). Thus, the preferred leader in Japanese organisations is high both on task commitments and relationship orientation (Misumi and Peterson, 1985). This can be contrasted to the Western style of task-oriented manager, who may be less demanding at work but is more interpersonally detached.

When considering data from mainland China, we must be aware that the responses given by participants, and the conclusions reached by researchers, may have been influenced by the political climate in which the work was conducted. Furthermore, Chinese societies are highly diverse, and organisational settings are likely to have different effects on leadership styles even within the same country (Smith and Wang, 1996). Nevertheless, certain characteristics of Chinese leadership emerge from a number of studies. Jones *et al.* (1990) found that praising a worker in front of others was seen as more rewarding by Chinese supervisors than North American supervisors. The maintenance of face and family loyalties, so important in Chinese societies, must also be considered by the successful Chinese leader, who must combine, as in Japan, an awareness of both task and interpersonal dimensions of leadership (Smith *et al.*, 1989). In addition, a further quality in a leader, that of making a 'moral contribution' to society, is highly valued in supervisors and managers (Lin *et al.*, 1987). A supervisor must therefore exhibit honesty, integrity and commitment to the work team.

Decision making

In some Western European countries, there are legal requirements to consult with the workforce, whereas in the US the emphasis is more on volunteeristic consultation and involvement. In Eastern Europe, the rapid changes that followed the fall of Communism have greatly reduced the nature of worker participation and union rights (Beardwell and Holden, 1994).

As is the case with studies of leadership, most organisational theories have been 'made in the US', and ignore cultural variations. Motivational techniques that fit with existing cultural values are most likely to be productive (Erez, 1994). For example, a classic North American study by Coch and French (1948) found that group participation in decision making led to greater worker commitment and better work performance than participation by a worker's representative or in a condition of no worker participation. This result failed to be replicated in Norway, possibly because union representatives were seen as the most legitimate way to liaise with managers in that more egalitarian country (Erez, 1994). In a similar study in Israel (Erez and Earley, 1986, cited in Erez, 1994), Israeli students reacted more negatively to being assigned goals without consultation than US students did, reflecting the lower power distance reported for Israel (Hofstede, 1983).

Another example of cross-cultural variation in decision making concerns the use of Quality Control Circles. These circles are small workshop groups that voluntarily undertake quality control activities and suggest improvements to their workplace (Erez, 1994). These groups are highly effective in Japan, and reflect the Shinto notion of *joge*, where group activities are preferred over individual actions and opinions, and where individuals feel much more comfortable discussing decisions with fellow workers (Love *et al.*, 1994; Maher and Wong, 1994). In another example of group participation, the *ringisei* system also practised in Japan involves the wide circulation of office documents. Officers each signify whether they have seen the documents and approved them, leading to a great deal of 'bottom-up' workforce participation. This means there is thorough consultation before a decision is reached (Reischauer, 1988). However, while quality circles and *ringisei* systems operate successfully in Japan, they may be less successful in the more individualistic US, where individual performance appraisals and decision making may be more successful (Lawler, 1986).

Peter Smith and his colleagues (Smith *et al.*, 1994; Smith *et al.*, 1996) have examined 'event management' across a number of cultures. They examine the way in which managers rely on their own experiences to deal with difficult situations, or turn instead to regulations or consult colleagues. In one study, Smith *et al.* (1993) examined sources of guidance in eight everyday organisational events, collecting data from private and public sector managers in five European countries (the UK, Germany, the Netherlands, Finland and Portugal). An example of such an event would be appointing a new subordinate, or dealing with someone who was performing consistently badly. In those countries highest on individualism and lowest on power distance, greater reliance was placed on the manager's own experience and training and on the responses of subordinates. In those countries lowest on individualism and highest on power distance, there was a greater reliance on formal rules and procedures. In countries which Hofstede (1980) coded as feminine, greater reliance was placed on 'unwritten rules as to how things are done'; in masculine countries, more reliance was placed on formal rules. Smith *et al.* (1993) also reported a trend towards greater reliance on specialists in high uncertainty avoidance cultures.

In an analysis of sixteen cultures, Smith *et al.* (1994) again found that managers relied more on their own experiences and training in individualist, low power-distance countries, while in collectivist, high power-distance countries such as China, managers were more likely to rely on superiors in handling events. In a further study, Smith *et al.* (1994) compared responses to familiar work events and unfamiliar work problems in Japan, the UK and the US, and related this to quality of team performance. They found that, in Japan, those work teams judged to be most effective by supervisors showed more reliance on their peers. Work teams judged to be most effective in the US made greater reference to their superiors, while in the UK those teams rated highly showed greater self-reliance.

Finally, Smith and Peterson (submitted) related the extent to which middle managers drew upon different sources in eight work events across thirty countries, once again tying this to the work of Hofstede (1980), the Chinese Culture Connection (1987) and Schwartz (1994). As in their earlier studies, Smith and Peterson reported a positive association between cultural individualism and low power distance and the extent to which managers relied on their own experience and training. In contrast, those from high power-distance cultures demonstrated a greater reliance on formal rules, reflecting their deference to superiors.

Laurent (1983) studied the attitudes of managers to a range of work situations in a number of Western European countries and in the US, Indonesia and Japan. National differences were found in responses to a number of items. One question asked respondents whether or not they agreed with the statement that 'the main reason for a hierarchical structure is so that everybody knows who has authority over them'. While 86 per cent of respondents in Indonesia agreed with this statement, only 18 per cent of respondents in the US concurred, preferring to see the main purpose of hierarchy as assisting in problem solving. This reflects those two countries' relative positions on Hofstede's (1980) power distance index: whereas Indonesia is one of the highest scorers on this dimension (eighth out of fifty-three nations) the US is ranked only thirty-eight on the index.

What effect might different industrial settings have on decision making processes? Wang and Heller (1993) examined decision making by eleven Chinese and ten British companies in both the manufacturing and service sectors. Both managers and trade union leaders from the companies participated. Wang and Heller gave respondents eighteen decision tasks concerning short-term judgements (such as the replacement of minor equipment), medium-term judgements (for example changing wage systems) and long-term decisions (such as the introduction of new products). Participants were then asked the extent to which different work groups could influence these decision processes. Wang and Heller (1993) found that decision-making power was contingent upon several factors, including the type of decision task, the system of management and the industry concerned. Decision making was less hierarchical in manufacturing (rather than service) industries in China, while the reverse was true for companies in the UK. Such findings demonstrate the importance of incorporating a number of local and sub-cultural factors into our analyses when considering decision making across cultures.

Disagreements within the workplace

Smith *et al.* (in press) examined the way in which managers from a range of organisations in twenty-three countries dealt with disagreement in their work unit. Due to the desire to maintain harmony often reported in collectivist societies, Smith and his colleagues hypothesised that *in-group* disagreements would be less frequent in collectivist societies. When disagreements arose, collectivists would also be more likely to rely on rules to avoid confronting other group members, while workers in individualist societies would be more likely to fall back on their own experiences and training. Given the importance of satisfying superiors in high power-distance societies, Smith and his colleagues also predicted that *out-group* disagreements would be greatest in those cultures. In such societies, workers would also be keen to consult their supervisors for advice, rather than relying on their peers or subordinates.

Smith *et al.* (in press) asked employees how much they dealt with intra-departmental differences in opinion (an in-group scenario) and failures by another department to provide required resources (an out-group event). They found that, while individualism–collectivism did not predict the occurrence of disagreements, high power distance did predict greater disagreement between out-groups, as hypothesised. Low power-distance nations were also most likely to deal with out-group disagreement by referring to co-workers and subordinates. Collectivism was associated with a greater reliance on the use of formal rules and procedures when confronting disagreements, while individualism was related to a greater use of the workers' own experiences and training. Smith and his colleagues suggest that these findings have a number of implications. Where North American or European companies operate in collectivist settings (such as in Asia or Latin America), expatriate managers who openly consult subordinates might aggravate disputes and be viewed as incompetent. Similarly, where Pacific Rim managers control companies in individualist cultures, their emphasis on the use of formal rules and procedures for dealing with disagreements may alienate local workers.

Even within apparently 'similar' cultures there is enormous room for national differences in communication and conflict resolution. Britain and the US are similarly ranked along the dimensions of individualism, power distance, uncertainty avoidance and masculinity–femininity (Hofstede, 1980, 1994b). Dunkerley (1997) questioned British and American managers working in Britain about similarities and differences in British and American workplace communications, and found the Americans preferred 'direct' communication at work, in contrast to the British preference for a more indirect form of communication. This can lead to problems: in the words of one American respondent: 'It's frustrating because the British never seem to want resolution; we Americans are seen as impatient, abrupt or rude when we try to resolve anything'.

American managers were also more likely to favour a style of criticism, which they saw as 'more direct and unambiguous' but which was judged as 'more harsh and destructive' by British management. Americans were also more optimistic in their outlook at work, a contrast to what they (the Americans) perceived as a confusing pessimism among British managers. Building on theories of achievement motivation and the fear of failure, Dunkerley (1997) links these cultural differences in optimism/pessimism to the strong economic position of the US, in contrast to the economic uncertainties of Britain in the latter half of the century.

Social loafing

'Social loafing' is a well-known phenomenon in social psychology, reflecting the tendency for individuals to reduce their performance when they are working with others (Harkins and Petty, 1983). Earley (1993) argued that such 'loafing' may be primarily a function of an individualist culture, where personal gains can be increased by social loafing. He examined cross-cultural differences in workplace performance by asking managers in Israel, China and the US to participate in simulated activities involving the processing of a 'basket' of items. Participants were led to believe they were working either as individuals, or as part of a ten-person in-group or out-group. Earley found that individualists who believed they were alone did better than individualists working in an in-group or out-group, while collectivists did best in an in-group context. Thus, while individualists may 'socially loaf', collectivists are more likely to engage in 'individual loafing', reducing performance when working alone. Earley (1993) concludes that incentive schemes based on individual performance may be less effective in countries such as Israel and China (where collectivism is higher than in the US) although much depends on whether the worker is working with an in-group or out-group. These findings underline the utility of team labour contracts in collectivist cultures (e.g. Wang, 1993, in China), and the importance of employing management teams who sufficiently understand the local cultural norms for collective activity and work performance.

Informal economies

In most countries throughout the world, informal, and sometimes illegal, economic arrangements form a second economy, sometimes referred to as a 'black' or 'grey' economy. Such second economies depend heavily on smooth interpersonal relationships to function successfully.

Sik (1988) illustrates how reciprocal exchange agreements in Hungary are vital for increasing efficiency and eliminating shortages when labour-intensive help is needed. Such 'non-market' labour transactions, in which one household exchanges its labour for another, are common in small-scale agriculture and for large household tasks such as house-building. Such exchanges are particularly essential when there is a shortage of services, or when labour prices are high and the working capacity of the average house-hold is too small to fulfil all the tasks necessary. From a personal relationships perspective, these exchanges require extended social networks, and the building of a highly functional set of liaisons. At the same time, although much of this labour is offered as 'a favour', there is an implicit understanding that reciprocation of a similar value will occur. This can, of course, lead to considerable costs, and as it is often difficult to value the different tasks performed, unequal reciprocation may give rise to conflicts between households. Sik (1988) suggests that reciprocal agreements only work because of the vitality of Hungarian social networks, and the long-established traditions of cooperation in Hungarian society.

In another former Communist country, Georgia, the second economy was (and is) a large and thriving part of national economic activity. Mars and Altman (1983) described how, in a highly masculine culture, the success of forbidden economic activity was highly dependent on an extensive social network, which became 'an individual's major resource' (p. 549). They described the case of a market trader, who was warned through his social network about a likely police raid on his market. Unable to afford to close his stall completely, he was caught by the police selling goods at above the controlled price, and arrested. However, goods held at his home were rapidly dispersed by relatives and friends (to counter a possible police raid on his house) and money was raised to 'pay off' the police and release the trader, with much of this money collected through loans made by other traders in the market. These loans had no guarantee or any specified time for return, but were based on the trust and honour of the trader and his family. Mars and Altman (1983) point to the contrast between formal Soviet values (which separated the specific spheres of private and work life and promoted universalist values) and the reality of a diffuse, closely entwined, nepotistic social network which encouraged strong obligations and reciprocation, particularly among those in the higher echelons of the business world. This pattern of cooperation may still be evident in the post-Communist era. In a comparative study of entrepreneurs in Georgia, Russia and Hungary (Goodwin, 1998), Georgian entrepreneurs reported the closest links between their entrepreneurial activities and their family lives. The economic problems caused by the recent civil war in Georgia are likely to make the informal economy a prominent feature of this society for years to come.

Summary

Work outside the family may fulfil important psychological needs, but the relationship between home life and the workplace varies across cultures and occupational groups. Hofstede and Trompenaars provide valuable cultural dimensions on which to locate personal relationships at work, with the emergence of specific corporate cultures largely predictable from a culture's positions on the dimensions of individualism–collectivism and power distance. Unlike their Western counterparts, Japanese and Chinese leaders are likely to combine task and emotional orientations, and, despite the hierarchical nature of Japanese corporations, decision making is made with the involvement of a wide range of workers. In high power-distance cultures, disagreements and ambiguities are likely to be resolved by consulting formal regulations, whereas individualist managers are more likely to rely on their own experiences and training. 'Social loafing' is common in individualist societies, whereas 'individual loafing' is more frequent in collectivist cultures. Finally, the success of 'informal economies' relies on close personal relationships which can offer vital information and protection in times of greatest need.

8 Friendship and the broader social network

Introduction

In the previous seven chapters, I have been discussing relationships with romantic partners, family members and work colleagues. All of these relationships form part of a wider social network which can act as a valuable psychological resource, one which has both a 'direct effect' on our well-being and operates as an important 'buffer' against life's stresses (Cohen and Wills, 1985; Sarason *et al.*, 1997). In this chapter, I begin by discussing some of the ways in which cultural differences in values influence social support, and considering how difficult social and economic conditions in a culture may serve to illustrate some of the more negative effects of social support. I also point to ethnic variations in social support, focusing in particular on our own work on Hindu Gujaratis in Britain. I then discuss cross-cultural variations in one particular supportive relationship – friendship – before turning to consider how a number of different cultural dimensions can help us understand cross-cultural variations in verbal and non-verbal communications. Good communication skills are, of course, essential for 'fitting in' to a society, and I go on to consider how we may 'self-monitor' our social performances in order to 'fit in with others'. I conclude the chapter by examining some of the cultural dimensions that underline loneliness and social isolation.

Social support and social networks

Social support and cultural values

The last twenty years have witnessed a great deal of research into social support, and there are now more than 5,000 papers dealing with this topic (Sarason *et al.*, 1997). Social support is generally perceived to be 'a good thing', with a recent public health campaign in California proclaiming that 'friends can be good medicine' (Basic Behavioral Science Research for Mental Health, 1996a). Social support both promotes and restores health, with a socially supportive environment being a major aid in the resistance to disease (Sternberg and Gold, 1998).

According to Vaux (1985: 90):

> Social support processes are interwoven with the fabric of society and are undoubtedly related to macro-system phenomena ... the extent, composition, and context of our social relationships are determined to some degree by cultural blueprints.

One portion of the social support literature has considered the impact of culture on support. Triandis (1994: 42ff) offers a model of the cultural antecedents of disease. In this model, stress can be reduced by the perception of social support, with such a perception most likely in a cohesive society. In collectivist cultures, of course, the 'in-group' is highly cohesive, and group loyalty is strong. Children are reared to value this group, and are rarely left alone. Network ties can form the 'building blocks' of social relationship in collectivist societies, smoothing social interactions and helping individuals enlarge their social networks. Not surprisingly, therefore, collectivists have been found to enjoy closer, more supportive networks (Triandis *et al.*, 1988; Triandis *et al.*, 1990). Collectivist relationships are also more enduring and networks are more likely to be shared (Gudykunst *et al.*, 1989). In cultures where the isolated nuclear family is rare, a couple's relationship may be secondary to that of the extended kinship network in providing support and caring (Moghaddam *et al.*, 1993). At the same time, sanctions exist to discourage disengagement from the network and, by 'playing down' in-group differences, the costs involved in network maintenance are reduced (Seginer, 1992).

We can find a number of examples of these strong social networks around the world. Confucian (primarily Chinese) cultures have a strong sense of shame, and a strong desire to maintain harmony and social obligations to in-group members (Schneider *et al.*, 1997). In Italy, which Triandis (1995) classifies as collectivist, there is strong loyalty to the extended family and neighbourhood, particularly in rural settings (Schneider *et al.*, 1997). In a collectivist Eastern Germany, Ostner (1996) describes the ideological notion of *Gemeinschaft* or community, an ideology enhanced in practice by a scarcity and austerity which necessitated the sharing of limited resources.

In contrast, the independence of individualists isolates them from more intimate personal relationships (Gudykunst *et al.*, 1989; Triandis, 1989, 1995). According to Bellah *et al.* (1985), an American culture that stresses individualism, privacy and independence makes a sense of community hard to attain. Triandis (1989) argues that, while originally individualism was linked to the concept of the common good, more recent individualism is hedonistic and exhibits little public concern. While entry and exit from a group may be easy for individualists (who may be skilled at providing compliments, or performing other 'superficial' rewarding behaviours), relationships between individualists may lack 'depth' (Triandis, 1994). Using the related personality values of idiocentrism (for individualism) and allocentrism (for collectivism), Triandis and his colleagues (Triandis *et al.*, 1985; Triandis *et al.*, 1988) have also reported that allocentrics enjoy fuller and more intimate social support networks. Allocentrics in the US report that they value cooperation and perceive social support to be of a higher quality, and are more likely to extend as well as expect social support. This is likely to contribute to the enhanced perceptions of happiness and subjective well-being reported by allocentrics (Sinha and Verma, 1994).

It is important here to distinguish between a collectivist belief in 'helping the in-group' and a broader notion of *equality* or *egalitarianism*. Doi (1986) argues that North American individualism contains a general belief in equality, which also requires that we must make our 'own way', without the help of others. This type of 'broad egalitarianism' is also encaptured in Schwartz's notion of egalitarianism, which he reports to be positively correlated with individualism (Schwartz, 1994). In line with this, in a three-country analysis, Goodwin, Nizharadze *et al.* (1997) found that social support was positively correlated with collectivism, but was *negatively* correlated with egalitarianism.

Recent research has differentiated between different sources of support (Sarason *et al.*, 1997). We may, for example, receive little support from friends, but may be compensated for this by receiving help from our family (Hobfoll, 1988). This 'balancing-out' of needed support may be highly culture-dependent: family integration, for example, is more highly valued in collectivist cultures (Han and Choe, 1994).

In some cultures, good social support can provide far more than just a sense of psychological well-being. In their study of malnutrition in Western Kenya, Whyte and Kariuki (1997) noted how neighbours and relatives serve to ensure the very survival of a family by helping care for the young when the mother is at work. While families and local communities in this society may not meet all the needs of their members, they can provide an essential form of social security in situations where no other help is available (Cattell, 1997).

The 'down-side' of social support

Relationships offer both opportunities and challenges, and social support can be seen as a fluid concept, having both its good and its bad aspects (Duck *et al.*, 1997). In recent years, a number of research projects have illuminated the 'down-side' of social support (Hobfoll and Stokes, 1988). Seeking support can make the seeker feel dependent and incompetent (House, 1981). This sense of dependency might cause particular discomfort in individualist societies, where a construal of the self as an 'independent' entity may be undermined (Markus and Kitayama, 1991). Other researchers have noted how supporters can also be distressed when they share their discomforts. Ashworth *et al.* (1976) found respondents felt uncomfortable when others discussed painful personal experiences. Derlega *et al.* (1990) reported that people anticipating a stressful event were more stressed if they discussed this event between themselves. In certain regions of the world, during periods of prolonged stress, there are particular reasons for questioning the benefits of support relationships. In a landmark study of Israeli women whose boyfriends, husbands or relatives were engaged in the 1982 Israel–Lebanon war, Hobfoll and London (1985) found that turning to others could lead to an exaggeration of the dangers faced by these men and only helped to perpetuate rumours and increase anxieties.

In the former Soviet Union (and indeed in most of Communist East and Central Europe), the considerable fear of betrayal by others led to a great reluctance to 'open up' and ask others for help (Shlapentokh, 1984). To investigate the psychological impacts of the economic and political uncertainties that followed the collapse of Communism, Goodwin *et al.* (1995) interviewed students, manual workers and entrepreneurs in the Russian cities of Moscow and Tver during 1992 and 1993. Given the shared uncertainties and stresses of this time, friends might have been expected to have provided the respondents with emotional support. Instead, however, it was found that the widespread material problems of everyday life meant that friends were unwilling to unburden themselves to others. In the words of one factory worker: 'Our friends have many problems ... I don't want to disturb them with my problems or pain'.

This is reminiscent of the words of Hobfoll *et al.* (1990: 473):

> ... we can only call on help so often before we tire the supporters and, since our supporters also have limited resources, we can only call upon them within the limits of their own resources. They cannot give us the time and energy they do not have!

Increasingly, our respondents suggested, friendship and family networks were used in an 'exchange' fashion, with support primarily focused around meeting material needs. In the words of one respondent,

> ... some time ago we used to have a deep psychological connection – one person said half of a word or a thought, and you would reply. But now ... friends are changing too ... people now call each other friends according to the principle of give and take only.
>
> (Goodwin *et al.*, 1995)

This particular respondent was a young entrepreneur, and his remarks are particularly representative of the entrepreneurs in our sample. Entrepreneurs represent a relatively new group in Russia. They live in a highly competitive (and increasingly dangerous) world, one which necessitates frequent travel and unsociable working hours if they are to succeed.

Such a group has little time or opportunity to build enduring social networks (Allan, 1993). They also maintain a belief in a psychological individualism that goes beyond the physical constraints of their daily lives, and seems to discourage the development of close relationships (Goodwin, 1995; Goodwin and Emelyanova, 1995a). Any expression of emotional needs could thus be seen as expressing a 'weakness' by a members of a group who feel primarily responsible for their own physical and psychological well-being.

Ethnic variations and migration

The implications of social support may differ across groups. In Thorpe *et al.*'s (1992) study of Greek and British pregnant women, social support was predictive of the emotional well-being of the British women but not the Greek women during pregnancy. At least two interpretations for these results are possible. One explanation is that the social relationships of Greek women were more stressful, and support therefore had a less positive impact overall. A second explanation is that support is assumed in the Greek culture and may thus be less appreciated by these Greek respondents. The greater support offered for pregnant women in Britain may be a welcome but novel experience.

Work using different ethnic groups within the US has also suggested that support availability has different effects for different ethnic groups. Here, degree of acculturation to the US may be a significant mediating variable (Dunkel-Schetter *et al.*, 1996). Research with Mexican-Americans has shown that recent immigrants to the US perceive less support from friends and relatives and are less satisfied than more established Mexican-Americans and European-Americans. These new immigrants are also at a greater risk of developing psycho-pathology (Vega and Kolody, 1985). In reviewing comparative studies of pregnant Hispanic-Americans, African-Americans and European-Americans, Dunkel-Schetter *et al.* (1996) concluded that, although there appears to be less support overall for Hispanic-Americans compared to other culture groups, they report less stress, less need for support and greater satisfaction with the support received. Other work on pregnancies among the Hispanic community in the US has shown that, although Mexican-Americans in general receive more family support than friendship or spousal support, newly arrived Mexican immigrants receive more spousal support. These immigrants rely heavily on spouses when they first arrive, with the family support network taking some time to establish (Dunkel-Schetter *et al.*, 1996).

Lewis (1989) reported that African-American mothers of young children have four major support networks: extended kin, religious groups, friends and current partners. Over three-quarters of these African-American mothers reported strong kin networks and partner support, and two-thirds were in a religious community that provided emotional support. However, less than a fifth of these respondents were members of extensive friendship networks, suggesting that, in line with the high levels of collectivism among this group, family relationships and the religious community are more significant than friends in helping with the trials of raising young children.

Schwarzer *et al.* (1994) examined levels of social integration and social support among East Germans at the time of the opening of the borders with Western Germany. In a three-wave longitudinal study, conducted between 1989 and 1991, 428 East Germans completed a range of measures assessing both their perceived levels of support and the actual support they had received. Over this two-year period these authors found that, rather than being passive victims of their changing lives, social bonding for those who migrated Westwards increased. Receiving social support was a significant buffer against the negative impacts of long-term unemployment, with some sub-groups, particularly women and the young, recipients of the greatest support.

Social support in a British Asian community

Previous research has stressed the close-knit and supportive aspects of Asian family life in Britain (Stopes-Roe and Cochrane, 1988, 1989). Stopes-Roe and Cochrane (1990b) asked respondents to state to whom they could turn if they had any of a range of problems (personal problems, health problems, family problems, or problems concerning money, job or employment). First-generation Asian parents named significantly more confidants and were significantly more satisfied with their support than either their offspring or a comparable group of British parents or young people. Asian parents and their children were also more likely to turn to family members for help than a comparable British sample, and were particularly likely to use their children for support. Thus, 70 per cent of household confidants named by Asian parents were their children, and only 25 per cent were their spouses: in comparison only 39 per cent of British parents cited their children as confidants and 59 per cent named spouses. The important supportive role of the second generation in the Asian family structure may be largely attributed to their ability to help solve many of the practical problems faced by first-generation immigrant parents.

Although the Asian younger generation may provide valuable material and informational aid, when it comes to dealing with complex problems (such as marital disagreement) the role of the younger generation is less certain. Asian marriage is very much a 'community event' (Menski, 1991), and turning to the children when a marriage has problems poses obvious difficulties (Stopes-Roe and Cochrane, 1990b). To examine how the Asian population in Britain might deal with emotional conflicts, seventy Hindu Gujarati couples living in a large city in the British Midlands were questioned (Goodwin, Adatia *et al.*, 1997). In general, these couples solved emotional problems between themselves, with half of the respondents claiming that all problems concerning their marriage would be solved by the partners concerned. The involvement of the family was seen to be very much a 'second step', once the partners had failed to resolve problems, and was seen to be likely to contribute to further tensions in the wider family. In particular, the position of the older generation as 'heads of the household' made it unlikely for them to seek advice or support from their family on marital issues. However, relating *minor* frustrations and grievances about the marriage was an important form of emotional support and a 'safety-valve' for the younger female respondents, with natal family members trusted far more than 'the other side' of the family. Here, a close sister or aunt was most frequently cited as a source of support for the wife, while a male or mutual friend of the couple was most cited by the husband. These were seen as like-minded individuals who would understand and not catastrophise the situation.

Most of Goodwin, Adatia *et al.*'s respondents' Asian friends had undergone similar life experiences, and could therefore empathise with the couple's concerns. Support from friends was seen as having the advantage of being free from obligation and coming from a source without a stake in 'one side' of the family. This was particularly valuable in cases where the marriage was arranged by the couple themselves, where support from the wider family was greatly reduced. In this instance, friends and very selected members of the informal network, usually of the same generation, were used for emotional support. However, although these Asian friends had some role as supporters, non-Asian friends were seen as unable to understand the Asian marriage and were very rarely consulted.

Finally, support from the wider community (such as caste or religious group) was rarely seen as a resource for Hindu Gujaratis facing marital problems. Personal and family honour was seen as something which must be maintained at all costs, with respondents emphasising the necessity to maintain a happy 'public face'. Thus, rather than supporting troubled couples, the wider community was seen as more likely to help contribute to dissolution through gossip and unwelcome interference.

Friendship

While our childhood or old age relationships may be based around the family unit, at other times in life our friends may be our most important personal relationships (Salamon, 1977). However, despite many thousands of research papers on friendships, there has been little systematic research on friendships outside of North America (Adams and Blieszner, 1994),

Many of the most obvious differences between friendships across cultures can be traced to the significance of hierarchy within a society. In Chinese societies, for example, we can see a sharp distinction between 'in-group' members (*zijiren* – typically kin, romantic partner and close friends) and the 'out-group' (*waijen* – all those not in the in-group). This distinction is far sharper in Chinese societies than in their Western counterparts (Gudykunst and Ting-Toomey, 1988; Triandis *et al.*, 1988). Yang (1995) divides Chinese relationships into three groups: *chia jen* (family members), *shou-jen* (relatives outside the family, friends, neighbours, classmates and colleagues) and *sheng-jen* (strangers). Group memberships dictate different social interactions. In *chia jen* relationships, behaviour is strictly demarcated by role and duty, while in *shou-jen* relationships there is a more moderate sense of reciprocity and independence. In the *sheng-jen* relationship, there is a stress on reciprocity and no interdependence between the actors. In Chinese societies, friendship is the only equal relationship within the Confucian system, and friendship between males is particularly valued (Won-Doornink, 1991). In a study of Chinese students, Cheung (1984) found that friends were sought for help with psychological problems before medical doctors.

How are everyday interactions with friends affected by the in-group/out-group distinction in Chinese societies? Wheeler (1988) found that Hong Kong Chinese students had fewer interactions than American students, with most interactions appearing to occur 'by chance'. The work of Goodwin and Lee (1994), suggests that Chinese friends are less willing than British friends to make disclosures in taboo areas. However, to conclude that the Chinese are simply secretive is misleading. Greater trust and disclosure is evident towards in-group rather than out-group members (Gudykunst *et al.*, 1992), and while Chinese close relationships may take some time to mature, they are highly intimate (Hui and Villareal, 1989). The apparent sociability of Westerners may therefore be less 'deep' than the close friendships of the Chinese (Triandis *et al.*, 1988).

Japanese associations are also not lightly formed. Casual contacts are often difficult to establish although, again, once a friendship has been secured it is likely to be particularly strong (Reischauer, 1988). Salamon (1977) compared friendship patterns in middle-class families in Japan and Germany. In Japan, she noted that as early as elementary school, children are expected to make intimate friends. These friendships – referred to as *shin' yu* relations – involve few barriers: 'one withholds nothing and is never suspicious of another's motives' (Salamon, 1977: 813). Such friendships are expected to last throughout life, and often an individual will feel closer – and disclose more – to these friends than to their partner or other members of their nuclear family (Kumar, 1991).

Such intimate friendship can also be found in a number of other collectivist societies and ethnic groups (Schneider *et al.*, 1997). In a study of North American ethnic groups, for example, Dunkel-Schetter *et al.* (1996) reported that, although Hispanic-Americans have less extensive friendships than European-Americans, friendships between members of this community are particularly deep. The closeness of these friendships in collectivist societies may also allow individuals to see the weakness in their friends. Roger Baumgarte and his colleagues (Baumgarte *et al.*, 1997) questioned college students in the US and Korea. Despite many similarities between the two cultures, they found that US students tended to idealise their friends, seeing them as admirable individuals who were similar to themselves and to whom they would happily self-disclose. Korean respondents, while warm and caring towards their friends, were more realistic about these friendships, noting where they differed from their friends. In a subsequent analysis of four cultures (the US, China, Korea and France), correcting or criticising a friend was seen as supportive and was valued by Korean students (Baumgarte *et al.*, 1998).

In individualist cultures, friendships may be more plentiful but less enduring. Western, individualistic friendship can be seen as a 'non-institutionalised institution', in which there are relatively few ritualistic ties and relationships are built on 'voluntary interdependence'. Salamon (1977), for example, failed to find the individualised relationship characterised by *shin' yu* in her West German comparison group. Here, instead, the marriage partner plays the part of the 'best friend', and married couples in North America self-disclose more on a variety of intimate topics than do Japanese (Gudykunst and Nishida, 1986) or Koreans (Won-Doornink, 1985). However, there may be evidence of changing patterns in some societies. Gao (1991) found that young people in both North America and more collectivist China stated that close, intimate, satisfying friendship with a partner was a prerequisite for marriage. Furthermore, although cultural and social norms may be important in the early stages of a relationship, as the relationship develops cultural differences in friendship may diminish (Baumgarte *et al.*, 1998; Gudykunst, 1994).

In Chapter 2, I discussed the values of universalism and particularism across cultures. Although particularism correlates significantly with collectivism (Smith, 1993), particularists choose their associates, while collectivists may be born into a network of obligation (Smith and Bond, 1998). Trompenaars (1993) asked respondents in thirty-eight cultures to imagine they were a passenger in a car driven by a close friend, when that car hits a pedestrian. The friend was speeding in a city area, but there were no witnesses. The friend's lawyer advises that if the passenger were to testify the friend was not speeding, it may save the friend from severe consequences. The question was: 'what right does the friend have to expect his passenger to protect him?' (Trompenaars, 1993: 34).

Trompenaars' (1993) results showed that North Americans and most Northern Europeans were 'universalist' in their approach, with 95 per cent giving a 'universalist' response, such as 'he has no right as a friend to expect me to testify he was not speeding'. In such universalist cultures, the moral rules about what is right and good apply in all circumstances. In contrast, those in particularist cultures such as South Korea were likely to defend their friend (particularly if the accident was serious), with only 36 per cent of respondents from this country giving a 'universalist' response. Here the assumption is that friendship has 'special obligations' which come before universal principles of justice.

The degree to which a culture embraces multi-culturalism may determine friendship between members of different ethnic groups. In Singh Ghuman's (1994) study of British and Canadian youth, there was a considerable amount of cross-ethnic friendship in Canada (where multi-culturalism is strongly encouraged), but practically no cross-ethnic friendship in England. In a diary study of North American students on a large, mixed-race campus, McLaughlin *et al.* (1997) asked respondents to record information about their social interactions. In this mixed-race campus setting, there was plenty of opportunity for inter-group contact, with contact resulting in substantial inter-group friendship. However, the degree to which such friendships will develop may be dependent on the opportunity for mixed-race interaction in later years. Rather pessimistically, research in a number of cultures has found ethnocentrism in friendships to increase with age as the opportunities for mixed-race interaction decrease (Schneider *et al.*, 1997).

Sex differences in relationship intimacy have been widely reported, with men usually found to be less willing to disclose intimately than women (e.g. Baumgarte *et al.*, 1998). For example, Salamon (1977) observed that *shin' yu* relationships are particularly important for women in their traditional role of homemaker, with Japanese women spending a great deal of time talking on the telephone with their *shin' yu* partners. Although men may have *shin' yu* relationships, the work group dominates so much of the man's waking time that he is likely to spend little time communicating with such intimates. In India, however, sex role differences in same-sex friendship is less evident, with men and women sharing similarly 'expressive' communication patterns (Berman *et al.*, 1988). This may reflect the relatively 'feminine' nature of this society (Hofstede, 1980), or it may stem from the problems that face opposite-sex friendships in a society where opposite-sex interactions are heavily supervised. This reinforces the observation that friendships must be viewed as part of a wider set of social relationships and norms which may encourage or prohibit particular allegiances.

Recently, the British sociologist Graham Allan (1998) has attempted to analyse the impacts of modernisation on friendships. He argues that, rather than seeing modernity as leading to the decline in relationships (as is implied by some of the theorists of modernisation discussed in Chapter 2), informal solidarities such as friendships have become *more* significant in recent years. From this perspective, friendships are an important source of psychological identity in a world where changes in employment are undermining established occupational identities, and where increasing divorce and family breakdown have dismantled traditional family allegiances. Allan's valuable contextualisation of friendships within their social and economic settings offers an important avenue for inter-disciplinary research into friendship and social structure across cultures.

Communication patterns

Verbal and non-verbal communications are vital for the development of romantic relationships, friendships and business relations, and there is now a large literature describing cultural differences in communication (see, for example, Argyle, 1988; Gudykunst *et al.*, 1996). There are significant differences in the uses and meanings of non-verbal communications across cultures, and inevitably this can lead to serious misunderstandings in cross-cultural interactions. An embrace from a close friend can mean something quite different from one culture to another (Krauss *et al.*, 1991). The wink of an eye can indicate a prospective romantic partner or just a nervous tic with great cultural knowledge often needed to decipher true meanings (Trompenaars, 1993). An Arab may be insulted by a person who crosses his or her legs and points the sole of their shoe towards them (Kannemeyer *et al.*, 1992), while a European-American teacher interacting with an African-American student may misinterpret the student's avoidance of eye-contact as disrespectful when it may in fact indicate respect (Gudykunst, 1994). In this brief review, I first discuss non-verbal communication before moving on to verbal communication and disclosure.

Non-verbal communications

While the human form may place some limit on the variety of non-verbal movements available, gestures and meanings are often particular to a specific region (Argyle, 1988). 'Neutral' cultures such as Japan show considerable self-constraint in their communications, while in highly affective cultures such as Italy interactants will reveal their thoughts and feelings both verbally and non-verbally, making great use of touch and dramatic gestures (Trompenaars, 1993). Morris *et al.* (1979) describe the distribution of twenty key gestures across forty European locations. While some of the gestures they examined could be found crossing national boundaries, many of these same gestures examined had multiple meanings. Thus a tap of the temple with the tip of the forefinger could mean either 'crazy' or 'intelligent', depending on the part of the world in which it was employed! Some of the gestures studied, such as the head toss, dated back at least two millennia, while others were likely to be popular for only a specific period. Within Britain, for example, few people now would use (or even recognise) the famous 'V for Victory' sign employed by Churchill during the Second World War. This led to the notorious instance in which the 'V' sign was given by Margaret Thatcher outside 10 Downing Street following a general election victory. In this case, the Prime Minister mistakenly put her hand in the reversed position, giving out a quite different (and rather more insulting) gesture to her country!

Several gestures are associated with speech in a number of cultures, and serve to illustrate or expand on what is being said (Argyle, 1988). However, the impact of these gestures on verbal fluency may vary across cultures. Graham and Argyle (1975) found that, while hand movements generally improved communication across cultures, this effect was particularly pronounced among Italians.

Hall (1976) discriminated between 'contact' and 'non-contact' cultures. Little (1968) found interacting members of Mediterranean ('contact') cultures stood closer distances than members of North European ('non-contact') cultures. Watson (1970) found Arab, Latin American and Southern European students touched more, stood closer, faced one another directly, and used more eye contact than students from 'non-contact' Asian and Northern European cultures. Lomranz (1976) asked Argentinian, Iraqi and Russian students to place imaginary interactants on a board. Argentinian and Russian students placed the interactants at greater distances, although the actual proximity of the figures depended on the relationship between these conversationalists. In Iraq, interactants were placed at the same distance, regardless of the relationship they enjoyed. Personal space was thus found to be a function of both culture and the nature of the interaction. Barnlund (1975) found that American college students touched their parents in more areas of their body than Japanese students, and were more likely to discriminate in their touch between same-sex and opposite-sex friends. However, as Lebra (1992) notes, the greater use of touch among the Americans should not indicate that the Japanese are socially isolated, as Japanese co-drinking and co-dining relationships may be very intimate even if they do not involve touch. Finally, it is important to remember that contact rules may vary within sub-groups, with caste systems in some countries (such as India) still having an impact on the proximity of interactants (Argyle, 1988).

Rules about personal space may be particularly important when inviting guests to a home. In Japan, for example, the home is a very private sphere, open only to a restricted few. Guests are expected to remain in certain guest rooms and not to wander freely in the house (Befu, 1974). Trompenaars (1993) notes how households in the 'diffuse' cultures of France and Germany use high hedges at the edge of their properties to demarcate clearly the private and public world.

Debates about the extent of universality in non-verbal behaviour have been particularly pronounced in the area of emotional expression. Ekman and Friesen (1971) argued that universal patterns were to be found in the relationship between distinctive patterns of facial muscles and particular emotions – happiness, sadness, anger, fear, surprise, disgust and interest. They examined respondents from a large number of cultures, including members of a remote tribal group that had experienced only minimal contact with Western cultures. In a series of studies, respondents were read stories describing particular emotions, and asked to indicate the facial photograph best illustrating the emotion. Respondents across cultures agreed on the facial expressions for happiness, sadness, anger and disgust, but had more difficulty distinguishing fear and surprise. The results for the most 'Westernised' respondents were almost identical to those for the least Westernised. This was taken to support the claim that there are constants across cultures in emotional facial behaviour. These findings are complemented by other work which found smiling to be an indicator of happiness across eleven cultures (Keating *et al.*, 1981).

More recently, some have argued that such universals in human facial expressions may be less evident than has previously been claimed (Russell and Fernandez-Dols, 1997). While they accept that similar patterns of facial movement may occur in all human groups, Russell and Fernandez-Dols re-analyse the work of Ekman and Friesen and argue that the attribution of emotions to particular facial expressions is proportional to the degree of Western influence on a culture. They also argue that there is no universal link between particular facial patterns and particular emotions – in other words, no evidence to suggest that in all societies happy people smile, angry people frown and so on. They thus conclude that there is likely to be only *minimal universality* in the way in which facial expressions are produced and interpreted. Thus, while physiological and neuro-chemical networks connecting the sensory signals from the face to the autonomic nervous system are largely unaffected by cultural differences, the subjective feelings associated with various expressions do vary across cultures (Basic Behavioral Science Research for Mental Health, 1996b).

Scherer *et al.* (1986) investigated broader sets of emotions by examining the antecedents of reported emotions among students in eight, primarily European, countries (Belgium, France, Great Britain, Israel, Italy, Spain, Switzerland and West Germany). Using a mixture of open-ended questions and rating scales, respondents provided detailed descriptions of emotional events and their physiological reactions to these events. They also reported the amount of control or coping they had used in these emotional situations.

Reactions to emotional events were analysed for four emotions: fear, anger, joy and sadness. Overall, Scherer *et al.* (1986) reported far more commonalties than differences in emotional expression and, where differences did emerge, they rarely followed national stereotypes. Belgians and French were the most non-verbally responsive, Spanish and Israeli respondents the least. British, Israeli, French and Belgian subjects reported the greatest amount of facial reaction and Italian and Spanish the least. Body movements were recorded most frequently by the English and French and least frequently by the Israelis. A high amount of control over their overt emotional responses was reported for joy, sadness and anger by Belgian and French subjects. British subjects reported a high amount of control for sadness and anger but less for joy. Italian subjects displayed less control for sadness and anger, while Swiss subjects were low on control for anger. Of course, as Scherer *et al.* (1986) recognise, self-reported emotions are not necessarily reliable – indeed, some reports might contradict 'real' behaviour (for example, British respondents might have exaggerated their degree of verbalisations because their baseline for verbal interaction was so low).

Unfortunately, Scherer *et al.* fail to provide a theoretical structure for their findings, and it is therefore difficult to know the extent to which their results might be replicated using different samples and more 'direct' methods of measurement of emotional expression.

Non-verbal rules are often combined into complex rituals which require a great deal of cultural knowledge from their actors. Befu (1974) describes the hierarchical ritual associated with the pouring of *sake*, the sacred Japanese alcoholic drink. First, the host pours the *sake* for the guest, and the guest then reciprocates. If a person of lower status wishes to drink with one of higher status, the lower status person must first pour for the other, who then reciprocates, with this exchange offering the opportunity for the lower status person to approach. A higher person can also offer up their own cup for *sake* to others. As can be imagined, interactions can become very complicated – to the outsider at least – as Befu explains:

> When a cup is offered to someone, he is not required to return it immediately. Since normally a person drains a cup in several sips, putting it on the table at intervals of a few minutes, often someone else comes along to offer another cup before he finishes the first. When one finishes the first cup offered, he might offer it to the second person ... The upshot of this is that the route a cup travels forms a complex pattern indicating social status, cliques, ulterior motives etc. ... after a while cups are unevenly distributed, some people having several in front of them – typically high status individuals to whom others have paid homage – leaving none in front of some of the lower ranking individuals. Since it is improper to leave people without cups to drink from, the *ryootei* (restaurant) management ... will bring extra cups and leave them in the centre of the table. High status persons should not hoard cups, however. They should try to drink up and redistribute them as fast as they can.
>
> (Befu, 1974: 117)

According to Befu, this explains why so many Japanese business executives are heavy drinkers. There is simply no socially accepted means for refusing *sake*.

Verbal communications

The study of self-disclosure – 'that which individuals reveal about themselves to others' (Derlega *et al.*, 1993: 1) has been a major topic of socio-psychological research for some three decades. In Western research, reciprocal disclosure has been seen as a major force in both the development of romantic relationships (Wintrob, 1987) and friendships (Altman and Taylor, 1973), and is a good predictor of marital satisfaction (Antill and Cotton, 1987) and of family cohesion (Vangelisti, 1994). By providing an important opportunity for obtaining social support, disclosure also acts as a mediator of stress, and in doing so becomes a significant contributor to physical health (e.g. Pennebaker *et al.*, 1987) and psychological well-being (e.g. Larson and Chastain, 1990).

Self-disclosure can be seen as a 'balance', where too much intimacy can be seen as threatening, not enough as rejection (Ting-Toomey, 1991). Altman and Taylor (1973) describe the development of a relationship as a process of *social penetration* during which interactants broaden the breadth of the topic and increase the depth at which topics are discussed. They liken the disclosure process to the peeling of an onion: at first interaction is superficial but, provided that previous exchanges have been rewarding, disclosure gradually moves towards the central, 'intimate' level. Self-disclosure has been seen as an interactive strategy aimed at uncertainty reduction (Berger and Bradac, 1982): as interactants question others, and thus strive to alleviate the unease associated with uncertainty (Gudykunst and Matsumoto, 1996), they gain the confidence to tell others their own thoughts and feelings. This desire for uncertainty reduction, and the use of disclosure to overcome it, is subject to cultural and demographic variation, however, and specific features of the environment or nature of the interactants serve to inhibit or accelerate the social penetration process (Berger and Bradac, 1982).

People from individualist cultures are expected to self-disclose more information about themselves than members of collectivist cultures (Gudykunst, 1994). While individualists are more likely to give personal information about themselves, collectivists provide and seek group membership information from their conversational partners (Gudykunst, 1994). In individualist societies, members tend to verbalise and negotiate their desires in an assertive manner: in collectivist societies, members are more circumspect in their desire to maintain harmonious relationships (Ting-Toomey, 1991). Thus, in Japan, a forceful 'American' personality is seen as neurotic, while cooperativeness and reasonableness are highly valued. To maintain the harmonic flow of personal relationships, collectivists are also more likely to send 'backchannel' signals such as small verbalisations to show the person is listening (Gudykunst, 1994). As we saw in our discussion of friends and support networks, collectivist cultures are also characterised by a smaller, but more intimate, circle of interactants (Gudykunst and Ting-Toomey, 1988). As early as 1936, Lewin observed disclosure differences between Americans and Germans, with the Americans disclosing more than the Germans but failing to achieve the high level of intimacy evident in Germany (Lewin, 1936). Greater collectivism is also associated with greater differences between in-groups and out-groups in the intimacy of communications (Gudykunst and Matsumoto, 1996).

Even the role of silence in a conversation might vary significantly across cultures. The Japanese word *haragei* ('the art of the belly') refers to the meeting of minds without clear verbal interaction (Reischauer, 1988). In collectivist cultures there is no compulsion to talk, but just to be with accepted others (Hofstede, 1994b). Collectivist groups such as the Chinese do not see 'small talk' as being as necessary as do individualists, as there is less need to develop relationships in collectivist societies (Gudykunst, 1994). In contrast, individualistic cultural groups see talk as enjoyable (Wiemann *et al.*, 1986). Individualists feel they 'must' communicate, and have a low tolerance for silence (Gudykunst, 1994)

M.S. Kim (1994) examined the use of five 'conversational constraints' among students in Korea (a collectivist culture), Hawaii (a moderately individualist culture) and the US (an individualist culture). These constraints described a concern for avoiding hurting the other's feelings, a desire to minimise imposing on the other, a concern for avoiding negative evaluations by the interactant; and a desire for clarity and effectiveness in communications. Participants were asked to rate the importance of each constraint in six situations. As Kim had anticipated, clarity was seen as more important in individualist cultures, while face-saving was more important in collectivist cultures. There were no cross-cultural differences in the avoidance of negative evaluation or concern for effectiveness in communication.

The distinction between low- and high-context communication styles parallels the distinction between individualism and collectivism (Gudykunst, 1994). In high-context (usually collectivist) cultures, little information is *explicitly* transmitted, but the situation and their role positions of those involved transmits a great deal of information (Hall, 1976). In low-context cultures, such as the US, there is little room for ambiguity and people are more direct in their communication styles. Consequently, when North Americans are indirect in their communications, it is usually only in areas of high sensitivity or nervousness (Condon, 1984).

A second of Hofstede's (1980) dimensions, uncertainty avoidance, has also been related to conversational disclosure, with people in high uncertainty avoidance cultures shunning ambiguous situations and seeking explicit rules and easily interpretable and predictable relationships (Gudykunst and Matsumoto, 1996; Hofstede, 1980). Those in high uncertainty avoidance cultures are more explicit in their communications, talking with their hands and showing emotions, and can thus appear aggressive to those from low uncertainty avoidance cultures (Hofstede, 1994b). Ting-Toomey (1991) combined a number of cultural dimensions in her analysis of Japanese, American and French students. As might have been anticipated from national positions on the individualism–collectivism dimension, American students talked most to their romantic partners, French students spoke an intermediate amount to their romantic partners, and the Japanese talked the least. However, the high degree of uncertainty avoidance in France meant that respondents avoided overt arguments. Furthermore, the femininity of French culture meant that, while Japanese females reported higher degrees of relational conflict than the males, and US females reported higher degrees of disclosure maintenance than males, there were no sex differences in disclosure among the French students. This research represents a real advance on previous work which has focused on just one dimension of values, offering a more complex analysis of the cultural influences on verbal communications.

Politeness formulas complement disclosure rules in regulating verbal communication. The Japanese have many graduations of politeness, carefully matched to the situation, with humble forms used for the self and polite forms used for those of higher status (Reischauer, 1988). Interpersonal address in Japan has specific and detailed status associations, with the wide-spread use of direct address forms such as *okusan* (or *okusama* for the lady of the house). The company president in Japan feels little desire to become 'one of the lads' or to associate himself with those of lower rank, while the graduate will address his or her former teachers in a respectful manner even once he or she has achieved a similar level of distinction (Reischauer, 1988). However, inter-personal frustrations are given a vent for release in parties and other social settings. Furthermore, in private conversation with friends, a Japanese may brag about success and accomplishments, while under other circumstances this same person may be far more humble (Lebra, 1992). This private/public division can also be seen in the contrast between the private relationship enjoyed by a man and woman in a Japanese marriage and the more public show of disdain for her by her husband when among his drinking colleagues (Suzuki, 1976).

As can be seen from the above, the great majority of previous research on conversational disclosure has focused on comparisons between Western nations (usually North America) and 'Eastern' nations such as Japan. In some totalitarian societies, where there is a great deal of monitoring of everyday life, disclosure may have very different, even life-threatening, implications (Markova, 1997; Shlapentokh, 1984). For example, within Communist Central and Eastern Europe, there were strict limits on the permissible topics for discussion (Buckley, 1989). In the words of Gilberg (1990: 272), Communist society was marked by

> ... a legacy of fear ... fuelled by the legacy of suspicion ... not merely a fear of officialdom and authorities but a fear of other people – neighbours, friends, work associates and even relatives.

Even in the more relaxed post-Stalinist era, 'every person (lived) with the assumption that there are squealers everywhere' (Shlapentokh, 1984: 242).

To investigate the effects of this history of repression on self-disclosure, Goodwin and colleagues examined self-disclosure in three former Communist states: Russia, Georgia and Hungary (Goodwin *et al.*, 1999). Building on previous research into disclosure and uncertainty reduction, a number of hypotheses were generated examining the importance of culture, demographic variables and individual differences in disclosure. Overall, disclosure rates were found to differ according to the culture in which the participants lived and the target of the disclosure. In line with previous work on individualism and collectivism, Hungarians (the most collectivist group in the sample) were the most willing to disclose to intimates, but not to casual acquaintances. Age also predicted disclosure rates (elder subjects disclosed less), as did degree of fatalism (fatalists were the most reluctant to disclose). Further analyses revealed that students were more likely to disclose to close friends than were manual workers or entrepreneurs, and that female respondents were less willing to disclose about their political beliefs than were their male counterparts. Goodwin *et al.*'s results suggest that future cross-cultural studies of disclosure should also incorporate major demographic factors as well as culture into their analyses, as such factors are likely to be highly influential in structuring the opportunities for interaction and social exchange (Allan, 1993).

Fitting in with others

Self-monitoring

'Self-monitoring' examines the relationship between attitudes and public behaviour. Low self-monitors are more likely to demonstrate a stronger correspondence between their attitudes and their behaviour than high self-monitors, who may instead be keener to 'fit in' with others around them (Snyder, 1974).

At first glance, the findings on self-monitoring across cultures seem to be contradictory. A number of writers (e.g. Yang, 1995) have pointed to a large amount of self-monitoring in Chinese societies, with Chinese people striving to change their behaviour to fit in with their situation. Even idiocentrics in these collectivist societies may exhibit behaviours that comply with the norms in order to avoid criticism and win approval (Han and Choe, 1994; Yang, 1995). However, other researchers have provided evidence to show that Chinese respondents might be *less* self-monitoring than their Western counterparts (Goodwin and Pang, 1994). This may result from a lesser concern with 'the self' in Chinese societies (Gudykunst *et al.*, 1987).

We can interpret these mixed findings more readily if we consider the differentiation between the 'public' and 'private' self (Markus and Kitayama, 1991; Yang, 1995). While the public self is highly visible, the private self is relatively unchanged by external circumstances (Triandis, 1989). Given the nature of in-group and out-group relationships in collectivist societies, Chinese individuals may only conform *superficially* to strangers, and their 'private selves' may be less influenced by out-group members. Goodwin and Pang examined the maladaptive effects of high self-monitoring among Singaporean (collectivist) and British (individualist) students (Goodwin and Pang, 1994). In this study it was found that high self-monitors in Britain had significantly poorer romantic relationships than high self-monitors in Singapore, suggesting that such superficial behavioural modifications might have 'less serious' consequences for enduring relationships in collectivist societies.

In Chapter 6, I discussed the psychological process described by Doi in Japan as *amae* or 'passive love'. This relationship of indulgence and dependence, usually described in the context of the mother–child relationship, becomes transformed into a socially contracted dependence in later social relationships, and is particularly evident in the relationship between leaders and subordinates (Moeran, 1984). Freedom for the individual thus becomes located in their significant relationships with others, with the Japanese more likely than Westerners to socialise in groups and to conform in dress and conduct (Reischauer, 1988). In Japanese culture, social conformity is thus not perceived as a weakness in the way it may be in the more individualist US (Tobin, 1992). When Japanese kinship-based networks decrease, individuals may seek new social networks both within and outside the community. While these new relationships are more informal than relationships with kin, they still continue to provide a form of 'social glue', highly functional for community life in this collectively oriented society (Moeran, 1984).

In a seven-nation study, Buunk and Hupka (1986) found individual autonomy in relationships to be lowest in countries assumed to be high on collectivism and power distance, such as Hungary and the former Soviet Union. This lack of autonomy was manifested through a preference for sharing friendships and leisure activities and a rejection of autonomy in social activities. Buunk and Hupka relate these findings to two indices of democracy developed by Vincent (1971) and Bollen (1980), suggesting that the more democratic a country the more students endorse autonomous beliefs. However, gender differences may interact significantly with the endorsement of autonomous beliefs. Thus, men valued autonomy more in Communist societies, while the opposite gender pattern was evident in more autonomous nations.

In Buunk and Hupka's (1986) analysis, subjects from the former Soviet Union were the least autonomous of their respondents. In Russia, 'fitting in' with the community was an important imperative in the peasant community during serfdom, where many agricultural tasks were performed by all members of the community (Alechina *et al.*, 1997). The heroes of Russian nineteenth-century literature were unassuming in their goals, quite distinct from the Western hero fighting for his or her own ends. Following the Communist revolution, Bolshevik ideology promised to make Russia one large happy family, with Lenin portrayed as 'everyone's grandfather'. However, as we have seen throughout this book, inconsistencies between public and private behaviours meant a perplexing array of beliefs and values, particularly confusing for young children raised in this society. The legacy of this 'split behaviour' seems to be a rather bewildered younger generation, who find the uncertainties of the post-Soviet world threatening and debilitating (Alechina *et al.*, 1997).

Loneliness

Loneliness can be seen as both a subjective feeling and a state of social isolation. Studies in Western cultures have found that a considerable proportion of adults suffer from at least occasional feelings of loneliness, with such loneliness correlated with suicide, poor health and alcohol abuse (Tornstam, 1992). At present, however, there has been little systematic research on loneliness and cultural values.

Nina (1996) examined the causes, motives and effects of loneliness among a hundred married couples from San Juan, Puerto Rico. In her study, women reported more frequent and intense loneliness experiences than men, with feelings of loneliness being particularly powerful during the early stages of marriage. These women's loneliness reflected a desire to return home to the family, in this highly family-centred and collectivist culture. Jylha and Jokela (1990) found that living alone can provoke greater loneliness in the southern (more collectivist) parts of Europe than in the more individualist north. Van Tilburg *et al.* (1998) examined more than 5,000 older adults in the Netherlands and Italy. They offered an inverse macro-level association hypothesis, suggesting that loneliness is most prevalent in regions where living alone was rarest and community bonds strongest. Thus, we might expect less *incidence* of loneliness in a collectivist society, but a *greater degree* of loneliness among the small number who are not socially involved.

Finally, in Tornstam's (1992) study of more than 2,700 Swedish adults, age was found to have a significant impact on gender differences in loneliness, with only married subjects aged between 20 and 49 exhibiting such gender differences. Basing his ideas on Maslow's (1954) need hierarchy, Tornstam (1992) suggests that, while older respondents have been traditionally more concerned with just 'getting by', younger respondents are more attuned to emotional, 'post-material' deficits and are thus more sensitive to subtle relationship factors which lead to loneliness in their relationships. Although Tornstam's study was limited to Sweden, his observations are consistent with other research from a number of cultures which reports a greater concern with emotional issues as societies become more affluent (Katakis, 1984).

Summary

Social support is generally seen as a 'good thing', and support is generally more available for members of collectivist societies. At the same time, shared stresses in a society can limit the degree of support available, restricting the opportunities for emotional help. Social support provision varies across ethnic groups, with British Asians relying heavily on other members of their family even when confronting difficulties with their own family relationships.

Friendship is a major component of all support networks, but friendships in collectivist societies are likely to differ from those in individualist cultures by being fewer in number but deeper and longer-lasting in nature. Friends may become increasingly significant in changing societies, where the opportunities for family support decrease. Non-verbal behaviours appear to vary substantially in both frequency and meanings across societies, and although some facial expressions seem to be common across cultures, the relationship between emotions and facial actions is culturally variable. Verbal disclosure is generally greater in individualist societies, although intimate disclose to in-group members may be greater in collectivist nations. In high uncertainty avoidance cultures such as Egypt, communication is explicit, and may often appear unduly 'emotional' to those from outside such cultures.

'Fitting in with others' is an important motivation in most societies, but such conformity may be dependent on the nature of the interaction and the politics of the society. A failure to integrate within a society may lead to loneliness, particularly in collectivist societies where 'breaking into' an established in-group may be particularly problematic.

9 Taking it further

Implications and future developments

Introduction

In this final chapter I begin by drawing together two constant themes of this book – the role of cultural values in understanding relationship behaviours, and the influence of social change on relationship adaptation and transition. I then go on to consider the implications of culture and cultural change for relationship interventions across cultures. Finally, I conclude this book by calling on relationship researchers to apply their knowledge beyond the confines of the academic journal, and to address the pressing relationship dilemmas which confront our modern world.

Making sense of cultural differences

In this book, I have argued that our social relationships, from their very inception, vary across cultures in a manner at least partly predictable from the cultural values held in those societies (e.g. Kohn, 1989; Triandis *et al.*, 1984). Although the origins of these values are, as yet, only poorly understood, geographical setting, historical and political events, economic developments and religion are all likely to influence the development of such values (Kim *et al.*, 1994; Schwartz, 1997; Triandis, 1995). Taken together with other important 'etic' factors (such as social class, education and age), these values can help us develop inclusive hypotheses about relationship behaviours and beliefs in different societies, and aid us in interpreting contradictory findings in different cultural settings. This is encapsulated in the model shown in Figure 9.1.

Such a framework inevitably raises a number of questions requiring further research. At present, we know a considerable amount about the cultural values of some nations (most 'Western' cultures, plus Japan, China, and some southern European states). We also know a great deal about the significance of one cultural dimension – individualism–collectivism (e.g. Kim *et al.*, 1994; Triandis, 1995) – but very little about the other dimensions identified by Hofstede (1980) and subsequent researchers, or the 'vertical' versus 'horizontal' axes of the individualism–collectivism divide (Singelis *et al.*,

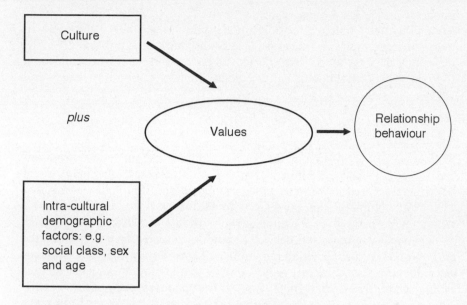

Figure 9.1 Culture, values and relationship behaviours

1995). The most complex set of values dimensions to date (Schwartz, 1997) has only recently been applied to the study of personal relationships, with this analysis focusing on just one culture, that of Israel (Lehmann, 1998).

Relationships researchers have also largely neglected the manner in which demographic variables may influence cultural values. At present, there is pitifully little interaction between epidemiologists and sociologists (who are traditionally interested in 'macro-level' analyses) and psychologists inter-ested in values and value development. Cross-cultural researchers in particular have failed to consider the relationship between culture and social class, despite the evidence that, in many key dimensions of social behaviour, social class and culture interact in a significant manner (see, for example, Goodwin, 1998; Kohn, 1989; Tudge *et al.*, 1997). Even ecological accounts of social development, which have been far more sensitive to issues of envi-ronment and the production of values, have largely neglected occupational variations in their focus on pre-literature societies (see Bronfenbrenner, 1988, for a critique).

The door is thus wide open for researchers to exploit the recent develop-ments in value research and to go beyond the simplistic and restricting paradigm of the simple individualism–collectivism divide. To do this, researchers should seek to extend both the countries analysed (there is, for example, practically no data on psychological values in Africa) and the range of relationship outcomes examined (we know, for example, very little about the interaction between cultural values and sexual behaviour, or cultural values and social isolation). Future researchers should explore the impact of values on a range of demographic factors, while at the same time recognising the complex relationship between values and behaviours in many societies. Such an integrative, inter-disciplinary approach offers the possibility of a far more sophisticated understanding of relationships, and the way they interact with culture, demographic factors and values and beliefs.

Changing cultures

Social change may be one of the constant features of our modern environment (Rice, 1992). Certainly, as we saw in Chapter 2, the majority of commentators see the world as an increasingly diminishing place dominated by the West. Numerous anecdotes serve to reinforce this image. Eriksen (1995: 278) cites the story of a tribe of camel nomads in North Africa whose traditional annual migration was delayed because they feared they might miss the final episodes of the television programme *Dallas*. Fukuyama, in his influential book *The End of History* (1993), argues that in modern societies there is no real alternative to liberal democracy as the major form of political organisation, and no alternative to the global capitalist marketplace as the primary form of economic organisation. Such economic and political inevitability is interpreted by most as leading to the inevitable homogenisation of family forms across the globe. Focusing primarily on changes in value structures, Hatfield and Rapson develop a Westernisation model, which they use to analyse personal relationships and social change (Hatfield and Rapson, 1996: 236ff). They examine several characteristics of Westernisation, including a greater belief in the equality of women and members of minority groups, a belief in the pursuit of happiness and the avoidance of pain, and a rejection of fatalism and the passive acceptance of traditional goals. These they relate to a decline in the condemnation of passionate and sexual love, a reduction in sexual and gender inequality, a greater acknowledgement and acceptance of homosexuality, a general shift from arranged to free-choice marriages, and the greater ease of divorce across cultures.

Allied to this, demographic changes can be seen as challenging traditional relationship practices across the globe. In the developed world, the success of health care measures, the reduction in fertility rates, and relative rises in economic levels have led to a significant increase in the proportion of elderly citizens (Sinha, 1991). The worldwide life expectancy rate of 46 years in 1950–55 has increased by eighteen years in the last four decades (United Nations, 1997). Projected increases in life expectancy are expected to be most dramatic in Africa and Asia: in South-east Asia, for example, only 5 per cent of the 1.05 billion people living in this region in 1980 were over 60 years of age. UN projections suggest that, by the year 2025, the total population of South-east Asia will have almost doubled, with more than 11 per cent of this region's population being aged 60 or over. Invoking the 'modernisation' hypothesis discussed in Chapter 2, Sinha (1991) suggests that a reduction in family size and the growth of schooling will lead to a decrease in emotional and economic family support for the elderly. He argues that there is an urgent need for the productive capacities of the able elderly to be recognised, so that this population continues to be valued by their families and the wider community.

At the other end of the life span, Kagitcibasi (1991) points to the implications of decreasing infant mortality rates across cultures. In 1960, only 83 per cent of majority world children lived beyond the age of one but by 1991 this had increased to 92 per cent (Myers, 1991). This, accompanied by increased schooling and the increasing participation of women in non-traditional occupations away from home, suggests the need for a greater focus on childhood development and care (Kagitcibasi, 1991). However, at present there is little evidence of the social reforms necessary to provide such support. Such changes in education offer an important challenge to traditional gender roles. In the European Union, for example, there are now 110 women with higher education qualifications to every 100 men, although there is considerable variation across nations: for example, Germany has 83 women for every 100 men, Portugal 170 women for every 100 men (Eurostat, 1998). Greater female participation in the workforce and changes in technology may be expected to lead to the adoption of more feminine values, with consequent implications for relationships attitudes and behaviours (Hofstede, 1994b).

For all this, as I have argued throughout this book, the impact of demographic and social transitions on personal relationships is likely to be complex, with even the most widespread of macro-level changes liable to have a range of implications for individuals' relationships and their families. Eriksen (1995) cites the case of the Trobriand Islanders, who have adapted to modernisation on their own terms. While modernisation has led to political and economic changes, both the kinship system and former ceremonial exchanges still exist, although the particular *meanings* they have for their participants may have changed. Similarly, Hviding (1994, cited in Eriksen, 1995) shows how Solomon Islanders, who formerly operated bilateral patterns of kinship descent, have moved to the patrilineal descent more appropriate for making land claims. Eriksen concludes that, rather than Globalisation/Westernisation/Modernisation meaning that we are all becoming the same, global symbols and information are now interpreted from a local vantage point, making people differ in new (and often unpredictable) ways. Thus, the 'modern' world appears in the most unlikely of places (for example, in a small suburb in India) while the 'West' is less evident in a Western city where a large proportion of the population come from non-Western societies (such as in Bradford, England). Such a 'mixing' of cultures has important outcomes for personal relationships, with Kagitcibasi (1996) arguing that a convergence towards emotional interdependence is as characteristic of the West as it is of the 'developing' world.

The complexity of these changes is best encaptured within a broad-systems perspective which considers the inter-relationship between individuals and their physical and social settings, such as the home, school and workplace (Bronfenbrenner, 1993). Bronfenbrenner's approach emphasises the link between broader contextual factors and the individual and is closely related to transactional approaches which examine the complex ways in which social change may be manifested in our personal lives (e.g. Wapner and Craig-Bray, 1992). From this viewpoint, actions must be made *comprehensible* in terms of the ways in which they impact on everyday life (Weber, 1921). Thus, structural circumstances are unlikely to 'mean' the same to all people, but are likely to vary with a particular individual's life circumstances, beliefs and motivations (Boudon, 1986).

Table 9.1 provides a first attempt to illustrate the ways in which 'macro-level' changes might influence some of the different spheres of personal relationships discussed in this volume. This framework can be seen as applicable to the process of acculturation (resulting from both voluntary and involuntary migration) as well as to rapid internal social transitions within a society. Broadly adapting Lazarus' (1991) theory of cognition and emotion, I have divided this framework into three sections: 'areas of adaptation' (relationships changes which have led to relatively little debate or conflict within a group or society), 'areas of challenge' (controversial changes in relationships which have activated considerable debate in these communities), and 'areas of conflict' (areas of relationships behaviour, attitudes or evaluation most negatively affected by social changes). This latter category is consistent with the observation of family theorists that, while some aspects of our social lives may readily adapt to new circumstances, other relationships changes may be more difficult and are less 'functional' for our daily lives (e.g. Boss, 1987).

First, consider the situation of the acculturating individual or family. The process of relationship formation is likely to be heavily influenced by the new culture into which an individual is moving, and we might expect a gradual adaptation by incoming groups to the dating *behaviours* of the new society (Feldman and Rosenthal, 1990; Rosenthal *et al.*, 1989). New, extended 'pseudo-kin' may be adopted, to allow for the smooth development of business arrangements and to help facilitate the formation of new social networks (Lau, 1981; Lee, 1985). Many relationships *values*, however, are more resistant to change (Horencyzk and Bekerman, 1993) and may form a contentious area for debate within the family. Actual marital choice, rather than dating behaviours, may be substantially influenced by more 'traditional' mate-selection practices, with, for example, many British Muslim families preferring to choose a marriage partner from 'back home' (Singh Ghuman, 1994). While some groups (particularly the young) may form new relationships, there is likely to be a weakening of existing support ties for elder respondents, who may lack the skills or facilities to establish relationships in this new country. Shifts in the 'balance of power' across generations following migration can also lead to inter-generational conflicts (Goodwin,

Table 9.1   The impact of acculturation and (internal) social change on close
relationships

Response to change	Acculturation	Rapid internal transitions
Areas of adaptation	Dating and mating *behaviours* 'Pseudo-kin' ties	Family and role relations Child-rearing values
Areas of challenge	Relationship *values* and marital choice	Support networks
Areas of conflict	Social support among the elderly Inter-generational relationships	Marital quality and mental health

Adatia *et al.*, 1997; Stopes-Roe and Cochrane, 1990a). Such conflicts are
likely to have important implications for the mental health of these migrant
groups (Berry, 1990).

In rapidly changing societies, we might expect different kinds of adaptation and conflict. When we consider relationship roles and family values,
economic realities create new modes of living and new sets of priorities.
Thus, in some societies women stop doing paid work due to the expense of
child care, which is no longer provided by the state (Ostner, 1996). Women
may also be the first to lose their jobs in times of growing unemployment.
While these social changes may be resisted by some groups within society (in
particular, by feminist groups) they may be bolstered by government policies
and proclamations (Vannoy, 1998). Different child-rearing values may also
emerge and be propagated by different segments of a society, and may serve
to reflect and reinforce the broader values of these social groups (Goodwin
and Emelyanova, 1995a; Kohn, 1989). Social support networks are also
likely to be structured by the material realities of the transient society, but
the costs associated with such networks are likely to lead to the renegotia-
tion of former alliances. Thus, while social support may become increasingly
important in a difficult economic environment, social networks may be
refashioned to meet the ecological demands of the situation and may now
provide informational rather than emotional support (Goodwin *et al.*, 1995).
Finally, the stresses experienced by many in transient societies may have a
direct and negative impact on mental health (Goodwin and Tang, 1998;
Schwarzer and Chung, 1996), which in itself has a bi-directional effect on
the quality of close relationships (Cramer *et al.*, 1996). This means that,
taken overall, rapid social change is likely to have a deleterious effect on
close personal relationships, at least in the early stages of a social transition.

Interventions across cultures

Given the complexities of the cultural, demographic and individual factors important in influencing relationship behaviour, and the changing nature of so many societies, how can the relationship researcher use his/her knowledge about culture to implement beneficial interventions within a society? Unfortunately, few examples of cultural-specific relationship intervention programmes have been reported, with the exception of the 'cultural assimilator' programmes available for instructing business people about inter-cultural encounters (Hofstede, 1994b). These programmes themselves, however, are still overwhelmingly North American in flavour and rarely provide in-depth information about a culture (Hofstede, 1994b). Needless to say, there are many pitfalls in 'superficial' interventions. For example, marriage counsellors who build their counselling on theories of independence and couple negotiation may soon alienate couples in societies where autonomy is less valued (Buunk and Hupka, 1986).

The Turkish psychologist Kagitcibasi (1996) argues that cross-cultural family interventions must be theory-based, and should incorporate pertinent and culturally-sensitive models of human relationships. In line with the work of Bronfenbrenner (1993) and other systems theorists, she argues it is necessary to 'unpack' lifestyle patterns in the environment, and to identify and build on the existing strengths of the family and wider cultural structures (Kagitcibasi, 1991). Thus, the counsellor in a collectivist society might involve family networks to help mediate in family problems. At the same time, researchers should not assume that all collectivist cultures (or indeed all families) are equal, and researchers should strive for a 'deep understanding' of a situation – or 'thicker' analysis (Geertz, 1973). In Goodwin, Adatia *et al.*'s research with a collectivist Hindu population, for example, family involvement in marital counselling was definitely *not* welcomed, with more 'objective' professional members of the community preferred as marriage mediators.

Interventions must also, of course, be seen against a backdrop of economic and social conditions. Working in India, Ujjwalarani (1992) argued that the very concepts, models and research tools used in counselling must be relevant to the Indian social milieu, where problems of poverty, overpopulation and the like are often more 'basic' than those generally found in the West. McIlwain (1997: 13), in her work with Aborigines in Australia, notes how 'good relationships are as important as a good research design'. She describes how sensitive information and appropriate question development might only be revealed once rapport has been established. In her case, it took the development of such rapport before she realised that asking 'how many children do you have' was less informative than 'how many children have you looked after?' Even terms such as 'love' can be interpreted in different ways in different communities (Goodwin, Adatia *et al.*, 1997). This means we must do much more than just ensure the careful translation of our questions. We must also require the full involvement of representative cultural members in order to avoid the pitfalls of irrelevant, misleading, or even offensive questioning (Goodwin, 1996).

Interventions in the personal relationships field almost inevitably involve making important value judgements. For Hatfield and Rapson (1996), many of the consequences of Westernisation are positive. They recognise that many of the 'traditional' ways so idealised in the West were less welcomed by those who lived under these systems, and often simply served the interests of a small but powerful elite. Kagitcibasi (1991) also warns against the patronising assumption that people should not seek to change traditional ways. Instead, she sees it is as necessary to find out what people *want*, and to use this to inform interventions. Boudon (1986: 49ff) gives the example of a Western observer astonished to find that families in the majority world still produce many offspring – despite the fact that the resultant population explosion has had collectively disastrous effects and reduced individual standards of living. However, a deeper look into the structure of the situation shows that the production of large families has considerable advantages, ensuring both emotional and economic support for the parents as they grow older. Such advantages are, of course, rarely acknowledged from the superficial perspective of the 'outsider'.

According to Kagitcibasi, once a 'deeper' understanding is obtained of the needs and resources available, the psychologist must then be prepared to accept his/her role as an agent of change, and must set standards for optimal development and change. Thus, in her Turkish Early Enrichment Project, Kagitcibasi (1996) studied children from rural families as they first attended formal schooling. To help parents deal with this change, maternal values and behaviours were addressed in group discussions designed to promote the development of appropriate 'school-relevant' cognitive and socio-emotional skills. This intervention led to a number of changes favourable to the children's development in their new school environment.

This active, moral commitment to understanding and acting on relevant cultural and social issues is an important advance over weak 'cultural relativism' (where 'everything is different so we can offer nothing'), or simple, often dangerous, 'moral absolutism' (Fowers and Richardson, 1996). Fowers and Richardson take a hermeneutic approach, arguing that we should actively consider our own moral values when judging others, and should continually revise these judgements as we confront new situations and cultures. Using the example of forced virginity tests on women in Turkey, Fowers and Richardson claim that we can neither dismiss these as simple examples of 'barbarous practices', nor sanction them by hiding behind cultural relativism. Instead, we must try to comprehend the social and moral motivations for such practices within the practitioners' own framework for actions, and we should defend our own standpoint in contrast to that of the other culture. In many instances, this active 'cultural conversation' can help us to learn from others, and to see our own views afresh. At the very least, such an approach helps us in understanding the evolution of others' behaviours and the cultural values that underpin this development.

Being of use ...

The above remarks bring me to my final considerations. Much of this book has been about *comparative* research, comparing social systems and societies/cultures in the light of Western theories and 'problems'. However, the degree to which these really are the key 'problems' for the study by the cross-cultural psychologist is questionable, and here again we must face important moral questions about the relevance of our work to the populations we are studying. Is an analysis of jealousy in relationships, or cross-cultural variations in personal advertisements, really of much utility to a society recovering from civil war? How relevant is the study of the similarity-attraction hypothesis in a time of mass famine or natural catastrophe? Although there may be, in Lewin's immortal words, 'nothing so practical as a good theory', the crises in personal lives that often follow societal upheavals demand action, and in many areas of personal relationships, interventions are desperately required. Unfortunately, the personal relationships journals offer relatively little advice as to how we can help families using existing social dynamics to cope with large-scale disasters, and even less information on how an understanding of cultural values can be used to aid some of the world's most needy peoples.

This does not mean that we have to abandon any form of relationships research outside the confines of middle-class Western life. It does, however, mean that relationships researchers should use their understanding of relationship interactions, and the range of methods they have at their disposal, to investigate some of the more major issues faced by the modern world – the spread of sexual disease, fertility and overpopulation, rape and violence – beyond the college setting. It also means that we need to move away from the study of middle-class students (on whichever campus in whichever country) to investigate a diversity of peoples and life conditions. This requires the embracing and development of indigenous theories (e.g. Gergen *et al.*, 1996; Heelas and Lock, 1981), the development of new techniques and methods, and the exploration of the way in which different approaches and insights may interact (Gergen *et al.*, 1996). Researchers should then come out from behind the cover of 'neutral theory generation' and use such theories and methods as practical tools to confront major problems in these societies (Gergen *et al.*, 1996).

Needless to say, this work is unlikely to be easy. While researchers in many non-Western countries may see some mainstream issues in personal relationships to be of both interest and relevance to their lives, they simply lack the time and resources for the development of valuable, indigenous theories. In his chapter on politics, ethics and cross-cultural research, Warwick (1980) discusses a range of potential hazards in conducting work across cultures, including the dangers of direct political interference, limitations in access to certain populations, restriction in the topics studied, and problems with the publication and usage of the data collected. During times of social transition, many of these ethical issues may be accentuated, as former sources of information and certainty become challenged. Confusion about the status of 'outsiders' coming to study in a culture means that 'academic entrepreneurs', with little commitment to a research team or institution, can be almost as destructive as the notorious economic entrepreneurs who proffer 'get-rich-quick' schemes and thrive in times of social change. Productive work means building up very special relationships, often with young and less experienced (but less 'institutionalised') colleagues, and being aware of the impact that the researchers themselves are likely to have on their respondents (Goodwin, 1998). Culturally sensitive practitioners, working with experts from the host country, can help guide 'best practice', while all the researchers involved need to be open-minded and actively interested in the political and economic climate of the country, rather than just trying to act as 'detached' scientists (Kukla, 1988). Trompenaars (1993: 177) sums this up neatly:

> We need a certain amount of humility and a sense of humour to discover cultures other than our own: a readiness to enter a room in the dark and stumble over unfamiliar furniture until the pain in our shins reminds us where things are.

Scholars of personal relationships have a lot to learn, but also a lot to offer in the cross-examination of their field. As Kohn (1993) notes, every aspect of cross-cultural work is profoundly affected by our personal experiences, but every modification we make as a result can provide us with important new insights into our subject. While the cross-cultural relationships road is a stony one, it is also replete with human warmth and excitement which makes it to me one of the most intellectually stimulating paths there is to follow.

Bibliography

Abramson, P.R. and Pinkerton, S.D. (1995). 'Nature, Nurture and In-Between', in P.R. Abramson and S.D. Pinkerton (eds), *Sexual nature, sexual culture*. Chicago: The University of Chicago Press.

Abu-Loghod, J. and Amin, L. (1961). 'Egyptian marriage advertisements: microcosm of a changing society', *Marriage and Family Living*, 23: 127–36.

Adams, J. (1965). 'Inequity in social exchange', in L. Berkowitz (ed.), *Advances in experimental social psychology*, vol. 2. New York: Academic Press.

Adams, R. and Blieszner, R. (1994). 'An integrative conceptual framework for friendship research', *Journal of Social and Personal Relationships*, 11: 163–84.

Alechina, I.E., Svejnevsky, P., Volovich, A.S. and Kerig, P.K. (1997). 'Through the Looking Glass: Reflections of Soviet Psychology and the Russian Psyche', *The Psychohistory Review: Studies of Motivation in History and Culture*, 24: 265–92.

Allan, G. (1993). 'Social structure and relationships', in S.W. Duck (ed.), *Social Contexts and Relationships* (pp. 1–25). Newbury Park: Sage.

—— (1998). 'Friendship, sociology and social structure', *Journal of Social and Personal Relationships*, 15: 685–702.

Al-Thakeb, F.T. (1985). 'The Arab family and modernity: Evidence from Kuwait', *Current Anthropology*, 26: 575–80.

Altman, I. and Taylor, D. (1973). *Social penetration: the development of interpersonal relationships*. New York: Holt, Rhinehart and Winston.

Amir, Y. and Sharon, I. (1987). 'Are social-psychological laws cross-culturally valid?', *Journal of Cross-Cultural Psychology*, 18: 383–470.

Amoateng, A.Y. and Heaton, T.B. (1989). 'The sociodemographic correlates of the timing of divorce in China', *Journal of Comparative Family Studies*, 20: 79–96.

Anderson, E. (1992). 'Chinese fisher families: Variations on Chinese themes', *Journal of Comparative Family Studies*, 23: 231–47.

Antill, J. and Cotton, S. (1987). 'Self-disclosure between husbands and wives: Its relationship to sex roles and marital happiness', *Australian Journal of Psychology*, 39: 11–24.

Archer, J. (1996). 'Sex differences in social behavior: Are the social role and evolutionary explanations compatible?', *American Psychologist*, 51: 909–17.

Argyle, M. (1982). 'Inter-cultural communication', in S. Bochner (ed.), *Cultures in Contact: Studies in Cross-cultural interaction*. Oxford: Pergamon.

—— (1987). *The psychology of happiness*. London: Methuen.

—— (1988). *Bodily communication* (2nd edn). New York: Methuen.

Argyle, M. and Henderson, M. (1984). 'The rules of relationships', in S. Duck and D. Perlman (eds), *Understanding Personal Relationships*. Beverly Hills, CA: Sage.

—— (1985). *The Anatomy of Relationships*. Harmondsworth, Middx: Penguin.

Argyle, M., Henderson, M., Bond, M., Iizuka, Y. and Contarello, A. (1986). 'Cross-cultural variations in relationship rules', *International Journal of Psychology*, 21: 287–315.

Ashworth, C., Furnham, G., Chaikin, A. and Derlega, V. (1976). 'Physiological response to self-disclosure', *Journal of Humanistic Psychology*, 16: 71–80.

Bailey, R.C. and Aunger, R.V. (1995). 'Sexuality, Infertility and Sexually Transmitted Disease among Farmers and Foragers in Central Africa', in P.R. Abramson and S.D. Pinkerton (eds), *Sexual nature, sexual culture*. Chicago: The University of Chicago Press.

Bakan, D. (1966). *The duality of human existence*. Chicago: Rand McNally.

Ballard, R. and Kalra, V. (1994). *The Ethnic Dimensions of the 1991 Census: a preliminary report*. Manchester: University of Manchester.

Banister, J. (1987). *China's changing population*. Stanford, CA: Stanford University Press.

Banks, I.W. and Wilson, P.I. (1989). 'Appropriate sex education for black teens', *Adolescence*, 24: 233–45.

Bar-Yosef, R.W. and Padan-Eisenstark, D. (1977). 'Role Systems Under Stress: Sex-Roles in War', *Social Problems*, 25: 135–45.

Bardi, A. and Schwartz, S.H. (1996). 'Relations among Sociopolitical Values in Eastern Europe: Effects of the Communist Experience?', *Political Psychology*, 17: 525–49.

Barnlund, D.C. (1975). *Public and private self in Japan and the United States*. Tokyo: Simul Press.

Barry, H., Child, I.L. and Bacon, M.K. (1959). 'Relation of child training to subsistence economy', *American Anthropologist*, 61: 31–3.

Basic Behavioral Science Research for Mental Health (1996a). 'Family Processes and Social Networks', *American Psychologist*, 51: 622–30.

—— (1996b). 'Sociocultural and environmental processes', *American Psychologist*, 51: 722–31.

Baumgarte, R., Kulich, S.J. and Lee, N. (1998). 'Friendship patterns among college students in four cultures'; paper presented at the 9th International Society for the Study of Personal Relationships, Saratoga Springs, June 1998.

Baumgarte, R., Lee, N.-M., Concilus, F. and Choi, B.M. (1997). 'Friendship patterns among college students in Korea and the U.S.'; paper presented at the International Network of Personal Relationships, University of Miami at Ohio, June 1997.

Beardsley, L.M. and Pedersen, P. (1997). 'Health and Culture-Centered Intervention', in J.W. Berry, M.H. Segall and C. Kagitcibasi (eds), *Handbook of Cross-Cultural Psychology, Volume 3: Social Behavior and Applications*. London: Allyn and Bacon.

Beardwell, I. and Holden, L. (1994). *Human resource management: A contemporary perspective*. London: Pitman.

Beck, U. and Beck-Gernsheim, E. (1995). *The normal chaos of love*. Cambridge: Polity Press.

Befu, H. (1968). 'Gift-Giving in a Modernizing Japan', in T.S. Lebra and W.P. Lebra (1988), *Japanese Culture and Behavior* (pp. 158–70). Honolulu: University of Hawaii Press.

—— (1974). 'An Ethnography of Dinner Entertainment in Japan', in T.S. Lebra and W.P. Lebra (1988), *Japanese Culture and Behavior* (pp. 108–20). Honolulu: University of Hawaii Press.

Behman, D. (1985). 'The Tunis Conference', *Current Anthropology*, 26: 555–6.

Bellah, R.N., Madsen, R., Sullivan, W.M., Swidler, A. and Tipton, S.M. (1985). *Habits of the heart: Individualism and commitment in American life*. Berkeley: University of California Press.

Berger, C.R. and Bradac, J.J. (1982). *Language and social knowledge: Uncertainty in Interpersonal Relations*. London: Edward Arnold.

Berk, R., Abramson. P.R. and Okami, P. (1995). 'Sexual activities as told in surveys', in P.R. Abramson and S.D. Pinkerton (eds), *Sexual nature, sexual culture*. Chicago: The University of Chicago Press.

Berman, J., Murphy-Berman, V. and Pachauri, A. (1988). 'Sex differences in friendship patterns in India and in the US', *Basic and Applied Social Psychology*, 9: 61–71.

Berman, J., Murphy-Berman, V. and Singh, P. (1985). 'Cross-cultural similarities and differences in perceptions of fairness', *Journal of Cross-Cultural Psychology*, 16: 55–67.

Berry, J.W. (1980). 'Social and cultural change', in H.C. Triandis and R.W. Brislin (eds), *Handbook of Social Psychology. Volume 5: Social Psychology*. Boston: Allyn and Bacon.

—— (1990). 'Psychology of Acculturation', in J. Berman (ed.), *Nebraska Symposium on Motivation 1989*. Lincoln: University of Nebraska Press.

—— (1994). 'Acculturation and Psychological Adaptation: An overview', in A.-M. Bouvy, F. van de Vijver, P. Bowski and P. Schmitz (eds), *Journeys into cross-cultural psychology* (pp. 129–41). Lisse: Swets and Zeitlinger.

—— (1997). 'Immigration, Acculturation and Adaptation', *Applied Psychology: An international review*, 56: 5–68.

Berscheid, E. (1994). 'Interpersonal relationships', *Annual Review of Psychology*, 45: 79–129.

Berscheid, E., Dion, E., Walster, E. and Walster, G. (1971). 'Physical attractiveness and dating choice: A test of the matching hypothesis', *Journal of Experimental Social Psychology*, 7: 173–89.

Berscheid, E. and Walster, E. (1978). *Interpersonal attraction* 2nd edn. New York: Random House.

Betancourt, H. and Lopez, S.R. (1993). 'The study of culture, ethnicity and race in American psychology', *American Psychologist*, 48: 629–37.

Betzig, L. (1989). 'Causes of conjugal dissolution: A cross-cultural study', *Current Anthropology*, 30: 654–76.

Bhachu, P. (1985). *Twice Migrants: East African Sikh Settlers in Britain*. London: Tavistock.

Blau, P., Ruan, D. and Ardelt, M. (1991). 'Interpersonal choice and networks in China', *Social Forces*, 69: 1037–62.

Blood, R. (1967). *Love match and arranged marriage*. New York: Free Press.

Bloor, D. and Bloor, C. (1976). 'An anthropological approach to industrial scientists: an empirical test of Mary Douglas' grid and group theory'; paper presented at the Mary Douglas Seminar, University College London, November 1976.

Blumstein, P. and Kollock, P. (1988). 'Personal relationships', *Annual Review of Sociology*, 14: 467–90.

Blumstein, P. and Schwartz, P.W. (1983). *American Couples*. New York: William Morrow.

Bollen, K.A. (1980). 'Issues in the comparative measurement of political democracy', *American Sociological Review*, 45: 370–90.

Bombar, M.L. (1996). 'Putting biological approaches in context', *ISSPR Bulletin*, 12: 3–6.

Bond, M.H. (1988a). 'Finding universal dimensions of individual variation in multicultural studies of values', *Journal of Personality and Social Psychology*, 55: 1009–15.

—— (1988b). 'Invitation to a Wedding: Chinese Values and Global Economic Growth', in D. Sinha and H. Kao (eds), *Social values and development: Asian Perspectives* (pp. 197–209). Sage: New Delhi.

Bond, R. and Smith, P. (1996). 'Culture and conformity: A meta-analysis of studies using Asch's line judgement task', *Psychological Bulletin*, 119: 111–37.

Borque, L. (1989). *Defining Rape*. Durham, NC: Duke University Press.

Boss, P. (1987). 'Family Stress', in M.B. Sussman and S.K. Steinmetz (eds), *Handbook of Marriage and the Family* (pp. 695–723). New York: Plenum Press.

Bosse, K. (1976). 'Social situation of persons with dermatoses as a phenomenon of interpersonal perception', *Zeitschrift für Psychosomatische Medizin und Psychoanalyse*, 22: 3–61.

Boudon, R. (1986). *Theories of social change*. Cambridge: Polity Press.

Box, S. (1983). *Power, Crime and Mystification*. London: Tavistock.

Bradbury, T.N. and Fincham, F.D. (1990). 'Attributions in marriage: Review and critique', *Psychological Bulletin*, 107: 3–33.

Bradley, C. and Weisner, T.S. (1997). 'Introduction: Crisis in the African family', in T.S. Weisner, C. Bradley and P.L. Kilbride (eds), *African families and the crisis of social change* (pp. xix–xxxii). Westport, CT: Bergin and Garvey.

Brehm, S.S. (1992). *Intimate Relationships* 2nd edn. New York: McGraw-Hill.

Bringle, R.G. and Buunk, B. (1986). 'Examining the causes and consequences of jealousy: Some recent findings and issues', in R. Gilmour and S. Duck (eds), *The emerging field of personal relationships* (pp. 225–40). Hillsdale, NJ: Erlbaum.

Brinton, M.C., Hang-Yue Ngo and Shibuya, K. (1991). 'Gendered mobility patterns in industrial economies: The case of Japan', *Social Science Quarterly*, 72: 807.

Brislin, R.W. (1990). *Applied Cross-cultural Psychology*. Newbury Park: Sage.

Brodbar-Nemzer, J.Y. (1986). 'Divorce and group commitment: The case of the Jews', *Journal of Marriage and the Family*, 48: 329–40.

Bronfenbrenner, U. (1970). *Two worlds of childhood: USA and USSR*. New York: Russell Sage.

—— (1988). 'Interacting systems in human development. Research paradigms: present and future', in N. Bolger, A. Caspi, G. Downey and M. Moorehouse (eds), *Persons in context: Development processes* (pp. 25–49). Cambridge: Cambridge University Press.

—— (1993). 'The ecological cognitive development: Research models and fugitive findings', in R. Wozniak and K. Fischer (eds), *Development in context: Acting and thinking in specific environments* (pp. 3–44). Hillsdale, NJ: Erlbaum.

Broude, G.J. (1983). 'Male–female relationships in cross-cultural perspective: A study of sex and intimacy', *Behavior Science Research*, 18: 154–81.

Brown, D.E. (1991). *Human Universals*. Philadelphia, PA: Temple University.

Brown, R.A. (1994). 'Romantic love and the spouse selection criteria of male and female Korean college students', *Journal of Social Psychology*, 134: 183–9.

Buckhart, B. and Fromuth, M. (1991). 'Individual and social psychological under-standings of sexual coercion', in E. Gruerholz and M. Koralewski (eds), *Sexual Coercion: A sourcebook on its Nature, Causes and Prevention*, Lexington, MA: Lexington Books.

Buckley, M. (1989). *Women and ideology in the Soviet Union*. Hertford, CT: Harvester Wheatsheaf.

Burgess, E.W. and Wallin, P. (1953). *Engagement and marriage*. Philadelphia: Lippin-cott.

Burgoyne, S. and Spitzberg, B. (1992). 'An examination of communication strategies and tactics used in potential date rape episodes'; paper presented at the Sixth International Conference on Personal Relationships, Maine, July 1992.

Burnett, R., McGhee, P., Clarke, D.D. *et al.* (1987). *Accounting for Relationships: Explanation, Representation, and Knowledge*. New York: Methuen.

Burton, S. (1990). 'Straight talk on sex in China', *Time*, 14 May 1990, p. 82.

Buss, D.M. (1984). 'Toward a Psychology of Person-Environment (PE) Correlation: The Role of Spouse Selection', *Journal of Personality and Social Psychology*, 47: 361–77.

—— (1987). 'Sex differences in human mate selection criteria: An evolutionary perspective', in C. Crawford., M. Smith and D. Krebs (eds), *Sociobiology and psychology: Ideas, issues and applications*. Hillsdale, NJ: Lawrence Erlbaum.

—— (1988). 'The evolution of human intrasexual competition: Tactics of mate attraction', *Journal of Personality and Social Psychology*, 54: 616–28.

—— (1989). 'Sex differences in human mate preferences: Evolutionary hypotheses tested in 37 cultures', *Behavioral and Brain Sciences*, 12: 1–14.

Buss, D.M. and Barnes, M.L. (1986). 'Preferences in human mate selection', *Journal of Personality and Social Psychology*, 50: 559–70.

Buss, D.M., Abbott, M., Angleitner, A. *et al.* (1990). 'International preferences in selecting mates', *Journal of Cross-Cultural Psychology*, 21: 5–47.

Buunk, B. (1980). 'Extramarital sex in the Netherlands: Motivations in social and marital context', *Alternative Lifestyles*, 3: 11–39.

Buunk, B. and Hupka, R.B. (1986). 'Autonomy in close relationships: A cross-cultural study', *Family Perspective*, 20: 209–21.

—— (1987). 'Cross-cultural differences in the elicitation of sexual jealousy', *The Journal of Sex Research*, 23: 12–22.

Byrne, D. (1971). *The attraction paradigm*. New York: Academic Press.

Byrne, D. and Kelley, K. (1992). 'Differential age preferences: The need to test evolu-tionary versus alternative conceptualizations', *Behavioral and Brain Sciences*, 15: 96.

Cameron, K. (1996). 'Individual and relational barriers to condom use: A cross-cultural study'; paper presented at the 6th ICPR, Banff, Calgary, August 1996.

Camilleri, C. (1967). 'Modernity and the family in Tunisia', *Journal of Marriage and the Family*, 29: 590–5.

Campbell, A. and Muncer, S. (1993). 'Men and the meaning of violence', in J. Archer (ed.), *Male Violence* (pp. 332–51). London: Routledge.

Carver, C.S., Scheier, M.F. and Weintraub, J.K. (1989). 'Assessing coping strategies: A theoretically based account', *Journal of Personality and Social Psychology*, 56: 267–83.

Cassidy, M.L. and Lee, G.R. (1989). 'The study of Polyandry: A critique and synthesis', *Journal of Comparative Family Studies*, 20: 1–11.

Cattell, M.G. (1997). 'The discourse of neglect: Family support for the elderly in Samia', in T.S. Weisner, C. Bradley and P.L. Kilbride (eds), *African families and the crisis of social change* (pp. 157–83). Westport, CT: Bergin and Garvey.

Cha, J-H (1994). 'Aspects of individualism and collectivism in Korea', in U. Kim, H.C. Triandis, C. Kagitcibasi, S.-C. Choi, and G. Yoon, *Individualism and collectivism: Theory, method and applications* (pp. 157–74). Thousand Oaks, CA: Sage.

Chang, H.C. and Holt, G.R. (1991). 'The concept of yuan and Chinese interpersonal relationships', in S. Ting-Toomey and F. Korzenny (eds), *Cross-cultural interpersonal communication* (pp. 28–57). Newbury Park: Sage.

Chang, W. (1976). 'Interpersonal attraction as a function of opinion similarity and opinion presentation sequence', *Bulletin of Educational Psychology*, 9: 73–84.

Chauvin, R. (1980). 'Sur le neo-darwinisme dans les sciences du comportement', *Annee biologique*, 19: 203–16.

Chen, N.Y., Shaffer, D.R. and Wu, C. (1997). 'On physical attractiveness stereotyping in Taiwan: A revised sociocultural perspective', *Journal of Social Psychology*, 137: 117–24.

Cheng, C.H., Bond, M.H. and Chan, S.C. (forthcoming). 'The perception of ideal best friends: Chinese adolescents', *International Journal of Psychology*.

Cheung, F. (1984). 'Preferences in help-seeking among Chinese students', *Culture, Medicine and Psychiatry*, 8: 371–80.

Chia, R., Chong, C. and Cheng, B. (1986). 'Attitude toward marriage roles among Chinese and American college students', *Journal of Social Psychology*, 126: 31–5.

Chiasson, N., Charbonneau, C. and Proulx, J. (1996). 'In-group-out-group similar information as a determinant of attraction toward members of minority groups', *The Journal of Social Psychology*, 136: 233–41.

Chinese Culture Connection (1987). 'Chinese values and the search for culture-free dimensions of culture', *Journal of Cross-Cultural Psychology*, 18: 143–64.

Christakopoulou, S. (1995). *Koinonikoi desmoi ston psyhologiko horo kai xrono tis koinotitas: Mia diapolitisiki meleti* (Social bonds in the psychological space and time of the community: A cross-cultural study); doctoral dissertation, University of Athens.

Christensen, H.T. (1973). 'Attitudes toward marital infidelity: A nine-cultural sampling of university student opinion', *Journal of Comparative Family Studies*, 4: 197–214.

Chu, G.C. (1985). 'The emergence of a new Chinese culture', in W. Tseng and D. Wu (eds), *Chinese culture and mental health*. New York: Academic Press.

Chu, G.C. and Ju, Y. (1993). *The great wall in ruins*. New York: State University of New York Press.

Coch, L. and French, J.R.P. (1948). 'Overcoming resistance to change', *Human Relations*, 1: 512–32.

Cohen, S. and Wills, T. (1985). 'Stress, social support and the buffering hypothesis', *Psychological Bulletin*, 98: 310–57.

Cole, M. (1990). 'Cultural Psychology: A once and future discipline?', in J. Berman (ed.), *Nebraska Symposium on Motivation, 1989*, (pp. 279–335). Lincoln: University of Nebraska Press.

Condon, J. (1984). *With respect to the Japanese*. Yarmouth, ME: Intercultural Press.

Condorcet, M.J. (1966). *Esquisse d'un tableau historique des progres de l'espirit humain*. Paris: Editions Sociales.

Cooper, M.H. (1992). 'Women and AIDS', *Congressional Quarterly Researcher*, 2: 1123–39.

Corwin, L.A. (1977). 'Caste, class and the love-marriage: Social change in India', *Journal of Marriage and the Family*, 39: 823–31.

Cowan, P.A., Field, D., Hansen, D., Skolnick, A. and Swanson, G. (eds) (1993). *Family, self and society: Toward a new agenda for family research*. Hillsdale, NJ: Erlbaum.

Cramer, D., Henderson, S. and Scott, R. (1996). 'Mental health and adequacy of social support: A four-wave panel study', *British Journal of Social Psychology*, 35: 285–95.

Cross, M. (1979). *Urbanization and urban growth in the Caribbean*. Cambridge: Cambridge University Press.

Cunningham, M.R. (1986). 'Measuring the physical in physical attractiveness: Quasi-experiments on the sociobiology of female facial beauty', *Journal of Personality and Social Psychology*, 50: 925–35.

Cunningham, M.R., Barbee, A.P. and Pike, G.L. (1990). 'What do women want? Facialmetric assessment of multiple motives in the perception of male facial physical attractiveness', *Journal of Personality and Social Psychology*, 59: 61–72.

Cunningham, M.R., Roberts, A.R., Barbee, A.P., Druen, P.B. and Wu, C.-H. (1995). ' "Their ideas of beauty are, on the whole, the same as ours": Consistency and Variability in the Cross-Cultural Perception of Female Physical Attractiveness', *Journal of Personality and Social Psychology*, 68: 271–9.

Daibo, I., Murasawa, H. and Chou, Y.-J. (1994). 'Attractive faces and affection of beauty – A comparison in preferences of feminine facial beauty in Japan and Korea', *The Japanese Journal on Emotions*, 1: 101–23.

Danziger, R. (1996). 'Compulsory testing for HIV in Hungary', *Social Science and Medicine*, 43: 1199–204.

Davenport, W.H. (1977). 'Sex in cross-cultural perspective', in F.A. Beach (ed.), *Human sexuality in four perspectives* (pp. 115–63). Baltimore: Johns Hopkins University Press.

—— (1987). 'An anthropological approach', in J.H. Geer and W.T. O'Donohue (eds), *Theories of human sexuality* (pp. 197–236). New York: Plenum Press.

Davis, J.A. and Smith, T.W. (1991). *General social surveys, 1972–1991*. Chicago: National Opinion Research Center, University of Chicago.

De Jong Gierveld, J. (1992). 'Living alone and single? Types of partner relationships among non-married older adults'; paper presented at the 6th ICPR, Maine, July 1992.

Denmark, F.L., Schwartz, L. and Smith, K.M. (1991). 'Women in the United States and Canada', in I.L. Adler (ed.), *Women in cross-cultural perspective* (pp. 1–18). New York: Praeger.

Derlega, V., Abdo, D., Winstead, B. and Swinth, H. (1990). 'Effects of topic of conversation and similarity of experience of coping with stress', unpublished manuscript, Old Dominion University USA.

Derlega, V.J., Metts, S., Petronio, S. and Margulis, S. (1993). *Self-disclosure*. Newbury Park: Sage.

De Vos, G. (1960). 'The Relation of Guilt toward Parents to Achievement and Arranged Marriage among the Japanese', in T.S. Lebra and W.P. Lebra (1988), *Japanese Culture and Behavior* (pp. 80–101). Honolulu: University of Hawaii Press.

Diaz-Guerrero, R. (1991). 'Historic-sociocultural premises (HSCPs) and global change', *International Journal of Psychology*, 26: 665–73.

Diener, E., Wolsic, B. and Fujita. F. (1995). 'Physical attractiveness and subjective well-being', *Journal of Personality and Social Psychology*, 69: 120–9.

Dion, K.K. (1986). 'Stereotyping on physical attractiveness: Issues and conceptual perspectives', in C.P. Herman, M.P. Zanna and E.T. Higgins (eds), *Appearance, stigma and social behavior: The Ontario Symposium on Personality and Social Psychology* (vol. 3, pp. 7–21). Hillsdale, NJ: Lawrence Erlbaum.

Dion, K.K. and Dion, K.L. (1991). 'Psychological individualism and romantic love', *Journal of Social Behaviour and Personality*, 6: 17–33.

—— (1993). 'Individualistic and collectivistic perspectives on gender and the cultural context of love and intimacy', *Journal of Social Issues*, 49: 53–69.

Dion, K.K., Berscheid, E. and Walster, E. (1972). 'What is beautiful is good', *Journal of Personality and Social Psychology* 24: 285–90.

Dion, K.K., Pak, A.W.-P. and Dion, K.L. (1990). 'Stereotyping physical attractiveness: A sociocultural perspective', *Journal of Cross-cultural Psychology*, 21: 158–79.

Dion, K.L. and Dion, K.K. (1988). 'Romantic love: Individual and cultural perspectives', in R. Sternberg and M. Barnes (eds), *The psychology of love* (pp. 264–92). New Haven: Yale University Press.

—— (1993). 'Gender and ethnocultural comparisons in styles of love', *Psychology of Women Quarterly*, 17: 463–73.

Doherty, R.W., Hatfield, E., Thompson, K. and Choo, P. (1994) 'Cultural and ethnic influences on love and attachment', *Personal Relationships*, 1: 391–8.

Doi, L.T. (1962). '*Amae*: A Key Concept for Understanding Japanese Personality Structure', in T.S. Lebra and W.P. Lebra (1988), *Japanese Culture and Behavior* (pp. 121–9). Honolulu: University of Hawaii Press.

Doi, T. (1986). *The anatomy of conformity: The individual versus society*. Tokyo: Kodansha.

Doise, W. (1987). *Levels of explanation in social psychology*. Cambridge: Cambridge University Press.

Doise, W., Clemence, A. and Lorenzi-Cioldi, F. (1993). *The Quantitative Analysis of Social Representations*. Hemel Hempstead: Harvester Wheatsheaf.

Doise, W., Clemence, A. and Spini, D. (1995). 'Human Rights and Social Psychology', *BPS Social Psychology Section Newsletter*, 35: 3–21.

Douglas, M. (1970). *Natural symbols*. London: Barrie and Rockliffe.

—— (1982). 'Introduction to grid/group analysis', in M. Douglas (ed.), *Essays in the Sociology of Perception* (pp. 1–8). London: Routledge and Kegan Paul.

Drigotas, S.M. and Rusbult, C.E. (1992). 'Should I stay or should I go? A dependence model of breakups', *Journal of Personality and Social Psychology*, 62: 62–87.

Driscoll, R., Davis, K.W. and Lipetz, M.E. (1972). 'Parental interference and romantic love', *Journal of Personality and Social Psychology*, 24: 1–10.

Duck, S.W. (1982). 'A topography of relationship disengagement and dissolution', in S. W. Duck (ed.), *Personal Relationships 4: Dissolving Personal Relationships*. London: Academic Press.

—— (1986). *Human Relationships: An introduction to social psychology*. London: Sage.

—— (ed.) (1997). *Handbook of personal relationships: Theory, research and interventions* 2nd edn. Chichester: John Wiley.

Duck, S.W., Hay, D.F., Hobfoll, S.E., Ickes, W. and Montgomery, B. (eds) (1988). *Handbook of Personal Relationships: Theory, research and interventions*. New York and Chichester: John Wiley.

Duck, S.W., West, L. and Acitelli, L.K. (1997). 'Sewing the field: the tapestry of relationships in life and research', in S.W. Duck (ed.), *Handbook of personal relationships: Theory, research and interventions* (2nd edn., pp. 1–23). Chichester: John Wiley.

Dunkel-Schetter, C., Sagrestano, L.M., Feldman, P. and Killingsworth, C. (1996). 'Social support and pregnancy: A comprehensive review focusing on ethnicity and culture', in G.R. Pierce, B.R. Sarason and I.G. Sarason (eds), *Handbook of Social Support and the Family* (pp. 375–412). New York: Plenum Press.

Dunkerley, K.J. (1997). 'Similarities and differences in the British and American styles of communicating within United Kingdom Cross-Cultural Companies'; MSc thesis, Department of Psychology, University of Bristol, UK.

Durkheim, E. (1898). 'Representation individuelles et representations collectives', *Revue de Metaphysique et de Morale*, 6: 273–302.

—— (1933). *The division of labor in society* (trans. G. Simpson). New York: Free Press.

Dyson, T. and Moore, M. (1983). 'Kinship structure, female autonomy and demographic behavior in India', *Population and Development Review*, 9: 35–60.

Eagly, A.H., Ashmore, R.D., Makhijani, M.G. and Longo, L.C. (1991). 'What is beautiful is good, but … : A meta-analytic review of research on the physical attractiveness stereotype', *Psychological Bulletin*, 110: 109–28.

Earley, P.C. (1993). 'East meets West meets Mideast: Further explorations of collectivistic and individualistic work groups', *Academy of Management Journal*, 36: 319–48.

Ebbinghaus, H. (1908). *Abriss der Psychologie*. Leipzig: Veit.

Ekman, P. and Friesen, W.V. (1971). 'Constants across cultures in the face and emotion', *Journal of Personality and Social Psychology*, 17: 124–9.

Ellis, G.J. and Petersen, L.R. (1992). 'Socialization values and parental control techniques: a cross-cultural analysis of child rearing', *Journal of Comparative Family Studies*, 23: 39–54.

Entwisle, B., Casterline, J.B. and Sayed, H.A.A. (1989). 'Villages as contexts for contraceptive behavior in rural Egypt', *American Sociological Review*, 54: 1019–34.

Epstein, S. (1962). *Economic development and social change in south India*. Manchester: Manchester University Press.

Erez, M. (1994). 'Work Motivation from a Cross-Cultural Perspective', in A-M Bouvy., F. van de Vijver, P. Bowski and P. Schmitz (eds), *Journeys into cross-cultural Psychology* (pp. 386–403). Lisse: Swets and Zeitlinger.

Eriksen, T.H. (1995). *Small Places, Large Issues*. London: Pluto Press.

Eurostat (1998). *Education in the EU*: Eurostat Report 9/98. Luxembourg: European Union.

Family Planning Association of Hong Kong (1987). *Adolescent sexuality study 1986*. Hong Kong: Family Planning Association.

Feingold, A. (1990). 'Gender differences in effects of physical attractiveness on romantic attraction: A comparison across five research paradigms', *Journal of Personality and Social Psychology*, 59: 981–93.

—— (1992a). 'Gender differences in mate selection preferences: A test of the parental investment model', *Psychological Bulletin*, 112: 125–39.

—— (1992b). 'Good-looking people are not what we think', *Psychological Bulletin*, 111: 304–41.

Feldman, S.S. and Rosenthal, D.A. (1990). 'The acculturation of autonomy expectations in Chinese high schoolers residing in two Western nations', *International Journal of Psychology*, 25: 259–81.

—— (1991). 'Age expectations of behavioural autonomy in Hong Kong, Australia and American youth. The influence of family variables and adolescent's values', *International Journal of Psychology*, 26: 1–23.

Fernandez, D.R., Carlson, D.S., Stepina, L.P. and Nicholson, J.D. (1997). 'Hofstede's Country Classification 25 Years Later', *Journal of Social Psychology*, 137: 43–61.

Ferri, E. and Smith, K. (1996). *Parenting in the 1990s*, report for the Joseph Rowntree Foundation, York, England.

Fijneman, Y., Willemsen, M.E., Poortinga, Y.H. *et al.* (1996). 'Individualism–Collectivism: An empirical study of a conceptual issue', *Journal of Cross-Cultural Psychology*, 27: 381–402.

Fine, M. (1994). 'An examination and evaluation of recent changes in Divorce Laws in Five Western Countries: The critical role of values', *Journal of Marriage and the Family*, 56: 249–63.

Fiske, A.P. (1991). *Structures of social life: The four elementary forms of human relations*. New York: Free Press.

—— (1992). 'The four elementary forms of sociality: Framework for a unified theory of social relations', *Psychological Review*, 99: 689–723.

Fitzpatrick, M.A. and Badzinski, D. (1985). 'All in the family', in G.R. Miller and M.L. Knapp (eds), *Handbook of interpersonal communication*. Beverly Hills, CA: Sage.

Fletcher, G. and Ward, C. (1988). 'Attribution theory and processes: A cross-cultural perspective', in M. Bond (ed.), *The Cross-Cultural Challenge to Social Psychology* (pp. 230–44). Newbury Park: Sage.

Flowers, P., Smith, J.A., Sheeran, P. and Beail, N. (1996). 'Health and romance: understanding unprotected sex in relationships between men'. MRC Medical Sociology Unit, Glasgow.

Foa, U.G. and Foa, E.B. (1974). *Societal Structures of the Mind*. Springfield: Charles Thomas.

Foa, U.G., Anderson, B., Converse, J. Jr., Urbansky, W.A., Cawley, M.J. III., Muhlausen, S.M. and Tornblom, K.Y. (1987). 'Gender-related sexual attitudes: Some cross-cultural similarities and differences', *Sex Roles*, 16: 511–19.

Fowers, B.J. and Richardson, F.C. (1996). 'Why is multiculturalism good?', *American Psychologist*, 51: 609–21.

Fox, G.L. (1975). 'Love match and arranged marriage in a modernizing nation: Mate selection in Ankara, Turkey', *Journal of Marriage and the Family*, 37: 180–93.

Frayser, S.G. (1985). *Varieties of sexual experience: An anthropological perspective on human sexuality*. New Haven, CT: HRAF Press.

Freeberg, A.L. and Stein, C.H. (1996). 'Felt obligation towards parents in Mexican-American and Anglo-American young adults', *Journal of Social and Personal Relationships*, 13: 457–71.

Freud, S. (1910). 'On sexuality: the psychology of love (I). A special type of object choice', *Pelican Freud Library*, vol. 7. Harmondsworth: Penguin.

—— (1912). 'On sexuality: the psychology of love (II). On the universal tendency to debasement in the sphere of love', *Pelican Freud Library*, vol. 7. Harmondsworth: Penguin.

—— (1914). 'On narcissism', *Pelican Freud Library*, vol. 7. Harmondsworth: Penguin.

Fromm, E. (1956). *The Art of Loving*. New York: Harper and Row.

Fukuyama, F. (1993). *The End of History and the Last Man*. Harmondsworth: Penguin.

Fuszara, M. (1997). 'Divorce in Poland: The effects in the opinion of the divorced', in J. Kurczewski and M. Maclean (eds), *Family law and family policy in the New Europe* (pp. 157–88). Dartmouth: Aldershot.

Gaines, S.O. (1997). 'Romanticism and Interpersonal Resource Exchange in Stigmatized Personal Relationships', *ISSPR Bulletin*, 14 (1): 4–6.

Gangestad, S.W., Thornhill, R. and Yeo, R.A. (1994). 'Facial attractiveness, developmental stability and fluctuating asymmetry', *Ethnology and Sociobiology*, 15: 73–85.

Gao, G. (1991). 'Stability of romantic relationships in China and the United States', in S. Ting-Toomey and F. Korkenny (eds), *Cross-Cultural interpersonal communication* (vol. 15, pp. 99–115). London: Sage.

Geertz, C. (1973). *The Interpretation of Cultures*. New York: Basic Books.

Georgas, J. (1997). 'Ecological approaches in cross-cultural psychology'; paper presented at the 5th European Congress of Psychology, Dublin, July 1997.

Georgas, J., Christakopoulou, S., Poortinga, Y.H., Angleitner, A., Goodwin, R. and Charalambous, N. (1997). 'The relationship of family bonds to family structure and function across cultures', *Journal of Cross-Cultural Psychology*, 28: 303–20.

Gergen, K.J., Gulerce, A., Lock, A. and Misra, G. (1996). 'Psychological Sciences in Cultural Context', *American Psychologist*, 51: 496–501.

Gil, A.G. and Vega, W.A. (1996). 'Two different worlds: Acculturation stress and adaptation among Cuban and Nicaraguan families', *Journal of Social and Personal Relationships*, 13: 435–56.

Gilberg, T. (1990). *Nationalism and communism in Romania*. Oxford: Westview Press.

Glass, S.P. and Wright, T.L. (1992). 'Justifications for Extramarital Relationships: The Association between Attitudes, Behaviors and Gender', *Journal of Sex Research*, 29: 361–87.

Glenn, N.D. (1989). 'Intersocial variation in the mate preferences of males and females', *Behavioral and Brain Sciences*, 12: 21–3.

Goffman, E. (1959). *Behavior in public places*. Harmondsworth: Penguin.

—— (1963). *Stigma: Notes on the management of spoiled identity*. Englewood Cliffs, NJ: Prentice Hall.

Goldstein, M.C., Schuler, S. and Ross, J.L. (1983). 'Social and economic forces affecting inter-generational relations in extended families in a third world country: A cautionary tale from South East Asia', *Journal of Gerontology*, 38: 716–24.

Goode, W.J. (1959). 'The theoretical importance of love', *American Sociological Review*, 24: 38–47.

—— (1963). *World revolution and family patterns*. New York: Free Press.

—— (1993). *World changes in divorce patterns*. New Haven, CT: Yale University Press.

Goodwin, R. (1989). 'Striking the perfect match: preferences for a partner as predictors of relationship initiation and quality'; unpublished doctoral thesis, University of Kent, UK.

—— (1990). 'Sex differences amongst partner preferences: Are the sexes really very similar?', *Sex Roles*, 23: 501–13.

—— (1995). 'The privatisation of the personal? I: Intimate disclosure in modern-day Russia', *Journal of Social and Personal Relationships*, 12: 21–31.

—— (1996). 'A brief guide to cross-cultural research', in J. Howath (ed.), *Psychological Research* (pp. 78–94). London: Routledge.

—— (1998). 'Personal relationships and social change: The "realpolitik" of cross-cultural research in transient cultures', *Journal of Social and Personal Relationships*, 15: 227–47.

Goodwin, R. and Emelyanova, T. (1995a). 'The privatisation of the personal? II: Attitudes to the family and child-rearing values in modern-day Russia', *Journal of Social and Personal Relationships*, 12: 32–9.

—— (1995b). 'The Perestroika of the Family? Gender and Occupational Differences in Family Values in Modern Day Russia', *Sex Roles*, 32: 337–51.

Goodwin, R., Adatia, K., Sinhal, H., Cramer, D. and Ellis, P. (1997). *Social support and marital well-being in an Asian community*. York: Joseph Rowntree Foundation.

Goodwin, R., Emelyanova, T. and Shunaeva, Y. (1995). 'Parents and friends as sources of support in modern Russia'; paper presented at the Social Section of the BPS, York, September 1995.

Goodwin, R. and Findlay, C. (1997). 'We were just fated together. Chinese love and the concept of *yuan* in Hong Kong and England', *Personal Relationships*, 4, 85–92.

Goodwin, R. and Lee, I. (1994). 'Taboo topics among Chinese and English friends', *Journal of Cross-Cultural Psychology*, 25: 325–8.

Goodwin, R., Nizharadze, G., Dedkova, N. and Emelyanova, T. (1999). '*Glasnost* and the art of conversation: a multi-level analysis of disclosure across three cultures', *Journal of Cross-Cultural Psychology*, 30, 72–90.

Goodwin, R., Nizharadze, G., Kosa, E., Nguyen Luu, L.A. and Emelyanova, T. (1997). *Trust and social support in a changing Europe*, final report, Soros Foundation, Prague.

Goodwin, R and Pang, A. (1994). 'Self-monitoring and relationship adjustment: A cross-cultural analysis', *Journal of Social Psychology*, 134: 35–9.

Goodwin, R and Tang, C. (1996). 'Chinese Personal Relationships', in M. Bond (ed.), *The Handbook of Chinese Psychology* (pp. 280–94). Hong Kong: Oxford University Press.

—— (1998). 'The transition to uncertainty? The impacts of Hong Kong 1997 on Personal Relationships', *Personal Relationships*, 5: 183–90.

Goodwin, R. and Tang, D. (1991). 'Preferences for friends and close relationship partners: Cross-cultural comparisons', *Journal of Social Psychology*, 131: 579–81.

Gordon, S. and Donat, P. (1992). 'Social exchange and influence strategies in dyadic communication: Applications to research on acquaintance rape'; paper presented at the 6th ICPR, Maine, July 1992.

Gouldner, A.W. (1960). 'The norm of reciprocity: a preliminary statement', *American Sociological Review*, 25: 161–78.

—— (1971). *The Coming Crisis of Western Sociology*. London: Heinemann.

Graham, J.A. and Argyle, M. (1975). 'A cross-cultural study of the communication of extra-verbal meaning by gestures', *International Journal of Psychology*, 10: 56–67.

Graziano, W.G., Jensen-Campbell, L.A., Shebilske, L.J. and Lundgren, S.R. (1993). 'Social influence, sex differences and judgements of beauty: Putting the *interpersonal* back in interpersonal attraction', *Journal of Personality and Social Psychology*, 65: 522–31.

Greeley, A., Michael, R. and Smith, Y. (1990). 'Americans and their sexual partners', *Society*, July, 36–42.

Greenberg, D.F. (1995). 'The pleasures of homosexuality', in P.R. Abramson and S.D. Pinkerton (eds), *Sexual nature, sexual culture*. Chicago: The University of Chicago Press.

Greenhalgh, S. and Li, J. (1995). 'Engendering reproductive policy and practice in peasant China: For a feminist demography of reproduction', *Signs*, 20: 601–40.

Gudykunst, W.B. (1994). *Bridging Differences: Effective Intergroup Communication* 2nd edn. Thousand Oaks, CA: Sage.

Gudykunst, W., Gao, G., Schmidt, K., Nishida, T. *et al.* (1992). 'The influence of individualism-collectivism, self-monitoring and predicted-outcome value on communication in ingroup and outgroup relationships', *Journal of Cross-Cultural Psychology*, 23: 196–213.

Gudykunst, W. and Matsumoto, Y. (1996). 'Cross-cultural variability of communication in personal relationships', in W.B. Gudykunst., S. Ting-Toomey and T. Nishida (eds), *Communication in Personal Relationships Across Cultures* (pp. 19–56). Thousand Oaks, CA: Sage.

Gudykunst, W.B. and Nishida, T. (1986). 'The influence of cultural variability on perceptions of communication behavior associated with relationship terms', *Human Communication Research*, 13: 147–66.

Gudykunst, W.B., Nishida, T. and Schmidt, K.L. (1989). 'The influence of cultural variability and uncertainty reduction in ingroup vs. outgroup and same vs. opposite sex relationships', *Western Journal of Speech Communication*, 53: 13–29.

Gudykunst, W. and Ting-Toomey, S. (1988). *Culture and interpersonal communication*. Newbury Park: Sage.

Gudykunst, W., Ting-Toomey, S. and Nishida, T. (1996). *Communication in Personal Relationships Across Cultures*. Thousand Oaks, CA: Sage.

Gudykunst, W., Yang, S. and Nishida, T. (1987). 'Cultural differences in self-consciousness and self-monitoring', *Human Communication Research*, 14: 7–34.

Gupta, G.R. (1976). 'Love, arranged marriage and the Indian Social Structure', *Journal of Comparative Family Studies*, 7: 75–85.

Gupta, U. and Singh, P. (1982). 'An exploratory study of love and liking and type of marriage', *Indian Journal of Applied Psychology*, 19: 92–7.

Haebich, K. (1997). 'Characteristics of men who aggress sexually and of men who imagine aggressing: A cross-cultural comparison'; paper presented at the 5th European Congress of Psychology, Dublin, July 1997.

Hall, E.T. (1976). *Beyond culture*. New York: Doubleday.

Han, G. and Choe, S-M. (1994). 'Effects of family, region and school network ties on interpersonal intentions and the analysis of network activities in Korea', in U. Kim, H.C. Triandis, C. Kagitcibasi, S.-C. Choi and G. Yoon, *Individualism and collectivism: Theory, method and applications* (pp. 213–24). Thousand Oaks, CA: Sage.

Hanassab, S. and Tidwell, R. (1989). 'Cross-cultural perspective on dating relationships of young Iranian women: A pilot study', *Counselling Psychology Quarterly*, 2: 113–21.

Hardin, E.E., Ridley, C.A., Feldman, C.M. and Cleveland, H.H. (1996). 'Assessing extreme romantic love beliefs among abusive men in Korea'; paper presented at the 8th ICPR, Banff, August 1996.

Harkins, S.G. and Petty, R.E. (1983). 'Social context effects in persuasion', in P. Paulus (ed.), *Basic group processes* (pp. 149–75). New York: Springer-Verlag.

Harrell, S. (1992). 'Aspects of marriage in three south-western villages', *The China Quarterly*, 130: 323–7.

Hart, I. and Poole, G.D. (1995). 'Individualism and collectivism as considerations in cross-cultural health research', *Journal of Social Psychology*, 135: 97–9.

Hatano, Y. (1990). 'Changes in the sexual activities of the Japanese youth'; paper presented at the International Conference on Sexuality in Asia, Hong Kong, May 1990.

—— (1991). 'Changes in sexual activities of Japanese youth', *Journal of Sex Education and Therapy*, 17: 1–14.

Hatfield, E. and Rapson, R.L. (1987). 'Passionate love: New directions in research', in W.H. Jones and D. Perlman (eds), *Advances in Personal Relationships* (vol. 1). Greenwich, CT: JAI Press.

—— (1996). *Love and Sex: Cross-Cultural Perspectives*. Boston: Allyn and Bacon.

Hatfield, E. and Sprecher, S. (1995). 'Men's and women's mate preferences in the United States, Russia and Japan', *Journal of Cross-cultural Psychology*, 26: 728–50.

Heath, D.T. (1995). 'Parents' Socialization of Children', in B.B. Ingoldsby and S. Smith (eds), *Families in Multicultural Perspective* (pp. 161–86). New York: The Guildford Press.

Heelas, P. and Lock, A. (1981). *Indigenous Psychologies: The Anthropology of the Self*. London: Academic Press.

Hendrick, C. and Hendrick, S. (1986). 'A theory and method of love', *Journal of Personality and Social Psychology*, 50: 392–402.

Herzlich, C. (1973). *Health and illness: A social psychological analysis*. London: Academic Press.

Hildenbrand, B. (1989). 'Tradition and modernity in the family farm: A case study', in K. Boh, G. Sgritta and M.B. Sussman (eds), *Cross-cultural perspectives on families, work and change*. New York: Haworth Press.

Hill, C.T. and Hicks, J. (1998). 'Attitudes about gender roles and marriage at four colleges in Japan'; paper presented at the 14th Congress of the International Association of Cross-Cultural Psychologists, Western Washington University, USA, August 1998.

Hill, C.T., Rubin, Z. and Peplau, O. (1976). 'Breakups before marriage: the end of 103 affairs', *Journal of Social Issues*, 32: 147–68.

Hillhouse, R.J. (1993). 'The individual revolution: The social basis for transition to democracy'; doctoral dissertation, Department of Political Sciences, University of Michigan.

Hinde, R.A. (1997). *Relationships: A dialectical perspective*. London: Psychology Press.

Ho, D. (1987). 'Fatherhood in Chinese culture', in M. Lamb (ed.), *The father's role: Cross-cultural perspectives* (pp. 227–45). Hillsdale, NJ: Erlbaum.

—— (1989). 'Continuity and variation in Chinese patterns of socialization', *Journal of Marriage and the Family*, 51: 149–63.

Ho, D. and Chiu, C.-Y. (1994). 'Component ideas of individualism, collectivism and social organization: An application in the study of Chinese culture', in U. Kim, H.C. Triandis, C. Kagitcibasi, S.-C. Choi and G. Yoon, *Individualism and collectivism: Theory, method and applications* (pp. 137–56). Thousand Oaks, CA: Sage.

Hobart, C.W. (1958). 'The incidence of romanticism during courtship', *Social Forces*, 36: 364–7.

Hobfoll, S.E. (1988). *The ecology of stress*. Washington, DC: Hemisphere.

Hobfoll, S., Freedy, J., Lane, C. and Geller, P. (1990). 'Conservation of social resources: Social support resource theory', *Journal of Social and Personal Relationships*, 7: 465–78.

Hobfoll, S. and London, P. (1985). 'The relationship of self-concept and social support to emotional distress among women during war', *Journal of Social and Clinical Psychology*, 3: 231–48.

Hobfoll, S. and Stokes, J. (1988). 'The process and mechanisms of social support', in S. Duck (ed.), *Handbook of personal relationships: Theory, research and interventions* (pp. 497–517). New York: Wiley.

Hoem, B. and Hoem, J.M. (1988). 'The Swedish family: Aspects of contemporary developments', *Journal of Family Issues*, 9: 397–424.

Hofstede, G. (1980). *Culture's consequences: International differences in work-related values*. Beverly Hills, CA: Sage.

—— (1983). 'Dimensions of national cultures in fifty cultures and three regions', in J.B. Deregowski., S. Dziurawiec. and R.C. Annis (eds), *Expiscations in cross-cultural psychology* (pp. 335–55). Lisse: Swets and Zweitlinger.

—— (1994a). 'Foreword', in U. Kim, H.C. Triandis, C. Kagitcibasi, S.-C. Choi and G. Yoon, *Individualism and collectivism: Theory, method and applications*. Thousand Oaks, CA: Sage.

—— (1994b). *Cultures and Organizations: Software of the Mind*. London: Harper-Collins.

—— (1996). 'Gender stereotypes and partner preferences of Asian women in masculine and feminine cultures', *Journal of Cross-Cultural Psychology*, 27: 533–46.

Homans, G. (1961). *Social Behavior: Its elementary form*. New York: Harcourt.

—— (1967). 'Basic social structures', in N. Smelsma (ed)., *Sociology*. New York: Wiley.

Hong, S.-M. (1986). 'Relationship between romantic love and length of time in love among Korean young adults', *Psychological Reports*, 59: 494.

Honig, E. and Hershatter G. (1988). *Personal voices: Chinese women in the 1980s*. Stanford, CA: Stanford University Press.

Horenczyk, G. and Bekerman, Z. (1993). 'Calibrating identities in the fast track of immigration: Acculturation attitudes and perceived acculturation ideologies'; paper presented at the conference on Changing European Identities: Social Psychological Analyses of Social Change, Farnham Castle, Surrey, May 1993.

Hortascu, N. and Karanci, A.N. (1987). 'Premarital breakups in a Turkish sample: Perceived reasons, attributional dimensions and affective reactions', *International Journal of Psychology*, 22: 57–74.

House, J. (1981). *Work stress and social support*. Reading, MA: Addison-Wesley.

Howard, J., Blumstein, P. and Schwartz, P. (1987). 'Social or evolutionary theories? Some observations on preferences in human mate selection', *Journal of Personality and Social Psychology*, 53: 194–200.

Hsu, F.L. (1981). *Americans and Chinese: Passage to differences* 3rd edn. Honolulu: University of Hawaii Press.

—— (1983). *Rugged Individualism Reconsidered*. Knoxville: University of Tennessee Press.

—— (1985). 'The self in cross-cultural perspective', in A. Marsella, G. DeVos and F. Hsu (eds), *Culture and self: Asian and Western perspectives* (pp. 24–55). London: Tavistock.

Hsu, J. (1985). 'The Chinese family: Relations, problems and therapy', in W. Tseng and D. Wu (eds), *Chinese culture and mental health* (pp. 95–112). New York: Academic Press.

Hui, C.H. and Triandis, H.C. (1986). 'Individualism–collectivism: A study of cross-cultural researchers', *Journal of Cross-Cultural Psychology*, 17: 225–48.

—— (1989). 'Effects of culture and response format on extreme response style', *Journal of Cross-Cultural Psychology*, 20: 296–309.

Hui, C. and Villareal, M. (1989). 'Individualism–collectivism and psychological needs: their relationship in two cultures', *Journal of Cross-Cultural Psychology*, 20, 310–23.

Hupka, R.B., Buunk, B., Falus, G., Fulgosi, A., Ortega, E., Swain, R. and Tarabrina, N.V. (1985). 'Romantic jealousy and romantic envy: A seven-nation study', *Journal of Cross-Cultural Psychology*, 16: 423–46.

Huston, T. and Levinger, G. (1978). 'Interpersonal attraction and relationships', *Annual Review of Psychology*, 29: 116–56.

Huston, T., Surra, C., Fitzgerald, N. and Cate, R. (1981). 'From courtship to marriage: Mate selection as an interpersonal process', in S. Duck and R. Gilmour (eds), *Personal Relationships 2: Developing Personal Relationships* (pp. 109–32). New York: Academic Press.

Hutter, M. (1988). *The changing family: Comparative persepectives*. New York: Macmillan.

Ingersoll-Dayton, B., Campbell, R., Kurokawa, Y. and Saito, M. (1996). 'Separateness and togetherness: Interdependence over the life course in Japanese and American Marriages', *Journal of Social and Personal Relationships*, 13: 385–98.

Ingoldsby, B.B. (1995a). 'The family in Western History', in B.B. Ingoldsby and S. Smith (eds), *Families in Multicultural Perspective* (pp. 36–58). New York: Guildford.

—— (1995b). 'Mate selection and marriage', in B.B. Ingoldsby and S. Smith (eds), *Families in Multicultural Perspective* (pp. 143–60). New York: Guildford.

—— (1995c). 'Marital Structure', in B.B. Ingoldsby and S. Smith (eds), *Families in Multicultural Perspective* (pp. 117–37). New York: Guildford.

Inkeles, A. (1977). 'Understanding and misunderstanding individual modernity', *Journal of Cross-Cultural Psychology*, 8: 135–76.

Jahoda, G. (1984). 'Do we need a concept of culture?', *Journal of Cross-Cultural Psychology*, 15: 139–52.

—— (1990). 'Our forgotten ancestors', in J. Berman (ed.), *Nebraska Symposium on Motivation, 1989*. Lincoln: University of Nebraska Press.

—— (1992). *Crossroads between culture and mind: continuities and change in theories of human nature*. New York: Harvester Wheatsheaf.

Jankowiak, W.R. and Fischer, E.F. (1992). 'A cross-cultural perspective on romantic love', *Ethology*, 31: 149–55.

Jodelet, D. (1989). *Folies et representations sociales*. Paris: Presses Universitaires de France.

Joffe, H. (1996). 'AIDS research and prevention: A social representation approach', *British Journal of Medical Psychology*, 69: 169–90.

Johnson, M. (1998). 'Love and Entrapment: Wife Beating in America'; paper given at the 9th International Conference on Personal Relationships, Saratoga Springs, June 1998.

Jones, A.P., Rozelle, R.M. and Chang, W.C. (1990). 'Perceived punishment and reward values of supervisor actions in a Chinese sample', *Psychological Studies*, 35: 1–10.

Jylha, M. and Jokela, J. (1990). 'Individual experiences as cultural: A cross-cultural study of loneliness among the elderly', *Ageing and society*, 10: 295–315.

Kagitcibasi, C. (1982). 'Old-age security value of children: Cross-national socio-economic evidence', *Journal of Cross-Cultural Psychology*, 13: 29–42.

—— (1988). 'Diversity of socialization and social change', in P. Dasen, J. Berry and N. Sartorius (eds), *Health and Cross-Cultural Psychology: Towards Applications*. Beverly Hills: Sage.

—— (1990). 'Family and socialization in cross-cultural perspective: A model of change', in J. Berman (ed.), *Nebraska Symposium on Motivation, 1989*. Lincoln: Nebraska University Press.

—— (1991). 'Decreasing infant mortality as a global demographic change: A challenge to psychology', *International Journal of Psychology*, 26: 649–64.

—— (1994). 'A critical appraisal of individualism and collectivism', in U. Kim, H.C. Triandis, C. Kagitcibasi, S.-C. Choi and G. Yoon (eds), *Individualism and collectivism: Theory, method and applications* (pp. 52–65). Thousand Oaks, CA: Sage.

—— (1996). *Family and human development across cultures: A view from the other side*. Hove: Lawrence Erlbaum.

Kamo, Y. (1993). 'Determinants of marital satisfaction: A comparison of the United States and Japan', *Journal of Social and Personal Relationships*, 10: 551–68.

Kannemeyer, K.C., Ritzer, G. and Yetman, N.R. (1992). *Sociology: Experiencing changing societies* 5th edn. Boston: Allyn and Bacon.

Kanungo, R.N. and Misra, S. (1988). 'The bases of involvement in work and family context', *International Journal of Psychology*, 23: 267–82.

Kashima, Y., Siegel, M., Tanaka, K. and Isaka, H. (1988). 'Universalism in lay conceptions of distributive justice: A cross-cultural examination', *International Journal of Psychology*, 23: 51–64.

Katakis, C.D. (1978). 'On the transaction of social change processes and the perception of self in relation to others', *Mental Health and Society*, 5: 275–83.

Katakis, H. (1984). *Oi tris tautotites tis hellenikis oikogenias* (The three faces of the Greek family). Athens: Kedros.

Keating, C.F., Mazur, A., Segall, M.H. *et al.* (1981). 'Culture and the perception of social dominance from facial expression', *Journal of Personality and Social Psychology*, 40: 615–26.

Keller, J.D. (1992). 'Schemes for schemata', in T. Schwartz, G. White and C. Lutz (eds), *New directions in psychological anthropology* (pp. 59–67). Cambridge: Cambridge University Press.

Kelley, H.H., Berscheid, E., Christensen, A. *et al.* (1983) *Close Relationships*. New York: Freeman.

Kelley, H.H. and Thibaut, J. (1978). *Interpersonal relations: A new theory of interdependence*. New York: Wiley.

Kelly, P. (1996). 'Metaphorical views of family interaction: A cross-cultural analysis', *Personal Relationships Issues*, 3: 17–23.

Kenny, D.A. (1988). 'The analysis of data from two person relationships', in S.W. Duck., D.F. Hay., S.E. Hobfoll, W. Ickes and B. Montgomery (eds), *Handbook of Personal Relationships: Theory, research and interventions* (pp. 57–77). New York and Chichester: John Wiley.

Kenrick, D.T. and Keefe, R.C. (1992). 'Age preferences in mates reflect sex differences in human reproductive strategies', *Behavioral and Brain Sciences*, 15: 75–133.

Kenrick, D.T., Sadelia, E.K., Groth, G. and Trost, T.R. (1990). 'Evolution, traits and the stages of human courtship: Qualifying the parental investment model', *Journal of Personality*, 58: 97–116.

Kephart, W.M. (1967). 'Some correlates of romantic love', *Journal of Marriage and the Family*, 29: 470–4.

Kephart, W.M. and Jedlicka, D. (1988). *The family, society and the individual.* New York: Harper and Row.

Kerig, P.K., Alyoshina, Y.Y. and Volovich, A.S. (1993). 'Gender-role socialization in contemporary Russia', *Psychology of Women Quarterly*, 17: 389–408.

Kibria, N. (1990). 'Power, patriarchy and gender conflict in the Vietnamese Immigrant Community', *Gender and Society*, 4: 9–24.

Kim, M.-S. (1994). 'Cross-cultural comparisons of the perceived importance of conversational constraints', *Human Communication Research*, 21: 128–51.

Kim, U. (1994). 'Significance of paternalism and communalism in the occupational welfare system of Korean firms: A national survey', in U. Kim, H.C. Triandis, C. Kagitcibasi, S.-C. Choi and G. Yoon, *Individualism and collectivism: Theory, method and applications* (pp. 251–66). Thousand Oaks, CA: Sage.

Kim, U., Triandis, H.C., Kagitcibasi, C., Choi, S.-C. and Yoon, G. (1994). *Individualism and collectivism: Theory, method and applications.* Thousand Oaks, CA: Sage.

King, A. and Bond, M. (1985). 'The Confucian paradigm of Man: A sociological view', in W. Tseng and D. Wu (eds), *Chinese culture and mental health* (pp. 29–46). New York: Academic Press.

Kitayama, S. (1992). 'Individualism and collectivism as social representation', review of J.J. Berman, 'Cross-Cultural Perspectives', Nebraska Symposium on Motivation, 1989, *Contemporary Psychology*, 37: 1322–4.

Klineberg, S.L. (1973). 'Parents, schools and modernity: an exploratory investigation of sex differences in the attitudinal development of Tunisian adolescents', *International Journal of Comparative Sociology*, 14: 221–44.

Klinger, E. (1977). *Meaning and void: Experience and incentives in people's lives.* Minneapolis: University of Minnesota Press.

Knox, D.H. and Sporakowski, J.J. (1968). 'Attitudes of college students towards love', *Journal of Marriage and the Family*, 30: 638–42.

Kohn, M.L. (1987). 'Cross-national research as an analytic strategy', *American Sociological Review*, 52: 713–31.

—— (1989). 'Social structure and personality: A quintessentially sociological approach to social psychology', *Social Forces*, 68: 26–33.

—— (1993) 'Doing social research under conditions of radical social change: The biography of an ongoing research project', *Social Psychology Quarterly*, 56: 4–20.

Kohn, M.L., Naoi, A., Schoenbach, C., Schooler, C. and Slomczynski, K.M. (1990). 'Position in the class structure and psychological functioning in the United States, Japan and Poland', *American Journal of Sociology*, 95: 964–1008.

Kok, L. (1990). 'Female sexual knowledge and attitude in Singapore'; paper presented at the International Conference on Sexuality in Asia, Hong Kong, May 1990.

Kontula, O. (1993). 'Sexual behavior changes in Finland during the last 20 years'; Meeting of the Society for the Scientific Study of Sex, Chicago, November 1993.

Kornadt, H., Eisler, A. and Tachibana, Y. (1998). 'Child-rearing and the development of social motives: A cross-cultural longitudinal study'; paper presented at the 14th Congress of the International Association of Cross-Cultural Psychologists, Western Washington University, USA, August 1998.

Krauss, R.M., Morrel-Samuels, P. and Colasante, C. (1991). 'Do conversational hand gestures communicate?', *Journal of Personality and Social Psychology*, 61: 743–54.

Kroeber, A.L. and Kluckhorn, C. (1952). *Culture: A critical review of concepts and definitions*. Cambridge, MA: Peabody Museum.

Kukla, A. (1988) 'Cross-cultural psychology in a post-empiricist era', in M. Bond (ed.), *The Cross-Cultural Challenge to Social Psychology* (pp 141–52). Newbury Park: Sage.

Kumagai, F. (1984). 'The life cycle of the Japanese family', *Journal of Marriage and the Family*, 46: 191–204.

Kumar, U. (1991). 'Life stages in the development of the Hindu woman in India', in L.L. Adler (ed.), *Women in cross-cultural perspective* (pp. 142–58). New York: Praeger.

Kurczewski, J. and Maclean, M. (1997). 'Introduction: The two Europes', in J. Kurczewski and M. Maclean (eds), *Family law and family policy in the New Europe* (pp. ix–xxvii). Dartmouth: Aldershot.

Laciak, B. (1997). 'The family in social policy of the days of transformation: Decentralization and scarcity', in J. Kurczewski and M. Maclean (eds), *Family law and family policy in the New Europe* (pp. 189–202). Dartmouth: Aldershot.

LaFrance, M. and Mayo, C. (1976). 'Racial differences in gaze behavior during conversations: Two systematic observational studies', *Journal of Personality and Social Psychology*, 33: 547–52.

Lam, D.J. and Yang, C.-F. (1989). 'Social behavior in *real* Hong Kong', *Personality and Social Psychology Bulletin*, 15: 639–43.

Lanaro, L.M., Doyle, A.B., Dayan, J. and Markiewicz, D. (1997). 'Parenting styles as predictors of self-esteem in children from individualist and collectivist cultures'; paper presented at the European Congress of Psychology, Dublin, July 1997.

Larson, D.G. and Chastain, R.L. (1990). 'Self-concealment: Conceptualization, measurement and health implications', *Journal of Social and Clinical Psychology*, 9: 439–55.

Lau, S. (1981). 'Chinese familism in an urban-industrial setting: The case of Hong Kong', *Journal of Marriage and the Family*, 43: 977–92.

Lau, S., Lew, W., Hau, K., Cheung, P. and Berndt, T. (1990). 'Relations among perceived parental control, warmth, indulgence and family harmony of Chinese in Mainland China', *Developmental Psychology*, 26: 674–7.

Lauman, E.O., Gagnon, J.H., Michael, R.T. and Michaels, S. (1994). *The social organization of sexuality: Sexual practices in the United States*. Chicago: University of Chicago Press.

Laurent, A. (1983). 'The cultural diversity of western conceptions of management', *International Studies of Management and Organization*, 13: 75–96.

Lawler, E.E. III (1986). *High involvement management*. New York: Jossey–Bass.

Lazarus, R.S. (1991) *Emotion and adaptation*. London: Oxford University Press.

Lebra, T.S. (1984). *Japanese Women: Constraint and Fulfillment*. Honolulu: University of Hawaii Press.

—— (1992). 'Self in Japanese culture', in N.R. Rosenberger (ed.), *Japanese sense of self* (pp. 105–20). Cambridge: Cambridge University Press.

Lee, G.R. (1982). *Family structure and interaction: A comparative analysis*. Mineappolis: University of Minnesota Press.

—— (1987). 'Comparative perspectives', in M.B. Sussman and S.K. Steinmetz (eds), *Handbook of Marriage and the Family* (pp. 59–80). New York: Plenum Press.

Lee, G.R. and Stone, L.H. (1980). 'Mate-selection systems and criteria: Variation according to family structure', *Journal of Marriage and the Family*, 42: 319–26.

Lee, J.A. (1973) *The Colors of Love: An exploration of the ways of loving.* Don Mills, Ontario: New Press.

Lee, R. (1985). 'Social stress and coping behaviour in Hong Kong', in W. Tseng and D. Wu (eds), *Chinese culture and mental health* (pp. 193–214). New York: Academic Press.

Lehmann, A. (1998). 'Motivations in Close Friendships'; paper given at the 9th International Conference on Personal Relationships, Saratoga Springs, June 1998.

Leung, K. and Bond, M.H. (1984). 'The impact of cultural collectivism on reward allocation', *Journal of Personality and Social Psychology*, 47: 793–804.

Leung, K. and Iwawaki, S. (1988). 'Cultural collectivism and distributive behavior: A cross-cultural study', *Journal of Cross-Cultural Psychology*, 19: 35–49.

Leung, K. and Park, H.J. (1986). 'Effects of interactional goals on choice of allocation rule: A cross-national study', *Organizational behaviour and human decision processes*, 37: 111–20.

Levine, R., Sato, S., Hashimoto, T. and Verma, I. (1995). 'Love and marriage in eleven cultures', *Journal of Cross-Cultural Psychology*, 26: 554–71.

Levinger, G. (1979). 'A social exchange view of the dissolution of pair relationships', in R.L. Burgess and T.L. Huston (eds), *Social exchange: Advances in theory and research* (pp. 169–93). New York: Academic Press.

Levinson, D. (1989). *Family values in cross-cultural perspective.* Newbury Park: Sage.

Levy, M. (1949). *The Family Revolution in Modern China.* Cambridge, MA: Harvard University Press.

Lewin, K. (1936). 'Some socio-psychological differences between the United States and Germany', *Character and Personality*, 4: 265–93.

Lewis, E.A. (1989). 'Role strain in African–American women: The efficacy of support networks', *Journal of Black Studies*, 20: 155–69.

Li, F. (1996). 'Relationship closeness and the perception of helping intentions'; paper presented at the 8th ICPR, Banff, August 1996.

Li, J. (1995). 'China's one-child policy: How and how well has it worked? A case study of Hebei Province, 1979–88', *Population and Development Review*, 21: 563–85.

Liao, C. and Heaton, T. (1992). 'Divorce trends and differentials in China', *Journal of Comparative Family Studies*, 23: 413–29.

Liebkind, K. (1996). 'Acculturation and stress: Vietnamese refugees in Finland', *Journal of Cross-Cultural Psychology*, 27: 161–80.

Liggett, J. (1974). *The Human Face.* New York: Stein and Day.

Lin, Y.-H.W. and Rusbult, C.E. (1995). 'Commitment to dating relationships and cross-sex friendships in America and China', *Journal of Social and Personal Relationships*, 12: 7–26.

Lin, W.Q., Chen, L. and Wang, D. (1987). 'The construction of the CPM scale for leadership assessment' (in Chinese), *Acta Psychologia Sinica*, 19: 199–207.

Little, K.B. (1968). 'Cultural variations in social schemata', *Journal of Personality and Social Psychology*, 10: 1–7.

Liu, D.L., Ng, M.L. and Chu, L.P. (1992). *Sexual Behaviour in Modern China: A Report of the Nationwide Sex Civilisation Survey of 20,000 Subjects in China* (in Chinese). Shanghai: SJPC Publishing Company.

Liu, J.H., Campbell, S.M. and Condie, H. (1995). 'Ethnocentrism in dating preferences for an American sample: the ingroup bias in social context', *European Journal of Social Psychology*, 25: 95–115.

Lockhart, L.L. (1987). 'A re-examination of the effects of race and social class on the incidence of marital violence: A search for reliable differences', *Journal of Marriage and the Family*, 49: 603–10.

Lomranz, J. (1976). 'Cultural variations in personal space', *Journal of Social Psychology*, 99: 21–7.

Long, S.O. (1987). *Family Change and the Life Course in Japan*. Ithaca, NY: Cornell University Press.

Love, K.G., Bishop, R.C., Heinisch, D.A. and Montei, M.S. (1994). 'Selection across two cultures: Adapting the selection of American assemblers to meet Japanese job performance demands', *Personnel Psychology*, 47: 837–46.

Lunin, I., Hall, T.L., Mandel, J.S., Kay, J. and Hearst, N. (1995). 'Adolescent sexuality in St. Petersburg, Russia', *AIDS*, 9 (Supplement 1): S53–S60.

Maclachlan, M. (1993). 'Sustaining human resource development in Africa: The influence of expatriates', *Management Education and Development*, 24: 167–71.

Maher, T.E. and Wong, Y.Y. (1994). 'The impact of cultural differences on the growing tensions between Japan and the United States', *SAM Advanced Management Journal*, 59: 40–6.

Man, P. (1991). 'The influence of peers and parents on youth life satisfaction in Hong Kong', *Social Indicators Research*, 24: 347–65.

Manderson, L. (1995). 'The pursuit of pleasure and the sale of sex', in P.R. Abramson and S.D. Pinkerton (eds), *Sexual nature, sexual culture*. Chicago: The University of Chicago Press.

Marin, G. and Triandis, H.C. (1985). 'Allocentrism as an important characteristic of the behavior of Latin Americans and Hispanics', in R. Diaz-Guerrero (ed.), *Cross-cultural and national studies in social psychology* (pp. 85–104). Amsterdam: North Holland.

Markova, I. (1997). 'The individual and the community: A post-Communist perspective', *Journal of Community and Applied Social Psychology*, 7: 3–17.

Markus, H. and Kitayama, S. (1991). 'Culture and self: Implications for cognition, emotion and motivation', *Psychological Bulletin*, 102: 72–90.

Mars, G. and Altman, Y. (1983). 'The cultural bases of Soviet Georgia's second economy', *Soviet Studies*, 25: 546–60.

Marshall, D.S. (1971). 'Sexual behavior in Mangaia', in D.S. Marshall and R.C. Suggs (eds), *Human sexual behavior: Variations in the ethnographic spectrum* (pp. 103–62). New York: Basic Books.

Maslow, A.H. (1954). *Motivation and Personality*. New York: Harper and Row.

Matsumoto, D., Weissman, M.D., Preston, K., Brown, B.R. and Kupperbusch, C. (1997). 'Context-specific measurement of individualism–collectivism on the individual level', *Journal of Cross-Cultural Psychology*, 28: 743–67.

McAllister, M.P. (1992). 'AIDS, medicalization and the news media', in T. Edgar, M.A. Fitzpatrick and V.S. Freimuth (eds), *AIDS: A communication perspective* (pp. 195–221). Hillsdale, NJ: Lawrence Erlbaum Associates.

McArthur, L.Z. and Berry, D.S. (1987). 'Cross-cultural consensus in perceptions of babyfaced adults', *Journal of Cross-Cultural Psychology*, 18: 165–92.

McCammon, S., Knox, S. and Schacht, C. (1993). *Choices in Sexuality*. Minneapolis: West.

McClelland, D.C. (1961). *The achieving society*. Princeton, NJ: Van Nostrand.

McGlone, F., Park, A. and Smith, K. (1998). *Families and Kinship*. London: Family Policy Studies Centre.

McIlwain, D. (1997). 'Relationships, Identity and the Flow of Knowledge: Aboriginal Cultures in Australia', *ISSPR Bulletin*, 14 (1): 12–14.

McKenry, P.C. and Price, S.J. (1995). 'Divorce: A comparative Perspective', in B.B. Ingoldsby and S. Smith (eds), *Families in Multicultural Perspective* (pp. 187–212). New York: The Guildford Press.

McKinney, C.V. (1992). 'Wives and sisters: Bajju marital patterns', *Journal of Comparative Family Studies*, 31: 75–87.

McLaughlin-Volpe, T., Arun, A. and Reis, H. (1997). 'The duality of daily social interactions with members of ethnic outgroups: A diary study', Paper presented at the International Network of Personal Relationships, University of Maine at Ohio, June.

Menski, W. (1991). 'Change and continuity in Hindu marriage ritual', in D. Killingley (ed.), *Hindu ritual and society*. Newcastle upon Tyne: Grevatt and Grevatt.

Meredith, W.H. and Abbott, D.A. (1995). 'Chinese Families in Later Life', in B.B. Ingoldsby and S. Smith (eds), *Families in Multicultural Perspective* (pp. 213–30). New York: The Guildford Press.

Merton, R.K. (1968). *Social Theory and Social Structure* enlarged edn. New York: The Free Press.

Millar, J. and Warman, A. (1996). *Family obligations in Europe*. London: Family Policy Studies Centre.

Mills, J. and Clark, M. (1982). 'Communual and exchange relationships', in L. Wheeler (ed.), *Review of Personality and Social Psychology*, vol. 3. Beverly Hills: Sage.

Minai, N. (1981). *Women in Islam: Tradition and transition in the Middle East*. New York: Seaview Books.

Minturn, L., Grosse, M. and Haider, S. (1969). 'Cultural patterning of sexual beliefs and behavior', *Ethnology*, 8: 301–13.

Mishra, R.C. (1994). 'Individualist and collectivist orientations across generations', in U. Kim, H.C. Triandis, C. Kagitcibasi, S.-C. Choi and G. Yoon, *Individualism and collectivism: Theory, method and applications* (pp. 225–38). Thousand Oaks, CA: Sage.

Misumi, J. and Peterson, M.F. (1985). 'The performance–maintenance (PM) theory of leadership – Review of a Japanese Research Programme', *Administration Science Quarterly*, 30: 198–223.

Modood, T., Beishon, S. and Virdee, S. (1994). *Changing Ethnic Identities*. London: Policy Studies Institute.

Moen, P. and Forest, K.B. (1990). 'Working parents, workplace supports and well-being: The Swedish experience', *Social Psychology Quarterly*, 53: 117–31.

Moeran, B. (1984). 'Individual, Group and *Seishin*: Japan's Internal Cultural Debate', in T.S. Lebra and W.P. Lebra (1988), *Japanese Culture and Behavior* (pp. 62–79). Honolulu: University of Hawaii Press.

Moghaddam, F.M., Taylor, D.M. and Wright, S.C. (1993). *Social psychology in cross-cultural perspective*. New York: W.H. Freeman.

Moore, S., Rosenthal, D. and Mitchell, A. (1996). *Youth, AIDS and sexually transmitted diseases*. London: Routledge.

Morgan, D.L. and Schwalbe, M.L. (1990). 'Mind and self in society: Linking social structure and social cognition', *Social Psychology Quarterly*, 53: 148–64.

Morris, D., Collett, P., Marsh, P. and O'Shaughnessy, M. (1979). *Gestures: Their Origins and Distribution*. London: Book Club Associates.

Moscovici, S. (1961). *La Psychoanalyse: son image et son public*. Paris: Presses Universitaires de France.

—— (1981). 'On social representations', in J.P. Forgas (ed.), *Social cognition: Perspectives on everyday life*. London: Academic Press.

—— (1984). 'The phenomenon of social representations', in R.M. Farr and S. Moscovici (eds), *Social representations*. Cambridge: Cambridge University Press.

—— (1988). 'Notes towards a description of social representations', *European Journal of Social Psychology*, 18: 211–50.

Moskoff, W. (1983). 'Divorce in the USSR', *Journal of Marriage and the Family*, 45: 419–25.

Munro, B. and Adams, G. (1978). 'Love American style: a test of role structure theory on changes in attitudes toward love', *Human Relations*, 3: 215–28.

Munroe, R.L. and Munroe, R.H. (1997). 'Logoli childhood and the cultural reproduction of sex differentiation', in T.S. Weisner, C. Bradley and P.L. Kilbride (eds), *African families and the crisis of social change* (pp. 299–316). Westport, CT: Bergin and Garvey.

Murdock, G.P. (1967). 'Ethnographic atlas: A summary', *Ethnology*, 6: 109–236.

Murdock, G.P. and White, D.R. (1969). 'Standard cross-cultural sample', *Ethnography*, 8: 329–69.

Murphy-Berman, V., Berman, J.J., Singh, P., Pachauri, A. and Kumar, P. (1984). 'Factors affecting allocation to needy and meritorious recipients: a cross-cultural comparison', *Journal of Personality and Social Psychology*, 46: 1267–72.

Murphy-Berman, V., Levesque, H.L. and Berman, J.J. (1996). 'U.N. Convention on the rights of the child', *American Psychologist*, 51: 1257–61.

Murstein, B. (1976). 'Qualities of desired spouse: A cross-cultural comparison between French and American College Students', *Journal of Comparative Family Studies*, 7: 455–69.

—— (1980). 'Mate selection in the 1980s', *Journal of Marriage and the Family*, 42: 777–93.

—— (1986). *Paths to marriage*. Beverly Hills: Sage.

Mwamwenda, T.S. and Monyooe, L.A. (1997). 'Status of Bridewealth in an African culture', *Journal of Social Psychology*, 137: 269–71.

Myers, R. (1991). *The twelve who survive*. London: Routledge.

Naltao, W. (1987). 'Divorce: Traditional ideas receding', *Beijing Review*, 11: 23–5.

Nassehi-Behman, V. (1985). 'Change and the Iranian family', *Current Anthropology*, 26: 557–62.

Ndeki, S., Klepp, K., Seha, A. and Leshabari, T. (1994). 'Exposure to HIV/AIDS information, AIDS knowledge, perceived risk and attitudes toward people with AIDS among primary school children in Northern Tanzania', *AIDS Care*, 6, 183–91.

Newcomb, M.D. (1987). 'Cohabitation and marriage: A quest for independence and relatedness', in S. Oskamp (ed.), *Social Psychology Annual: Vol. 7: Family Processes and problems: Social psychological aspects* (pp. 128–56). Beverly Hills: Sage.

Nina, R. (1996). 'Loneliness in Puertorican married couples'; paper presented at the 6th ICPR, Banff, Calgary, August 1996.

Ocholla-Ayayo, A.B.C. (1997). 'HIV/AIDS risk factors and changing sexual practices in Kenya', in T.S. Weisner, C. Bradley and P.L. Kilbride (eds), *African families and the crisis of social change* (pp. 109–24). Westport, CT: Bergin and Garvey.

Oppong, C. (1980). 'From love to institution: Indications of change in Akan marriage', *Journal of Family History*, 5: 197–209.

Orbuch, T.L. and Eyster, S.L. (forthcoming). 'Division of household labor among black couples and white couples', *Social Forces*.

Orbuch, T.L. and Veroff, J. (1997). 'The Cultural Context of Early Marriage: Findings from the Early Years of Marriage Project', *ISSPR Bulletin*, 14 (1): 10–12.

Orlick, T., Zhou, Q.Y. and Partington, J. (1990). 'Co-operation and conflict within Chinese and Canadian kindergarten settings', *Canadian Journal of Behavioral Science*, 22: 20–5.

Ostner, I. (1996). 'Families and family policies in transition: The case of post-unification Germany', in H. Jones and J. Millar (eds), *The politics of the family* (pp. 33–44). Aldershot: Avebury.

Parker, S. (1976). 'The precultural basis of the incest taboo: toward a biosocial theory', *American Anthropologist*, 78: 285–305.

Parsons, T. (1943). 'The kinship system of the contemporary United States', *American Anthropologist*, 45: 22–38.

Patterson, J. and Kim, P. (1991). *The Day America Told the Truth*. New York: Prentice-Hall.

Patzer, G.L. (1985). *The physical attractiveness phenomena*. New York: Plenum Press.

Payne, M. and Vandewiele, M. (1987). 'Attitudes toward love in the Caribbean', *Psychological Reports*, 60: 715–21.

Pearson, K. and Lee, A. (1903). 'On the laws of inheritance in man. I: Inheritance of physical characteristics'. *Biometrika*, 2: 372–7.

Pennebaker, J.W., Hughes, C.F. and O'Heeron, R. (1987). 'The psycho-physiology of confession: Linking inhibitory and psychosomatic processes', *Journal of Personality and Social Psychology*, 52: 781–93.

Pepitone, A. and Triandis, H.C. (1987). 'On the universality of social psychological theories', *Journal of Cross-Cultural Psychology*, 18: 471–98.

Peplau, A. (1998). 'Looking for Love in All The Wrong Places: Misguided Theories about Women's Sexual Orientation'; paper given at the 9th International Conference on Personal Relationships, Saratoga Springs, June 1998.

Perevedentsev, V.I. (1978). 'The Soviet family today', *Sociology and Social Research*, 67: 245–59.

Peterson, M.F., Smith, P.B., Akande, A. *et al.* (1995). 'Role conflict, ambiguity and overload by national culture: A 21 nation study', *Academy of Management Journal*, 38: 429–52.

Phalet, K. and Claeys, W. (1993). 'A comparative study of Turkish and Belgian youth', *Journal of Cross-Cultural Psychology*, 24: 319–43.

Philbrick, J. and Opolot, J. (1980). 'Love style: comparison of African and American attitudes', *Psychological Reports*, 46: 286.

Phizacklea, A. (1997). 'Migration and the Domestication of Labour'; paper presented at the Conference on Economy, Ethnicity and Social Change, University of Bristol, September 1997.

Pillai, V.K. and Roy, L.C. (1996). 'Attitudes toward sexual behavior among unmarried Zambian secondary school females', *Journal of Social Psychology*, 136: 111–12.

Pollay, R., Tse, D. and Wang, Z. (1990). 'Advertising, propaganda and value change in economic development: The new cultural revolution in China and attitudes toward advertising', *Journal of Business Research*, 20: 83–95.

Popenoe, D. (1988). *Disturbing the Nest: Family Change and Decline in Modern Societies*. New York: Aldine de Gruyter.

Ramu, G.N. (1991). 'Changing Family Structure and Fertility Patterns: An Indian Case', *Journal of Asian Studies*, 26: 189–206.

Rechtien, J.G. and Fiedler, E. (1988). 'Contributions to psychohistory: XIII. Courtly love today: Romance and socialization in interpersonal scripts', *Psychological Reports*, 63: 683–95.

Reik, T. (1941). *Of love and lust*. New York: Jason Aronson.

Reischauer, E. (1988). *The Japanese today: Change and continuity*. Cambridge: Harvard University Press.

Reykowski, J. (1994). 'Why did the collectivist state fail?', *Theory and Society*, 23: 233–52.

Rice, P.L. (1992). *Stress and Health* 2nd edn. Pacific Grove, California: Brooks/Cole.

Ridley, C.A., Hardin, E.E., Cleveland, H.H. and Feldman, C.M. (1996). 'Relational qualities and beliefs among abusive men in Korea'; paper presented at the 8th International Conference on Personal Relationships, Banff, August 1996.

Ritzer, G. (1993). *The McDonaldization of Society*. Thousand Oaks, CA: Pine Forge Press.

Rodman, H. (1972). 'Marital power and the theory of resources in cultural context', *Journal of Comparative Family Studies*, 3: 50–69.

Rodriguez, M.L. (1990). 'Efectos del tiempo historico en el tradicionalism de la familia mexicana medidas a traves de las premisas historico–socioculturales en dos communidades Nahutl'. Mexico: Tesis de Maestria, Universidad Iberoamericana.

Rogoff, B. and Chavajay, P. (1995). 'What's become of research on the cultural basis of cognitive development?', *American Psychologist*, 50: 859–77.

Rohner, R. (1984). 'Toward a conception of culture for cross-cultural psychology', *Journal of Cross-Cultural Psychology*, 15: 111–38.

Rosenberger, N.R. (1992a). 'Introduction', in N.R. Rosenberger (ed.), *Japanese sense of self* (pp. 1–20). Cambridge: Cambridge University Press.

—— (1992b). 'Tree in summer, tree in winter: movement of self in Japan', in N.R. Rosenberger (ed.), *Japanese sense of self* (pp. 67–92). Cambridge: Cambridge University Press.

Rosenblatt, P.C. and Anderson, R.M. (1981). 'Human sexuality in cross-cultural perspective', in M. Cook (ed.), *The bases of human sexual attraction*. London: Academic Press.

Rosenblatt, P.C. and Unangst, D. (1979). 'Marriage ceremonies: An exploratory cross-cultural study', in G. Kurian (ed.), *Cross-cultural perspectives of mate-selection and marriage* (pp. 227–42). Westport, CT: Greenwood Press.

Rosenstein, E. (1985). 'Cooperativeness and advancement of managers: An international perspective', *Human Relations*, 38: 1–21.

Rosenthal, D.A., Bell, R., Demetriou, A. and Efklides, A. (1989). 'From collectivism to individualism? The acculturation of Greek immigrants in Australia', *International Journal of Psychology*, 24: 57–71.

Ruan, F. and Matsumura, M. (1991). *Sex in China: Studies in sexology in Chinese culture*. New York: Plenum Press.

Ruble, D.N., Fleming, A.S., Hackel, L.S. and Stangor, C. (1988). 'Changes in the marital relationship during the transition to first motherhood: Effects of violated expectations concerning division of household labor', *Journal of Personality and Social Psychology*, 55: 78–87.

Rugh, A.B. (1984). *Family in contemporary Egypt*. Syracuse, NY: Syracuse University Press.

Rusbult, C. (1983). 'A longitudinal test of the investment model: the development (and deterioration) of satisfaction and commitment in heterosexual involvements', *Journal of Personality and Social Psychology*, 45: 101–17.

—— (1987). 'Responses to dissatisfaction in close relationships: The EVLN model', in D. Perlman and S. Duck (eds), *Intimate Relationships: Development, Dynamics and Deterioration*. Newbury Park: Sage.

Rusbult, C., Morrow, G. and Johnson, D. (1986). 'Predicting satisfaction and commitment in adult romantic involvements: An assessment of the generalizability of the investment model', *Social Psychology Quarterly*, 49: 81–9.

Russell, J.A. and Fernandez-Dols, J.M. (1997). *The Psychology of Facial Expression*. Cambridge: Cambridge University Press.

Rutledge, P.J. (1992). *The Vietnamese Experience in America*. Bloomington: Indiana University Press.

Safilios-Rothschild, C. (1976). 'A macro- and micro-examination of family power and love: An exchange model', *Journal of Marriage and the Family*, 38: 355–62.

Sagiv, L. and Schwartz, S.H. (1995). 'Value priorities and readiness for out-group social contact', *Journal of Personality and Social Psychology*, 69: 437–48.

Saks, M.J. (1996). 'The Role of Research in Implementing the U.N. Convention on the Rights of the Child', *American Psychologist*, 51: 1262–6.

Salamon, S. (1977). 'Family bounds and friendship bonds: Japan and West Germany', *Journal of Marriage and the Family*, 39: 807–20.

Saluter, A.F. (1996). 'Marital Status and Living Arrangements: March, 1994', *Current population reports: Population characteristics*, U.S. Bureau of the Census, Feb. 1996.

Sanday, P. R. (1981). *Female power and male dominance: On the origins of sexual inequality*. New York: Cambridge University Press.

—— (1992). 'The socio-cultural context of rape: a cross-cultural study', *Journal of Social Issues*, 37: 5–27.

Sarason, B.R., Sarason, I.G. and Gurung, R.A.R. (1997). 'Close personal relationships and health outcomes: A key to the role of social support', in S.W. Duck (ed.), *Handbook of personal relationships: Theory, research and interventions* 2nd edn (pp. 547–73). Chichester: John Wiley.

Scherer, K.R. and Wallbott, H.G. (1994). 'Evidence for universality and cultural variation of differential emotion response patterning', *Journal of Personality and Social Psychology*, 66: 310–28.

Scherer, K.R., Wallbott, H.G. and Summerfield, A.B. (1986). *Experiencing emotion: A cross-cultural study*. Cambridge: Cambridge University Press.

Schlegel, A. (1995). 'The cultural management of adolescent sexuality', in P.R. Abramson and S.D. Pinkerton (eds), *Sexual nature, sexual culture*. Chicago: The University of Chicago Press.

Schlegel, A. and Barry, H. III (1986). 'The cultural consequences of female contribution to subsistence', *American Anthropologist*, 88: 142–50.

—— (1991). *Adolescence: An anthropological inquiry*. New York: Free Press.

Schmitz, P.G. (1994). 'Acculturation and adaptation processes among immigrants to Germany', in A.-M. Bouvy, F. van de Vijver, P. Bowski and P. Schmitz (eds), *Journeys into Cross-Cultural Psychology*. Lisse: Swets and Zeitlinger.

Schneider, B.H., Smith, A., Poisson, S.E. and Kwan, A.B. (1997). 'Cultural dimensions of children's peer relations', in S.W. Duck (ed.), *Handbook of personal relationships: Theory, research and interventions* 2nd edn (pp. 121–46). Chichester: John Wiley.

Schooley, M. (1936). 'Personality resemblances among married couples', *Journal of Abnormal and Social Psychology*, 31: 340–7.

Schumpeter, J. (1954). *History of Economic Analysis*. Oxford: Oxford University Press.

Schuster, E. and Elderton, E. (1906). 'The inheritance of psychical characteristics', *Biometrika*, 5: 460–9.

Schwartz, S. (1992). 'Universals in the content and structure of values: Theoretical advances and empirical tests in 20 countries', in M.P. Zanna (ed.), *Advances in Experimental Social Psychology* (vol. 25, pp. 1–65). New York: Academic Press.

—— (1994). 'Beyond Individualism–Collectivism: New Cultural dimensions of values', in U. Kim., H.C. Triandis, C. Kagitcibasi, S.-C. Choi and G. Yoon (eds), *Individualism and Collectivism: Theory, method and application* (pp. 81–119). Newbury Park: Sage.

—— (1997). 'Values and Culture', in D. Munro, S. Carr and J. Schumaker (eds), *Motivation and Culture* (pp. 69–84). New York: Routledge.

Schwartz, S.H. and Bilsky, W. (1990). 'Toward a theory of the universal content and structure of values extensions and cross-cultural replications', *Journal of Personality and Social Psychology*, 58: 878–91.

Schwarzer, R. and Chung, R. (1996). 'Anticipating stress in the community: Worries about the future of Hong Kong', *Anxiety, Stress and Coping*, 9: 163–78.

Schwarzer, R., Hahn, A. and Schroder, H. (1994). 'Social integration and social support in a life crisis: Effects of macrosocial change in East Germany', *American Journal of Community Psychology*, 22: 685–706.

Schwertfeger, M. (1982). 'Interethnic marriage and divorce in Hawaii: A panel study of 1968 first marriages', *Marriage and Family Review*, 5: 49–59.

Scott, K.D. and Taylor, G.S. (1985). 'An examination of conflicting findings on the relationship between job satisfaction and abstenteeism: A meta-analysis', *Academy of Management Journal*, 28: 599–612.

Segall, M.H. (1984). 'More than we need to know about culture but are afraid not to ask', *Journal of Cross-Cultural Psychology*, 15: 153–62.

—— (1988). 'Psychocultural antecedents of male aggression', in P. Dasen, J. Berry and N. Sartorius (eds), *Health and cross-cultural psychology: Towards applications*. Beverly Hills: Sage.

Segall, M.H., Dasen, P.R., Berry, J.W. and Poortinga, Y.H. (1990). *Human behavior in global perspective*. Pergamon Press: New York.

Seginer, R. (1992). 'Support adolescents obtain from family and friends: The cross-cultural context of benefits and costs'; paper presented at the 6th International Conference on Personal Relationships, Orono, Maine, July 1992.

Sengoku, T. (1990). 'A comparative study in family education and sexual consciousness between Japan and China'; paper presented at the International Conference on Sexuality in Asia, Hong Kong, May 1990.

Shaikh, T. and Kanekar, S. (1994). 'Attitudinal similarity and affiliation need as determinants of interpersonal attraction', *Journal of Social Psychology*, 134: 257–9.

Shaver, P.R., Hazan, C. and Bradshaw, D. (1988). 'Love as attachment: The integration of three behavioural systems', in R.J. Sternberg and M.L. Barnes (eds), *The psychology of love* (pp. 68–99). New Haven, CT: Yale University Press.

Shaver, P.R., Wu, S. and Schwartz, J.C. (1992). 'Cross-cultural similarities and differences in emotion and its representation: A prototype approach', in M.S. Clark (ed.), *Review of personality and social psychology. Vol. 13: Emotion* (pp. 175–212). Newbury Park: Sage.

Shenkar, U. and Ronen, S. (1987). 'The cultural context of negotiations: The implications of Chinese interpersonal norms', *Journal of Applied Behavioral Science*, 23: 263–75.

Shibazaki, K. and Brennan, K.A. (1997). 'When birds of different feathers flock together: A preliminary comparison of intra- and inter-ethnic dating relationships'; paper presented at the International Network on Personal Relationships, Oxford, Ohio, July 1997.

Shieh, Y. (1990). 'A survey of female sexuality in Taiwan'; paper presented at the International Conference on Sexuality in Asia, Hong Kong, May 1990.

Shlapentokh, V. (1984). *Love, marriage and friendship in the Soviet Union: Ideals and practices*. New York: Praeger.

Sik, E. (1988). 'Reciprocal exchange of labour in Hungary', in R. Pahl (ed.), *On Work*. Oxford: Basil Blackwell.

Sillars, A.L. (1995). 'Communication and Family Culture', in M.A. Fitzpatrick and A.L. Vangelisti (eds), *Explaining Family Interactions*. Thousand Oaks, CA: Sage.

Simmel, G. (1971). *On Individuality and Social Forms*. Chicago: University of Chicago Press.

Simmons, C., Von Kolke, A. and Shimizu, H. (1986). 'Attitudes toward romantic love among American, German and Japanese students', *Journal of Social Psychology*, 126: 327–36.

Simmons, C., Wehner, E.A. and Kay, K.A. (1989). 'Differences in attitudes toward romantic love of French and American college students', *Journal of Social Psychology*, 129: 793–9.

Simpson, J.A. (1990). 'Influence of attachment styles on romantic relationships', *Journal of Personality and Social Psychology*, 59: 971–80.

Simpson, J.A., Campbell, B. and Berscheid, E. (1986). 'The association between romantic love and marriage: Kephart (1967) twice revisited', *Personality and Social Psychology Bulletin*, 12: 363–72.

Singelis, T.M. and Brown, W.J. (1995). 'Culture, self and collectivist communication: Linking culture to individual behavior', *Human Communication Research*, 21: 354–89.

Singelis, T.M., Triandis, H.C., Bhawuk, D.S. and Gelfand, M. (1995). 'Horizontal and vertical dimensions of individualism and collectivism: A theoretical and measurement refinement', *Cross-Cultural Research*, 29: 240–75.

Singh Ghuman, P.A. (1994). *Coping with two cultures: British Asian and Indo–Canadian Adolescents*. Clevedon: Multilingual Matters.

Sinha, D. (1988). 'The family scenario in a developing country and its implications for mental health: The case of India', in P. Dasen, J. Berry and N. Sartorius (eds), *Health and Cross-Cultural Psychology: Towards Applications*. Beverly Hills: Sage.

—— (1991). 'Rise in the population of the elderly, familial changes and their psychosocial implications: The scenario of the developing countries', *International Journal of Psychology*, 26: 633–47.

Sinha, D. and Tripathi, R.C. (1994). 'Individualism in a collectivist culture: A case of coexistence of opposites', in U. Kim, H.C. Triandis, C. Kagitcibasi, S.-C. Choi and G. Yoon, *Individualism and collectivism: Theory, method and applications* (pp. 123–36). Thousand Oaks, CA: Sage.

Sinha, J.B.P. and Verma, J. (1987). 'Structure of collectivism', in C. Kagitcibasi (ed.), *Growth and progress in cross-cultural psychology* (pp. 123–9). Lisse: Swets and Zeitlinger.

—— (1994). 'Social support as a moderator of the relationship between allocentrism and psychological well-being', in U. Kim, H.C. Triandis, C. Kagitcibasi, S.-C. Choi and G. Yoon, *Individualism and collectivism: Theory, method and applications*. Thousand Oaks, CA: Sage.

Smith, P.B. (1993). 'Some technical aspects of the Trompenaars Data Bank', in F. Trompenaars, *Riding the Waves of Culture*. London: Nicholas Brealey.

Smith, P.B. and Bond, M.H. (1998). *Social Psychology Across Cultures* 2nd edn. New York: Harvester Wheatsheaf.

Smith, P., Dugan, S. and Trompenaars, F. (1996). 'National culture and managerial values: A dimensional analysis across 43 nations', *Journal of Cross-Cultural Psychology*, 27: 231–64.

Smith, P.B., Misumi, J., Tayeb, M.H., Peterson, M.F. and Bond, M.H. (1989). 'On the generality of leadership styles across cultures', *Journal of Occupational Psychology*, 62: 97–110.

Smith, P.B. and Peterson, M.F. (submitted). 'Beyond value comparisons: Sources used to give meaning to management work events in thirty countries'.

Smith, P.B., Peterson, M.F., Akande, D. *et al.* (1994). 'Organizational Event Management in Fourteen Countries: A comparison with Hofstede's Dimensions', in

A.-M. Bouvy, F. van de Vijver, P. Bowski and P. Schmitz (eds), *Journeys into Cross-Cultural Psychology* (pp. 364–73). Lisse: Swets and Zeitlinger.

Smith, P.B., Peterson, M., Hofmann, K., and Ropo, A. (1993). 'European National Cultures as Defined by Managerial Behaviour'; paper presented at the 'Conference on Changing Identities', Farnham Castle, UK, May 1993.

Smith, P.B., Peterson, M.F., Leung, K. and Dugan, S. (forthcoming). 'Individualism–collectivism and the handling of disagreement: A 23 country study'. To appear in *International Journal of Intercultural Relations*.

Smith, P.B., Peterson, M.F. and Misumi, J. (1994). 'Event management and work team effectiveness in Japan, Britain and USA', *Journal of Occupational and Organizational Psychology*, 67: 33–43.

Smith, P.B., Peterson, M.F., Misumi, J. and Bond, M. (1992). 'A cross-cultural test of the Japanese PM Leadership theory', *Applied Psychology: An international review*, 41: 5–19.

Smith, P.B. and Schwartz, S.H. (1997). 'Values', in J.W. Berry, M.H. Segall and C. Kagitcibasi (eds), *Handbook of Cross-Cultural Psychology* 2nd edn, vol. 3. Boston: Allyn and Bacon.

Smith, P.B., Trompenaars, F. and Dugan, S. (1995). 'The Rotter Locus of Control Scale in 43 Countries: A test of cultural reliability', *International Journal of Psychology*, 30: 377–400.

Smith, P.B. and Wang, Z.-M. (1996). 'Chinese Leadership and Organizational Structures', in M. Bond (ed.), *The Handbook of Chinese Psychology* (pp. 322–37). Hong Kong: Oxford University Press.

Snyder, M. (1974). 'Self-monitoring of expressive behaviour', *Journal of Personality and Social Psychology*, 30: 526–37.

Social Science Research Council (1954). 'Acculturation: An exploratory formulation', *American Anthropologist*, 56: 973–1002.

Sorensen, S. and Siegel, J. (1992). 'Gender, ethnicity and sexual assault: findings from a Los Angeles study', *Journal of Social Issues*, 48: 93–104.

Sow, F. (1985). 'Muslim Families in Contemporary Black Africa', *Current Anthropology*, 26: 563–73.

Sperber, D. (1985). 'Anthropology and psychology: toward an epidemiology of representations', *Man*, 20: 73–89.

Sprecher, S., Aron. A., Hatfield, E., Cortese, A., Potapova, E. and Levitskaya, A. (1994). 'Love: American style, Russian style and Japanese style', *Personal Relationships*, 1: 349–69.

Sprecher, S. and Chandak, R. (1992). 'Attitudes about arranged marriages and dating among men and women from India', *Free Inquiry in Creative Sociology*, 20: 1–11.

Sprecher, S. and Duck, S. (1994). 'Sweet talk: The importance of perceived communication for romantic and friendship attraction experienced during a get-acquainted date', *Personality and Social Psychology Bulletin*, 20: 391–400.

Sprecher, S. and Hatfield, E. (1996). 'Premarital sexual standards among U.S. college students and a comparison with those of Russian and Japanese students', *Archives of Sexual Behavior*, 25: 261–88.

Sprecher, S. and Metts, S. (1989). 'Development of the "Romantic Beliefs scale" and examination of the effects of gender and gender-role orientation', *Journal of Social and Personal Relationships*, 6: 387–411.

Stanton, M.E. (1995). 'Patterns of Kinship and Residence', in B.B. Ingoldsby and S. Smith (eds), *Families in Multicultural Perspective* (pp. 97–116). New York: The Guildford Press.

Staples, R. (1982). *Black masculinity*. San Francisco: The Black Scholar Press.

Steinberg, L., Elmen, J.D. and Mounts, N.S. (1989). 'Authoritative parenting, psychosocial maturity and academic success among adolescents', *Child Development*, 60: 1424–36.

Stephan, W.G. (1992). 'Sexual motivation, patriarchy and compatibility', *Behavioral and Brain Sciences*, 15: 111–12.

Stephens, W. (1963). *The family in cross-cultural perspective*. New York: Holt, Rhinehart and Winston.

Stephenson, N., Breakwell, G. and Fife-Schaw, C. (1993). 'Anchoring social representations of HIV protection: The significance of individual biographies', in P. Aggleton, P. Davies and G. Hart (eds), *Aids: Facing the second decade*. London: Falmer Press.

Sternberg, M. and Gold, P.W. (1998). The Mind–Body Interaction in Disease, *Scientific American: Special Edition on the Mind*, 8–15.

Sternberg, R.J. (1988). 'Triangulating love', in R.J. Sternberg and M.L. Barnes (eds), *The psychology of love* (pp. 119–38). New Haven, CT: Yale University Press.

Stevens, G. (1992). 'Mortality and age-specific patterns of marriage', *Behavioral and Brain Sciences*, 15: 112–13.

Stones, C.R. (1986). 'Love styles revisited: A cross-national comparison with particular reference to South Africa', *Human Relations*, 39: 379–82.

Stopes-Roe, M. and Cochrane, R. (1980). 'Mental health and integration: A comparison of Indian, Pakistani and Irish immigrants to England', *Ethnic and Racial Studies*, 3: 316–41.

—— (1988). 'Marriage in two cultures', *British Journal of Social Psychology*, 27: 159–69.

—— (1989). 'Traditionalism in the Family: A comparison between Asian and British cultures and between generations', *Journal of Comparative Family Studies*, 20: 141–58.

—— (1990a). 'The child-rearing values of Asian and British parents and young people: An inter-ethnic and inter-generational comparison in the evalution of Kohn's 13 qualities', *British Journal of Social Psychology*, 29: 149–60.

—— (1990b). 'Support networks of Asian and British families: Comparisons between Ethnicities and between Generations', *Social Behaviour*, 5: 71–85.

Strange, H. (1976). 'Continuity and change: Patterns of mate selection and marriage ritual in a Malay village', *Journal of Marriage and the Family*, 38: 561–71.

Suda, J.D. (1978). *Religions in India*. New Delhi: Stirling.

Sudhir, M.A. and Sailo, L. (1989). 'Parent–child interaction and academic achievement among secondary school students in Aizawi', *Indian Journal of Psychometry and Education*, 20: 19–28.

Sung, B. (1990). 'Chinese American intermarriage', *Journal of Comparative Family Studies*, 21: 337–52.

Super, C.M. and Harkness, S. (1997). 'Modernization, family life and child development in Kokwet', in T.S. Weisner, C. Bradley and P.L. Kilbride (eds), *African families and the crisis of social change* (pp. 341–53). Westport, CT: Bergin and Garvey.

Suzuki, T. (1976). 'Language and Behavior in Japan: The Conceptualization of Personal Relations', in T.S. Lebra and W.P. Lebra (1988), *Japanese Culture and Behavior* (pp. 142–57). Honolulu: University of Hawaii Press.

Symons, D. (1995). 'Beauty is in the adaptations of the beholder: The evolutionary psychology of human female sexual attractiveness', in P.R. Abramson and S.D. Pinkerton (eds), *Sexual nature, sexual culture*. Chicago: The University of Chicago Press.

Tang So-Kum, C., Critelli, J.W. and Porter, J.F. (1993). 'Motives in sexual aggression: The Chinese context', *Journal of Interpersonal Violence*, 8: 435–45.

Tanomura, Y. (1990). 'Sex education in Japanese public school'; paper presented at the International Conference on Sexuality in Asia, Hong Kong, May 1990.

Tashakkori, A. and Thompson, V. (1988). 'Cultural change and attitude change: an assessment of postrevolutionary marriage and family attitudes in Iran', *Population Research and Policy Review*, 7: 3–27.

—— (1991). 'Social change and change in intentions of Iranian youth regarding education, marriage and careers', *International Journal of Psychology*, 26: 203–17.

Taylor, P.L. and Tucker, M.B. (1997). 'Interethnic dating patterns and marital attitudes in 21 cities'; paper presented at the International Network on Personal Relationships, Oxford, Ohio. July 1997.

Teays, W. (1991). 'The Burning Bride: The Dowry Problem in India', *Journal of Feminist Studies in Religion*, 7: 29.

Thakerar, J.N. and Iwawaki, S. (1979). 'Cross-cultural comparisons in interpersonal attraction of females toward males', *Journal of Social Psychology*, 108: 121–2.

Tharp, R. (1963). 'Psychological patterning in marriage', *Psychological Bulletin*, 60: 97–117.

Thibaut, J. and Kelley, H. (1959). *The Social Psychology of Groups*. New York: Wiley.

Thiessen, D. and Gregg, B. (1980). 'Human assortative mating and genetic equilibrium: An evolutionary perspective', *Ethology and Sociobiology*, 1: 111–40.

Thornhill, N.W. and Thornhill, R. (1987). 'Evolutionary theory and rules of mating and marriage pertaining to relatives', in C. Crawford, M. Smith and D. Krebs (eds), *Sociobiology and Psychology: Issues and Applications*. Hillsdale, NJ: Lawrence Erlbaum.

Thornhill, R. and Gangestad, S.W. (1993). 'Human facial beauty: Averageness, symmetry and parasite resistance', *Human Nature*, 4: 237–70.

Thorpe, K.J., Dragonas, T. and Golding, J. (1992). 'The effects of psychosocial factors on the emotional well-being of women during pregnancy: A cross-cultural study of Britain and Greece', *Journal of Reproductive and Infant Psychology*, 10: 191–204.

Ting-Toomey, S. (1991). 'Intimacy expressions in three cultures: France, Japan and the United States', *International Journal of Intercultural Relations*, 15: 29–46.

Tobin, J. (1992). 'Japanese preschools and the pedagogy of selfhood', in N.R. Rosenberger (ed.), *Japanese sense of self* (pp. 21–39). Cambridge: Cambridge University Press.

Tonnies, F. (1957). *Community and Society* (trans. C.P. Loomis). East Lansing: Michigan State University Press.

Topalova, V. (1997). 'Individualism/Collectivism and Social Identity', *Journal of Community and Applied Psychology*, 7: 53–64.

Tornstam. L. (1992). 'Loneliness in marriage', *Journal of Social and Personal Relationships*, 9: 197–217.

Tower, R.K., Kelly, C. and Richards, A. (1997). 'Individualism, collectivism and reward allocation: A cross-cultural study in Russia and Britain', *British Journal of Social Psychology*, 36: 331–45.

Towianska, A., Rozlucka, E. and Dabrowski, J. (1992). 'Prevalence of HIV antibodies in maritime workers and in other selected population groups in Poland', *The bulletin of the institute of maritime and tropical medicine in Gdynia*, 43: 19–24.

Triandis, H.C. (1989). 'Self and social behavior in differing cultural contexts', *Psychological Review*, 96: 269–89.

—— (1994). *Culture and Social Behavior*. New York: McGraw-Hill.

—— (1995). *Individualism and Collectivism*. Boulder, CO: Westview Press.

Triandis, H.C., Bontempo, R., Betancourt, H. *et al.* (1986). 'The measurement of etic aspects of individualism and collèctivism across cultures', *Australian Journal of Psychology*, 38: 257–67.

Triandis, H.C., Bontempo, R., Villareal, M.J., Asai, M. and Lucca, M. (1988). 'Individualism and collectivism: Cross-cultural perspectives on self–ingroup relationships', *Journal of Personality and Social Psychology*, 54: 323–38.

Triandis, H.C., Chen, X.P. and Chan, D.K.S. (1998). 'Scenarios for the measurement of collectivism and individualism', *Journal of Cross-Cultural Psychology*, 29: 275–89.

Triandis, H., Hui, C.H., Albert, R.D., Leung, S.-M., Lisansky, J., Diaz-Loving, R., Plascencia, L., Marin, G. and Betancourt, H. (1984). 'Individual models of Social Behavior', *Journal of Personality and Social Psychology*, 46: 1389–404.

Triandis, H.C., Leung, K., Villareal, M. and Clack, F. (1985). 'Allocentric vs. idiocentric tendencies: Convergent and discriminant validation', *Journal of Research in Personality*, 19: 395–415.

Triandis, H.C., McCusker, C. and Hui, C.H. (1990). 'Multimethod probes of individualism and collectivism', *Journal of Personality and Social Psychology*, 59: 1006–20.

Triandis, H.C., Marin, G., Lisansky, J. and Betancourt., H. (1984). 'Simparia as a cultural script of Hispanics', *Journal of Personality and Social Psychology*, 47: 1363–75.

Triandis, H.C., Villareal, M.J. and Clack, F.L. (1984). 'Allocentric vs. idiocentric tendencies: Convergent and discriminant validation' (Tech. rep. ONR–33). Champaign: Department of Psychology, University of Illinois.

Trickett, E.J. and Buchanan, R.M. (1997). 'The role of personal relationships in transitions: Contributions of an Ecological Perspective', in S. Duck (ed.), *Handbook of Personal Relationships: Theory, Research and Interventions* 2nd edn. (pp. 575–93). Chichester: John Wiley.

Trompenaars, F. (1993). *Riding the waves of culture: Understanding cultural diversity in business*. London: Nicholas Brealey.

Tseng, W.-S. and Wu, D. (1985). 'Directions for future study', in W. Tseng and D. Wu (eds), *Chinese culture and mental health*. New York: Academic Press.

Tsoi, W. (1985). 'Mental health in Singapore and its relation to Chinese culture', in W. Tseng and D. Wu (eds), *Chinese culture and mental health*. New York: Academic Press.

Tsui, M. (1989). 'Changes in Chinese Urban Family Structure', *Journal of Marriage and the Family*, 51: 737–47.

Tucker, M.B. and Taylor, R.J. (1989). 'Demographic correlates of relationship status among Black Americans', *Journal of Marriage and the Family*, 51: 655–66.

Tudge, J., Hogan, D., Lee, S., Tammeveski, P., Meltsas, M., Kulakova, N., Snezhkova, I. and Putman, S. (1997). 'Cultural heterogeneity: Parental values and beliefs and their preschoolers' activities in the United States, South Korea, Russia and Estonia', in A. Goncu (ed.), *Children's engagement in the world*. New York: Cambridge University Press.

Tully, M. (1995). *Ram Chander's story*. Harmondsworth: Penguin.

Tuzin, D. (1995). 'Discourse, intercourse and the excluded middle: Anthropology and the problem of sexual experience', in P.R. Abramson and S.D. Pinkerton (eds), *Sexual nature, sexual culture*. Chicago: The University of Chicago Press.

Tylor, E.B. (1889). On a method of investigating the development of institutions. *Journal of the Royal Anthropological Institute of Great Britain and Ireland*, 18: 245–72.

Udomaratn, P. (1990). 'Some aspects of Sexual Behaviour in Thai Society'; paper presented at the International Conference on Sexuality in Asia, Hong Kong, May 1990.

Udry, J. (1981). 'Marital alternatives and marital disruption', *Journal of Marriage and the Family*, 43: 889–97.

Ujjwalarani, M.V. (1992). 'Need and scope of counselling psychology in India', *Indian Journal of Behaviour*, 16: 8–11.

United Nations (1995). *United Nations Demographic Yearbook*. New York: UN.

United Nations (1997). *United Nations Demographic Yearbook*. New York: UN.

United Nations General Assembly (1989). *Adoption of a convention on the rights of the child* (UN Doc. A/Res/44/25. Nov 1989). New York: UN.

Vandewiele, M. and Philbrick, J.L. (1983). 'Attitudes of Senegalese students toward love', *Psychological Reports*, 52: 915–18.

Van de Vliert, E. and Huismans, S.E. (1998). 'Climate and masculinity'; paper presented at the 14th Congress of the International Association of Cross-Cultural Psychologists, Western Washington University, USA, August 1998.

Vangelisti, L. (1994). 'Family secrets: forms, functions and correlates', *Journal of Social and Personal Relationships*, 11: 113–35.

Vannoy, D. (1998). 'The Patriarchal Legacy in Russian Marriages'; paper given at the 9th International Conference on Personal Relationships, Saratoga Springs, June 1998.

Van Tilburg, T., De Jong Gierveld, J., Lecchini, L. and Marsiglis, D. (1998). 'Social integration and loneliness: A comparative study among older adults in the Netherlands and Tuscany, Italy', *Journal of Social and Personal Relationships*, 15: 740–54.

Vaux, A. (1985). 'Variations in social support associated with gender, ethnicity and age', *Journal of Social Issues*, 41: 89–110.

Vega, W.A. and Kolody, B. (1985). 'The meaning of social support and the mediation of stress across cultures', in W.A. Vega and M. Miranda (eds), *Stress and Hispanic mental health*. Washington, DC: DHHS Publication No. 85–1410. Rockville, MD: National Institute of Mental Health.

Vergin, N. (1985). 'Social change and the family in Turkey', *Current Anthropology*, 26: 571–4.

Vincent, J.E. (1971). 'Scaling the universe of states on certain useful multivariate dimensions', *The Journal of Social Psychology*, 85: 261–83.

Visser, A.P. and Ketting, E. (1994). 'Sexual health: Education and counseling perspectives on contraceptive use, HIV and sexuality', *Patient Education and Counseling*, 23: 141–5.

Voland, E. (1998). 'Sources of variability in mate preferences, mate choice and marriage patterns: A Darwinian perspective'; paper presented at the 14th Congress of the International Association of Cross-Cultural Psychologists, Western Washington University, USA, August 1998.

Wagels, K. and Roemhild, R. (1998). 'The German Way: Dissolving the Significance of Marriage'; paper presented at the 14th Congress of the International Association of Cross-Cultural Psychologists, Western Washington University, USA, August 1998.

Wallach, M.A. and Wallach, L. (1983). *Psychology's sanction for selfishness: The error of Egoism in Theory and Therapy*. San Francisco: W.H. Freeman.

Wallen, K. (1989). 'Mate Selection: Economics and affection'; commentary on D. Buss (1989), 'Sex differences in human mate preferences', *Behavior and Brain Sciences*, 12: 37–8.

Walster, E. and Walster, G. (1978). *A new look at love*. Reading, MA: Addison-Wesley.

Wandibba, S. (1997). 'Changing roles in the Bukusu family', in T.S. Weisner, C. Bradley and P.L. Kilbride (eds), *African families and the crisis of social change* (pp. 332–40). Westport, CT: Bergin and Garvey.

Wang, Z.M. (1993). 'Culture, economic reform and the role of industrial and organizational psychology in China', in M.D. Dunnette and L.M. Hough, *Handbook of Industrial and Organizational Psychology, vol. 4*. Palo Alto: Consulting Psychologists Press Inc.

Wang, Z.M. and Heller, F. (1993). 'Patterns of power distribution in managerial decision making in Chinese and British industrial organizations', *The International Journal of Human Resource Management*, 4: 113–28.

Wapner, S. and Craig-Bray, L. (1992). 'Person-in-Environment: Theoretical and Methodological Approaches', *Environment and Behavior*, 24: 161–88.

Warwick, D. (1980) 'The politics and ethics of cross-cultural research', in H. Triandis (ed), *Handbook of Cross-Cultural Psychology* (vol. 1, pp. 319–71). Boston: Allyn and Bacon.

Waterman, A.S. (1981). 'Individualism and psychological independence', *American Psychologist*, 36: 762–73.

Watson, J.L. (1998). *Golden Arches East: McDonald's in East Asia*. Cambridge: Cambridge University Press.

Watson, O.M. (1970). *Proxemic Behavior: A cross-cultural study*. The Hague: Mouton.

Weber, M. (1921/1968). *Economy and society*. Totowa, NJ: Bedminster Press.

Wellings, K., Fields, J., Johnson, A.M. and Wadsworth, J. (1994). *Sexual Behaviour in Britain*. London: Penguin.

Wen, J. (1995). 'Sexual beliefs and problems in contemporary Taiwan', in T.Y. Lin, W.S. Tseng and E.H. Yeh (eds), *Chinese Societies and Mental Health*. Hong Kong: Oxford University Press.

Wen-Shing, T. and Jing, H. (1991). *Culture and family: Problems and therapy*. New York: Haworth Press.

West, S., Newsom, J. and Fenaughty, A. (1993). 'Publication trends in JPSP: Stability and change in topics and theories across two decades', *Personality and Social Psychology Bulletin*, 18: 473–84.

Wheeler, L. (1988). 'My year in Hong Kong: Some observations about social behaviour', *Personality and Social Psychology Bulletin*, 14: 410–20.

—— (1989). 'A reply to Lam and Yang', *Personality and Social Psychology Bulletin*, 15: 644–7.

Wheeler, L. and Kim, Y. (1997). 'What is beautiful is culturally good: The physical attractiveness stereotype has different content in collectivistic cultures', *Personality and Social Psychology Bulletin*, 23: 795–800.

White, J. and Sorensen, S. (1992). 'A sociocultural view of sexual assault: from discrepancy to diversity', *Journal of Social Issues*, 48: 187–95.

Whiting, B.B. (1973). 'The Kenyan career woman: Traditional and modern', *Annals of the New York Academy of Sciences*, 208: 71–5.

Whiting, B.B. and Whiting, J.W. (1975). *Children of six countries: A psychocultural analysis*. Cambridge, MA: Harvard University Press.

Whyte, M.K. (1990). *Dating, mating and marriage*. New York: Aldine de Gruyter.

—— (1992). 'Introduction: Rural economic reforms and Chinese family patterns', *The China Quarterly*, 130: 317–22.

Whyte, M.K. and Parish, W.L. (1984). *Urban life in contemporary China*. Chicago: University of Chicago Press.

Whyte, S.R. and Kariuki, P.W. (1997). 'Malnutrition and gender relations in Western Kenya', in T.S. Weisner, C. Bradley and P.L. Kilbride (eds), *African families and the crisis of social change* (pp. 135–56). Westport, CT: Bergin and Garvey.

Wiemann, J.M., Chen, V. and Giles, H. (1986). 'Beliefs about talk and silence in cultural context'; paper presented at the Speech Communication Association Convention, September 1986.

Wilkinson, D. (1987). 'Ethnicity', in M.B. Sussman and S.K. Steinmetz (eds), *Handbook of Marriage and the Family*. New York: Plenum Press.

Williams, J.E. and Best, D.L. (1982). *Measuring sex stereotypes: A thirty nation study*. Beverly Hills: Sage.

—— (1990). *Sex and psyche: Gender and self viewed cross-culturally*. Newbury Park: Sage.

Wilson, D., Greenspan, R. and Wilson, C. (1989). 'Knowledge about AIDS and self-reported behaviour among Zimbabwean secondary school pupils', *Social Science and Medicine*, 28: 957–61.

Wilson, D., Manual, A. and Lavelle, S. (1991). 'Psychological predictors of condom use to prevent HIV transmission among Zimbabwean students', *International Journal of Psychology*, 26: 703–21.

Wilson, D. and Marindo, R. (1989). 'Erotophobia and Contraception among Zimbabwean students', *Journal of Social Psychology*, 129: 721–3.

Winarick, K. (1985). 'The "chemistry" of personal attraction', *The American Journal of Psychoanalysis*, 45: 380–8.

Winch, R. (1955). 'The theory of complementary needs in mate selection: Final results on the test of the general hypothesis', *American Sociological Review*, 20: 552–5.

—— (1958). *Mate Selection*. New York: Harper.

Wintrob, H. (1987). 'Self-disclosure as a marketable commodity', *Journal of Social Behavior and Personality*, 2: 77–88.

Wolf, R. (1996). *Marriages and Families in a Diverse Society*. New York: Harper-Collins.

Woll, S. (1987). 'Improper linear models of matchmaking'; paper presented at the Iowa Conference on Personal Relationships, Des Moines.

Won-Doornink, M. (1985). 'Self-disclosure and reciprocity in conversation: A cross-national study', *Social Psychology Quarterly*, 48: 97–107.

—— (1991). 'Self-disclosure and reciprocity in South Korean and U.S. Male Dyads', in S. Ting-Toomey and F. Korzenny (eds), *Cross-cultural interpersonal communication*. Newbury Park: Sage.

World Health Organisation (1995). *Weekly Epidemiological Record*, 70 (15 December 1995: 50), 353–60.

World Health Organisation (1997). *Causes of death: the developed and developing world*. Geneva: WHO.

Wu, S. and Shaver, P.R. (1993). 'American and Chinese love conceptions: Variations on a Universal Theme'; paper presented at the 101st APA Convention, Toronto, Ontario, August 1993.

Wyatt, G.E. (1993). 'Sociocultural influences on sexuality'; invited address at the 19th Annual Meeting of the International Academy of Sex Research, Pacific Grove, California, July 1993.

Xiantian, L. (1985). 'The effect of family on the mental health of the Chinese people', in W. Tseng and D. Wu (eds), *Chinese culture and mental health*. New York: Academic Press.

Xiaohe, X. and Whyte, M. (1990). 'Love matches and arranged marriages: A Chinese replication', *Journal of Marriage and the Family*, 52: 709–22.

Yamaguchi (1994) 'Collectivism among the Japanese', in Kim, U., Triandis, H.C., Kagitcibasi, C., Choi, S.-C. and Yoon, G., *Individualism and collectivism: Theory, method and applications* (pp. 175–88). Thousand Oaks, CA: Sage.

Yang, C.-F. (1988). 'Familism and development: An examination of the role of family in contemporary China Mainland, Hong Kong and Taiwan', in D. Sinha and H. Kao (eds), *Social values and development: Asian perspectives*. New Delhi: Sage.

Yang, K.S. (1981). 'Social orientation and individual modernity among Chinese students in Taiwan', *Journal of Social Psychology*, 113: 159–70.

—— (1986). 'Chinese personality and its change', in M.H. Bond (ed.), *The psychology of the Chinese people*. Hong Kong: Oxford University Press.

—— (1988). 'Will societal modernization eventually eliminate cross-cultural psychological differences?', in M.H. Bond (ed.), *The Cross-cultural Challenge to Social Psychology*. Newbury Park: Sage.

—— (1995). 'Chinese social orientation: An integrative analysis', in W. Tseng, T.Y. Lin and Y.K Yeh (eds), *Chinese Societies and Mental Health*. Hong Kong: Oxford University Press.

—— (1996). 'The psychological transformation of the Chinese people as a result of societal modernization', in M.H. Bond (ed.), *The Handbook of Chinese Psychology* (pp. 479–98). Hong Kong: Oxford University Press.

Yang, K.S. and Ho, D. (1988). 'The role of yuan in Chinese social life: A conceptual and empirical analysis', in A.C. Panajpe, D. Ho and R.C. Reiber (eds), *Asian contributions to psychology* (pp. 261–81). New York: Praeger.

Ying, Y. (1991). 'Marital satisfaction among San Francisco Chinese-Americans', *International Journal of Social Psychiatry*, 37: 201–13.

Zessen, G. van and Sandfort, T. (1991). *Seksualiteit in Nederland*. Amsterdam: Swets and Zeitlinger.

Zhou, M. (1990). 'Sex viewpoint of women college students in continental China today'; paper presented at the International Conference on Sexuality in Asia, Hong Kong, May 1990.

Index

UNIVERSITY OF WOLVERHAMPTON
LEARNING RESOURCES